ASP.NET MVC 2 Cookbook

Over 70 clear and incredibly effective recipes to get
the most out of the many tools and features of
the ASP.NET MVC framework

Andrew Siemer

Richard Kimber

BIRMINGHAM - MUMBAI

ASP.NET MVC 2 Cookbook

First published: January 2011

Production Reference: 1100111

Published by Packt Publishing Ltd.
32 Lincoln Road
Olton
Birmingham, B27 6PA, UK.

ISBN 978-1-849690-30-0

www.packtpub.com

Cover Image by Faiz Fattohi (faizfattohi@gmail.com)

Credits

Authors
Andrew Siemer
Richard Kimber

Reviewers
Tim Cromarty
Buu Nguyen
Baskin I. Tapkan

Acquisition Editor
David Barnes

Development Editor
Wilson D'souza

Technical Editor
Namita Sahni

Copy Editor
Laxmi Subramanian

Indexer
Rekha Nair

Editorial Team Leader
Aditya Belpathak

Project Team Leader
Priya Mukherji

Project Coordinator
Sneha Harkut

Proofreaders
Kelly Hutchinson
Susan Stevens

Production Coordinator
Shantanu Zagade

Cover Work
Shantanu Zagade

About the Authors

Andrew Siemer is currently a Senior Technical Architect for Perficient in Austin, Texas. He has worked as a software engineer, architect, trainer, and author since 1998 when he left the military. He is a frequent contributor to `DotNetSlackers.com`, host of `DotNetRadio.com`, author of *ASP.NET 3.5 Social Networking*, and a member of the ASP Insiders group. Andrew has provided consultancy to many companies on the topics of e-commerce, social networking, and various other business systems. He has worked with eUniverse, Point Vantage, Callaway Golf, Guidance Software, Intermix Media, Fox Interactive, Lamps Plus, and Lender Processing Services, to name a few. In addition to his daily duties, he also conducts classes in .NET, C#, and other web technologies, blogs on numerous topics (`blog.andrewsiemer.com`), and works on various community projects such as `MvcCookbook.com`. You can find Andrew Siemer on Twitter at `@asiemer`, as well as Facebook, LinkedIn, and various other social sites.

To my wife Jessica—I love you! Thank you for standing with me through yet another book project.

Richard Kimber has been working with web technologies for over 15 years. Primarily a .NET developer, Richard has worked in a broad range of development environments, from the financial services industry to new media and marketing. He now runs a web and mobile consultancy company called Dogma Creative with his wife Katie.

Katie, thank you for your constant support and encouragement. To my Granddad who passed away earlier this year, thank you for showing me what can be achieved.

About the Reviewers

Tim Cromarty has been working in IT for well over 20 years in a variety of positions and responsibilities. In the late '80s' he was an Oracle developer, and worked for a variety of companies including Oracle UK, ITV, Banks and Local Government. Then, in the late '90s'-he became involved in Java and web development working primarily for the European offices of US-based organizations. More recently, Tim has held a number of director level positions managing large multi-million pound global organizations.

As a developer, he enjoys learning new programming languages, techniques, and practices. He has been using .NET since the first version and has also spent plenty of time developing in C, Java, Perl, PHP, SQL, PL/SQL (he could go on...), but his current focus is .NET—especially MVC.

Based in Hampshire, England, Tim is currently an independent software consultant and technologist providing technical and managerial consultancy in Microsoft ASP.NET, MVC, jQuery, JavaScript and AJAX, as well as managing multiple web development projects, e-commerce, and community websites.

His blog can be found at http://blog.clicktricity.com.

I am married with an amazing 4-year-old son. My ambition is to stop lying about my age when I reach 30... My wife thinks I'm a nerd because my idea of relaxing is to read a programming manual!

Buu Nguyen is a Microsoft MVP in ASP.NET. He is currently the Vice President of Technology at *KMS Technology*—a global software services company. During his past seven years of experience in software development, he has been involved in the development of multiple applications ranging from Java and .NET enterprise applications to Ruby on Rails web applications.

Buu is an active community participant who has conducted training for Microsoft, published technical articles, developed open source software, and been a frequent speaker at technical conferences, including those organized by Microsoft.

Besides his industrial and community engagement, Buu is a part-time university lecturer who teaches courses in software architecture, J2EE, and ASP.NET.

Baskin I. Tapkan has recently joined Verifications, Inc—a consumer reporting agency specializing in systems integrations—as a senior software/web developer/architect. Baskin is a technology evangelist and has been programming for over 20 years, starting with Turbo Pascal and QBasic. He has been coding in the .NET framework since its release and now focuses on the ASP.NET MVC and WCF Services. Prior to joining the Verifications Inc., he has been a software architect at Healthland, Inc., a consultant with Magenic, and a systems design engineer at Imation Corporation. He has over 12 years of industry experience in manufacturing, healthcare, education, and consumer services, working on various database-driven applications. Baskin holds a Master's Degree in Electrical Engineering from the University of Wyoming. Baskin is an avid windsurfer and an upcoming kite boarder currently residing in Twin Cities, MN. He enjoys his few weeks of vacation at the Columbia River Gorge.

www.PacktPub.com

Support files, eBooks, discount offers, and more

You might want to visit www.PacktPub.com for support files and downloads related to your book.

Did you know that Packt offers eBook versions of every book published, with PDF and ePub files available? You can upgrade to the eBook version at www.PacktPub.com and as a print book customer, you are entitled to a discount on the eBook copy. Get in touch with us at service@packtpub.com for more details.

At www.PacktPub.com, you can also read a collection of free technical articles, sign up for a range of free newsletters, and receive exclusive discounts and offers on Packt books and eBooks.

http://PacktLib.PacktPub.com

Do you need instant solutions to your IT questions? PacktLib is Packt's online digital book library. Here, you can access, read, and search across Packt's entire library of books.

Why Subscribe?

- ► Fully searchable across every book published by Packt
- ► Copy & paste, print and bookmark content
- ► On demand and accessible via web browser

Free Access for Packt account holders

If you have an account with Packt at www.PacktPub.com, you can use this to access PacktLib today and view nine entirely free books. Simply use your login credentials for immediate access.

Table of Contents

Preface

Ten years ago, ASP.NET provided software developers with a means to write complex web applications with their existing Windows Forms skillsets. Today, it continues to be a robust framework for writing scalable applications, from small e-Commerce to enterprise-level CRM. But ten years later, with many business critical applications existing solely on the Web, the Forms paradigm is less relevant.

ASP.NET MVC, based on Ruby On Rails, is now in its second release, with a third around the corner—a powerful framework based on new and old ideas, ASP.NET MVC allows the developer to work with web protocols and standards, while still making use of the industry-standard development environment—Visual Studio.

By example, this book will take you through the key areas of ASP.NET MVC. We'll look at the MVC structure, data access, and ASP.NET MVC's compatibility with client scripting and dependency injection. With a minimal knowledge of web development, this book will help you build scalable web applications with relative ease.

What this book covers

Chapter 1, Working with the View... The view is possibly the most recognizable component of ASP.NET to a web forms developer, with its familiar ASPX extension. However, the differences are significant; we will explore the concepts of `ViewData`, strongly typed Views, and helpers in this chapter.

Chapter 2, Taking Action in Your Controllers... For every view there is an action and a controller to host it, for it is the action that you navigate to in your browser. The view is merely a template to be called upon. In this chapter, we will learn about controllers and their actions, particularly the resulting types that are not necessarily HTML.

Chapter 3, Routing... If the action is a destination, routing is how you get there. The structure of a URL is an important aspect of a site's navigation; it should read like a map, showing you where you are and give hints as to where you can go. We'll look at how you can manage URLs to create user-friendly site maps, control errors, and provide a hackable API into the current view.

Chapter 4, Master Pages... Don't Repeat Yourself; every good developer should keep things DRY. Master Pages are one of many conventions for doing just that. Here, we'll look at creating a site-wide look and feel, nesting, and shared functions.

Chapter 5, Working with Data in the View... The difference between static HTML and dynamically generated sites is usually the data. In this chapter, we'll look at how easy it is to manage data in this powerful new framework and how it reintroduces old concepts to powerful effect.

Chapter 6, Working with Forms... Forms are the heart of the interactive Web, working at the browser's most basic level; they can be enhanced to provide a rich and intuitive experience. ASP.NET MVC provides extraordinary control over these elements; we'll see how we can capitalize on this control with client scripting and templates.

Chapter 7, Simplifying Complex Applications... ASP.NET MVC has been designed from the ground up to be tested, extended, and improved. Here we'll see how third-party libraries can be used to extend existing functionality or provide a completely new set of options.

Chapter 8, Validating MVC... Validation is the key to any application that accepts input of any kind, but where should it be implemented—on the client where it is most responsive, in the business logic where it is most central, or in the data layer where it is most secure? ASP.NET MVC provides a simple yet powerful framework for defining validation from a central location that is decoupled from the data layer; validation that makes use of client scripting without being dependent on it; and with all this, keeping the validation DRY. In this chapter, we'll look at data annotations, client-side scripting, and remote validation.

Chapter 9, Data Access and Storage... With so many options for storage these days, you might find that you don't want to tie yourself to just one. In this chapter, we'll look at the repository pattern and how, when used in conjunction with dependency injection, we can create an application that, with minimal work, can be connected to XML, SQL, or test data sources.

Chapter 10, Application, Session, Cookies and Caching... Application optimization has never been easier with ASP.NET MVC. In this chapter, we'll look at session management using session and cookies, and how to cache different aspects of the application to provide the best performance.

What you need for this book

This book assumes that you're using ASP.NET MVC 2, but most recipes will work in version 1 and the latest release candidates of version 3 with only minor modification. To run ASP.NET MVC 2, you will need at least Microsoft Visual Studio 2008 or Visual Web Developer 2008, for which ASP.NET MVC 2 is available as a separate download. If you're already using VS 2010 or VWD 2010, ASP.NET MVC 2 is already installed. If you're not using any version at the moment, I would recommend downloading and installing Visual Web Developer 2010, it's free and pretty great. A few of the chapters have dependencies on free third-party libraries, which are described in the chapters. However, Chapter 9 also assumes the installation of SQL Server Express (2008 or above); this was likely part of your original Visual Studio installation, but if not, it is also a free download.

Who this book is for

This book is particularly written for web developers looking to transfer their knowledge from the ASP.NET web forms way of doing things to the ASP.NET MVC framework. As this book targets readers of various experience levels, you should be able to find recipes of a basic, intermediate, and advanced nature. Regardless of your experience level, each recipe will walk you through the solution in a step-by-step manner that anyone should be able to follow.

Conventions

In this book, you will find a number of styles of text that distinguish among different kinds of information. Here are some examples of these styles, and an explanation of their meaning.

Code words in text are shown as follows: "Next, we'll add a function to the CModel class that will allow us to set a given effect to any given mesh part."

A block of code is set as follows:

```
public ActionResult ReportComplete(string reportName,
  int fromYear, int fromMonth, int fromDay, int toYear,
  int toMonth, int toDay)
{
  return View("Report");
}
```

When we wish to draw your attention to a particular part of a code block, the relevant lines or items are set in bold:

```
<asp:Content ID="Content2" ContentPlaceHolderID="MainContent"
  runat="server">
<h2>Report</h2>
<%: ViewData["report"] %>
</asp:Content>
```

New terms and important words are shown in bold. Words that you see on the screen, in menus or dialog boxes for example, appear in the text like this: " In this recipe, we will take a look at a way to easily handle that pesky Page cannot be found error."

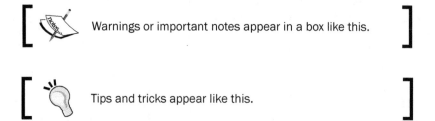

Warnings or important notes appear in a box like this.

Tips and tricks appear like this.

Reader feedback

Feedback from our readers is always welcome. Let us know what you think about this book—what you liked or may have disliked. Reader feedback is important for us to develop titles that you really get the most out of.

To send us general feedback, simply send an e-mail to feedback@packtpub.com, and mention the book title via the subject of your message.

If there is a book that you need and would like to see us publish, please send us a note in the SUGGEST A TITLE form on www.packtpub.com or e-mail suggest@packtpub.com.

If there is a topic that you have expertise in and you are interested in either writing or contributing to a book, see our author guide on www.packtpub.com/authors.

Customer support

Now that you are the proud owner of a Packt book, we have a number of things to help you to get the most from your purchase.

Downloading the example code for this book

You can download the example code files for all Packt books you have purchased from your account at http://www.PacktPub.com. If you purchased this book elsewhere, you can visit http://www.PacktPub.com/support and register to have the files e-mailed directly to you.

Errata

Although we have taken every care to ensure the accuracy of our content, mistakes do happen. If you find a mistake in one of our books—maybe a mistake in the text or the code—we would be grateful if you would report this to us. By doing so, you can save other readers from frustration and help us improve subsequent versions of this book. If you find any errata, please report them by visiting http://www.packtpub.com/support, selecting your book, clicking on the errata submission form link, and entering the details of your errata. Once your errata are verified, your submission will be accepted and the errata will be uploaded to our website, or added to any list of existing errata under the Errata section of that title. Any existing errata can be viewed by selecting your title from http://www.packtpub.com/support.

Piracy

Piracy of copyright material on the Internet is an ongoing problem across all media. At Packt, we take the protection of our copyright and licenses very seriously. If you come across any illegal copies of our works, in any form on the Internet, please provide us with the location address or website name immediately so that we can pursue a remedy.

Please contact us at copyright@packtpub.com with a link to the suspected pirated material.

We appreciate your help in protecting our authors, and our ability to bring you valuable content.

Questions

You can contact us at questions@packtpub.com if you are having a problem with any aspect of the book, and we will do our best to address it.

1
Working with the View

In this chapter, we will cover:

- ▶ Using magic strings and the `ViewData` dictionary
- ▶ Creating a strongly typed view
- ▶ Decoupling a strongly typed view with a View Model
- ▶ Centralizing display logic with templated helpers
- ▶ Using a partial view to segment view code
- ▶ Rendering a child view with `Html.RenderAction`
- ▶ Building a view from the database with NVelocity
- ▶ Consuming a JSON view with jQuery

Introduction

In this chapter, we will take a look at the easiest part of the whole ASP.NET MVC framework—the **View**. We will get started by looking at how data is passed out to the view in the simplest of ways using the `ViewData` dictionary and magic strings. From there, we will work towards better ways of getting data in and out of the view. Then we will take a look at some of the other view engines that you have at your disposal, which can easily be plugged into the ASP.NET MVC framework. Finally, we will take a look at other things that you can do with the view.

In our examples, we will be working with the basic concept of products and categories as though we were building a simple e-commerce site. We will be using an open source product called **NBuilder** to fake our data access layer. NBuilder will be used to quickly generate some product and category data for us to use in our views.

 NBuilder is a great open source product that can be used to quickly generate test instances of a particular .NET class. This works great when knocking together your views such as we are doing in this chapter. You can find more data about NBuilder at `NBuilder.org`. I also wrote a tutorial on how to get NBuilder running on `DotNetSlackers.com` at `dotnetslackers.com/articles/aspnet/Using-NBuilder-to-mock-up-a-data-driven-UI-Part1.aspx`.

Using magic strings and the ViewData dictionary

The most basic way to pass data from the controller into the view is through the use of magic strings and a convenient dictionary called `ViewData`. In this recipe, we will see how to use this easy, but dangerous, duo to shuttle data out to the far edges of our presentation layer. We will then take a quick look at why the use of magic strings and the `ViewData` container put us in a fragile state and should be kept away from, if at all possible.

 Magic Strings? A **magic string** is a string that represents an object or a block of code within your source. An example of this is when referencing an action or controller name in a link. As the name of the action is string-based, refactoring the action method name might get missed in the string references. This is usually thought to be a brittle way of pointing at your code. For that reason, not using magic strings, when possible, is considered to be a more stable manner of programming in MVC (or any other framework for that matter).

Getting ready

The most important part of any of these recipes is to create an **ASP.NET MVC 2** web application. Once that is created, we will need to do two more things—create a `Product` class, and get NBuilder up and running.

The `Product` class will be quite simple. We will create a new `Product.cs` file and place it in the `Models` folder of your MVC application.

Models/Product.cs:

```
public class Product
{
  public string Sku { get; set; }
  public string ProductName { get; set; }
  public string Description { get; set; }
  public double Cost { get; set; }
}
```

Getting NBuilder installed is almost as simple as the creation of the `Product` class. Go to `NBuilder.org/Download` and download the latest version of NBuilder (I am using 2.1.9 currently). Then extract the `FizzWare.NBuilder.dll` into your MVC application's `bin` directory. Then add a reference to that DLL (right-click on the project, add reference, browse, and locate the `FizzWare.NBuilder.dll` file in the `bin` directory). That's it!

How to do it...

1. The first step for us to get a product displayed on a page is to create a new view page. To do this, open the `Views` folder and then open the `home` folder. Right-click on the `home` folder and select **Add | View**. When the **Add View** window pops up, enter **Product** in the **View name** box. Then click on **Add**.

2. Once we have our new view page in place, we need to open the Home controller and add a new `Product` action so that we can handle requests for our `Product` view. To do this, open the `Controllers` folder and then open the `HomeController.cs` file. Just inside the class, you can create your new `Product` action method.

Controllers/HomeController.cs:

```
public class HomeController : Controller
{
  public ActionResult Product()
  {
    return View();
  }

  public ActionResult Index()
  {
    ViewData["Message"] = "Welcome to ASP.NET MVC!";
    return View();
  }

  . . .
}
```

3. Now hit *F5* to verify that your `Product` action is correctly wired to your `Product` view.

   If you see the **Debugging Not Enabled** pop-up, go ahead and click on **OK**!

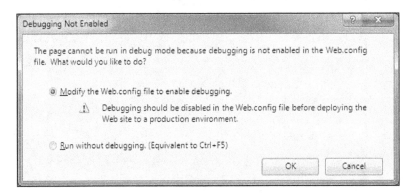

4. Then add `Home/Product` to the end of the URL. Your URL should look something like this: `http://localhost:63241/Home/Product`.

The port number in your URL is most likely different from the one you see here, as they are dynamically generated by default.

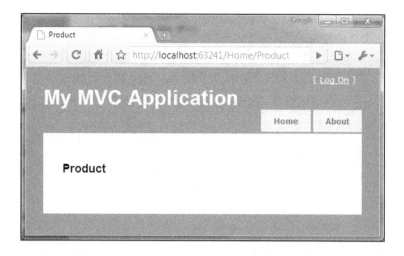

5. Now let's quickly wire up a product and throw it out to the view. To start, you can close the browser window. Click on the square icon in Visual Studio to stop the debugging process. Then go back to your home controller and `Product` action. Add these `using` statements to the top of your `HomeController.cs` file.

Controllers/HomeController.cs:

```
using FizzWare.NBuilder;
using WorkingWithTheView.Models ; WorkingWithTheView.Models;
```

6. Then in your `Product` action you can add this line.

Controllers/HomeController.cs:

```
public ActionResult Product()
{
    ViewData["ProductName"] = Builder<Product>
        .CreateNew()
        .Build()
        .ProductName;
    return View();
}
```

7. With this code in place you can now switch to your `Views/Home/Product.aspx` file. In here, all you need to do is render the `ProductName` to the view. Add this code to your view.

Views/Home/Product.aspx:

```
. . .
 <h2>Product</h2>
  <%= ViewData["ProductName"] %>
. . .
```

8. Now you should be able to hit *F5* again and see the generated product name rendered in the view.

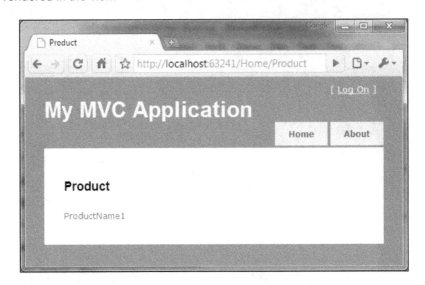

How it works...

In this recipe, we created a `Product` view that renders a `Products` name. This was done by adding a new product view file to the `Views/Home` folder. We then added a corresponding `Product` action to the Home controller. The MVC framework automatically maps any requests to `/Home/Product` to a `Product` action on the Home controller, which then routes the user to a `Product` view if no other view is specified. With that completed, we used NBuilder to generate an instance of a `Product`. The `Name` property of this `Product` instance is used to populate the `ViewData` dictionary. The `ViewData` dictionary is provided by the MVC framework as a mechanism to pass data from the controller down to the view. In the view, we were then able to access the data and render it in one fell swoop by using the shorthand for `Response.Write <%= %>`.

There's more...

In the beginning of this section, I had mentioned that we would use *magic strings* and `ViewData` to shuttle data from the controller to the view. As we saw earlier, the `ViewData` dictionary is a collection that is used as a sort of data-transfer object to shuttle data between an action in a controller down to the view. However, you may still be wondering what a magic string is. A magic string is not really magic. This is more a name that says by using this string (ProductName, for example) I expect you to go off and figure out what I really want. This is not magical in any way.

And this is where the fragility part of the conversation comes into play. If you reference something like `Product.ProductName` in all sorts of `ViewData` dictionary calls, you will find that everything works magically as expected. But then one day you will need to use a cool tool such as *ReSharper* to refactor `Product.ProductName` to just `Product.Name`. Refactoring tools don't always parse magic strings (though some do). While the tool that you used to refactor the `ProductName` property to just `Name` will pick up all strongly typed instances of that property, it may not find the magic strings. This will effectively break your code in such a way that you might end up with a handful of runtime errors that can be quite difficult to locate. We will cover the solution to this problem in the *Creating a strongly typed view* recipe.

See also

▶ *The recipe, Creating a strongly typed view, explains how to create a strongly typed view.*

Creating a strongly typed view

Now that we have looked at how to pass data around in your view using the `ViewData` dictionary, we can take a look at how to pass data around without the `ViewData` dictionary. Specifically, we want to take a look at how to do this using a strongly typed view.

Getting ready

This recipe will use the `Product` class that we created in the last recipe. It will also use NBuilder to generate `Product` data in the same way that we did earlier. You can copy the last project over for this recipe and build from where you left off in the last recipe (or start a new project and grab what you need from the previous recipe as we go).

How to do it...

1. The first thing that we need to do is open the `Views/Home` folder and then open the `Product.aspx` file.

2. Now we will modify the `Inherits` page attribute. We need to change our view so that it inherits from `System.Web.Mvc.ViewPage<Product>`. By doing this we are telling the view that it will be working with an instance of `Product`. In order for us to gain access to this `Product` instance, the MVC framework will provide us with a `Model` property that exposes the `Product` instance, which is passed down to the view by the controller.

   Views/Home/Product.aspx:
   ```
   <%@ Page Title="" Language="C#"
    MasterPageFile="~/Views/Shared/Site.Master"
    Inherits="System.Web.Mvc.ViewPage<Product>" %>
   <%@ Import Namespace="{project name}.Models" %>
   ```

Also notice that the previous listing has an `Import` statement to reference our `Product` class.

3. Now you can go to your `HomeController`. In the `Product` action we will change from passing a `Product` instance into `ViewData` and the `ViewData` out to the view. Instead, we will just pass that `Product` instance directly to the view. Do this by creating a `Product` variable (p) and remove the property reference to `ProductName`.

Controllers/HomeController.cs:

```
public ActionResult Product()
{
    Product p = Builder<Product>
        .CreateNew()
        .Build();
        //remove the reference to the ProductName here!

    return View(p);
}
```

4. With that completed, you can switch back to your `Product.aspx` view. We now need to change the way we refer to the data that is passed to the view by the controller. Instead of using the built-in `ViewData` dictionary directly, we will now reference the `Model` property that is exposed by a strongly typed view.

Views/Home/Product.aspx:

```
<h2>Product</h2>
<%= Model.ProductName %>
```

When typing this you should now have full blown IntelliSense to the specified `Model` of your strongly typed view.

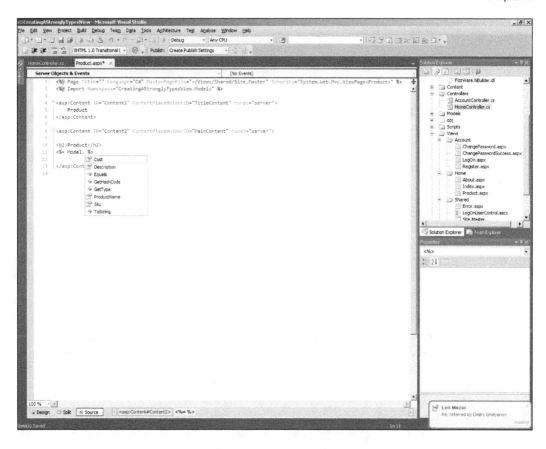

5. You should now be able to hit _F5_ and build and run your site. It should look identical to the previous recipe.

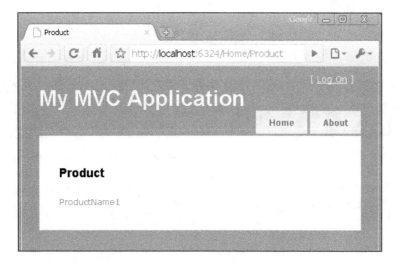

How it works...

What we did here was to remove our dependence on magic strings. We told the view to expect a `Product` to be passed in by inheriting from generic `ViewPage` of type `Product`. This doesn't mean that the `ViewData` will stop working. It can still be used. However, not only do you have IntelliSense, you now also have strongly typed code that can be refactored without worry.

There's more...

Now, while this is better than the first recipe where we used the `ViewData` dictionary to pass data around, this method still has some issues. In this case, we have a strongly typed reference to our domain model. This means that when our domain model changes by way of a good refactoring, our view will also need to change. This sounds like a good thing at first pass. However, this should scream to you: "Houston, we have a problem!". Our View should not know so much about our domain model that a small change in our object structure somehow forces our presentation layer to also undergo a code refactor.

There is another reason that using our domain directly from the model isn't that great. The view's Model can only be one object referenced by the generic type passed into the view base class from which the view is inheriting. If you want to expand your current view from showing just one product to showing the product, the category that the product is in, and the user that is currently logged in, you can't (or shouldn't) pass that data through your `Product` class. For these reasons, we will take a look at yet another way to pass data down to our view that will allow us to be strongly typed, easily refactorable, and allow our presentation layer (the view) to be fairly decoupled from our application layer. And the view model method will also allow us to move more than one type of data out to our view.

See also

- ▶ *Using magic strings and the ViewData dictionary*
- ▶ *Decoupling a strongly typed view with a View Model*

Decoupling a strongly typed view with a View model

Now that we have seen how to work with the `ViewData` dictionary and strongly typed views and have learned the shortcomings of each method, let's take a look at another approach. We will now use what is called a view model to pass our data from our controller to our view.

Getting ready

This recipe will build on the code from the last recipe. In this case, we will use the `Product` class, as well as NBuilder, to generate some `Product` data for us. In this recipe, we also want to pass a `Category` object to our view. To do this, we will need to add one more layer of abstraction between our business layer (currently our controller) and the presentation layer (the view) using a new view model class that can hold the current `Category` and a `Product` from that `Category`.

How to do it...

1. The first thing we are going to do is create a simple `Category` class in the `Models` directory.

   Models/Category.cs:

   ```
   public class Category
   {
     public string Name { get; set; }
     public int Id { get; set; }
   }
   ```

2. Next we need to create a view model. Generally, a view model is named for the view that uses it. In this case, we will be passing the view model out to our `Product` view, so we will call this view model the `ProductView` (or we can call it `ProductViewModel`). It will be responsible for carrying our `Product` and `Category` objects. Create a new `ProductView` class in the `Models` directory.

   Models/ProductView.cs:

   ```
   public class ProductView
   {
     public Product CurrentProduct { get; set; }
     public Category CurrentCategory { get; set; }
   }
   ```

3. With these two new classes created, we can open up our `Product.aspx` view page. We need to update it so that the view page inherits from the `System.Web.Mvc.ViewPage<ProductView>`.

   Views/Home/Product.aspx:

   ```
   <%@ Page Title="" Language="C#"
    MasterPageFile="~/Views/Shared/Site.Master"
    Inherits="System.Web.Mvc.ViewPage<ProductView>" %>
   <%@ Import Namespace="{project name}.Models" %>
   ```

4. Next, we need to update our `Product.aspx` view so that, instead of trying to display the `ProductName` directly off of the view's Model, we instead call the `Product` class in the Model and then the `ProductName`. Then we can output the current category's name too.

Views/Home/Product.aspx:

```
<h2><%= Model.CurrentCategory.Name %></h2>
<%= Model.CurrentProduct.ProductName %>
```

5. Finally, we need to wire up the data that will be passed from our `HomeController` to our view. Do this by opening up the `HomeController.cs` file. Then add code to instantiate a new `Category`. After this, add the new `Category` and `Product` to a new instance of a `ProductView` object and return that `ProductView` instance to the view.

Controllers/HomeController.cs:

```
public ActionResult Product()
{
    Product p = Builder<Product>
        .CreateNew()
        .Build();

    Category c = Builder<Category>
        .CreateNew()
        .Build();

    ProductView pv = new ProductView();
    pv.CurrentCategory = c;
    pv.CurrentProduct = p;

    return View(pv);
}
```

6. Now you can hit *F5* and see your site open up and display the current category and current product.

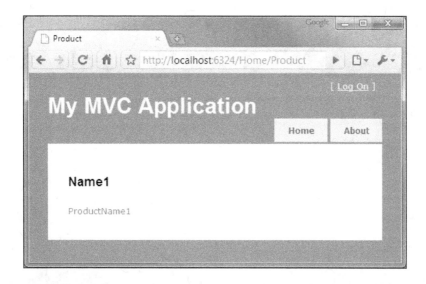

How it works...

This recipe wasn't so much about how something specifically worked, but more about explaining a specific design pattern that allows you to decouple your presentation layer away from knowing too much about your domain. Generally speaking, I would pass only view-specific objects to my view. For the most part, there is never a need for the view to know everything about a specific domain object.

Take a real life product for example; it would have name, price, and description—sure. Those are normal properties to expose to the view. But your business layer would also need to know the product's cost, weight, vendor, amount in stock, and so on. None of this information ever needs to make it out to your public site.

Also, if the view knows too much about specific domain knowledge, you will run into an issue—in that when you go to refactor your domain, you will be required to update any code referencing it. Generally speaking, you don't want information to leak across your layers (separation of concerns).

There's more...

`ViewModel` is not really a new pattern. You may have also heard of a **Data Transfer Object** or **DTO**. The idea of a DTO object's purpose in life is to shuttle data from one layer to another. Think of this as a contract between two layers. As long as the contract doesn't need to change, code in a specific layer can be refactored all day long with limited ripple effect throughout your code.

Centralizing display logic with templated helpers

In this recipe, we are going to look at how we can get some reuse out of our display code by using templated helpers.

Getting ready

To continue our e-commerce example, we are going to look at how to control the format of bits of our `Product` class from the previous recipe. Specifically, we will take a look at how to centralize the display of our product's cost.

How to do it...

1. First, we need to go into the `Views/Home` folder and create a new folder called `DisplayTemplates`.

2. Next, we need to create a partial view that will hold the display logic for the product's `cost` property. Right-click on the `DisplayTemplates` folder in the `Views/Home` folder and select **Add View**.

3. Name your view `Product.Cost` and then select the **Create a partial view (.ascx)** checkbox.

 You can call this control whatever you like. You will reference the name you choose directly in an upcoming step.

4. Now open up your new partial view and add some code to format the cost of a product (a `Double`). The Model reference in this code will be whatever value you feed this snippet later.

   Views/Home/DisplayTemplates/Product.Cost.ascx:
   ```
   <%@ Control Language="C#"
     Inherits="System.Web.Mvc.ViewUserControl" %>
   <%= String.Format("{0:C}", Model)%>
   ```

5. Now open up your `Product.aspx` view page. Under the place where the `ProductName` is currently displayed, we will display the `Cost` property and specify with a hint which template we want to use.

   Views/Home/Product.aspx:
   ```
   <h2><%= Model.CurrentCategory.Name %></h2>
   <%= Model.CurrentProduct.ProductName %>
   <%= Html.DisplayFor(Double=>Model.CurrentProduct.Cost,
       "Product.Cost") %>
   ```

6. Hit *F5* and see your `cost` property formatted appropriately!

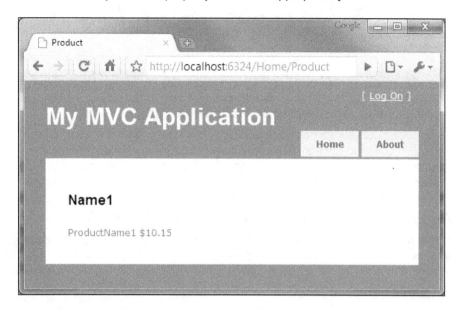

How it works...

The rendering engine noticed your hint of `Product.Cost`. It then looked in the `DisplayTemplates` folder to see if there were any templates with the same name as the `Product.Cost` hint. When it found the `Product.Cost.ascx` partial view, the call to `Html.DisplayFor` used the partial view to render the property.

Notice that in the `DisplayFor` method we used a *lambda* expression to pass only the `Cost` property (a `Double`) to the partial view. This is the only sticky part of how these templates work. The caller needs to know what the partial view expects.

There's more...

There are a few other things to know about templated helpers. Rather than using hints to specify how you want to render things, you could instead build templates based purely on data types. Also, you don't have to put the `DisplayTemplates` folder in the `Home` view subdirectory. You could instead create a template for usage by a view in any of the view folders. And if you did want to use hints but didn't want to specify them in the presentation code, that can be done too!

Type-specific templated helpers

Templated helpers, by default, can be based on the data type that is passed into the `Html.DisplayFor` method. If you were to create a `Double.ascx` partial view and place it in the `DisplayTemplates` folder and you then passed in the `Cost` property to the `DisplayFor` method, it would have worked just as well. Expand this thought to creating a template for the `Product` type and this can quickly simplify the creation of a website!

Where to put the DisplayTemplates folder?

The `DisplayTemplates` folder can be in both a specific view folder or in the shared folder. The `DisplayFor` method will first look in the current controller's corresponding view folder for any appropriate `DisplayTemplates` folder. If it doesn't find an appropriate partial view for the current rendering, it will look to the shared folder for an appropriate display template.

DataAnnotations on your model to specify UIHints

To utilize this method, the mechanics of using the `Html.DisplayFor` and the creation of the partial view in a `DisplayTemplates` folder are identical as mentioned earlier. The only thing different here is that you would specify a `UIHint` attribute on the `Product` class like this:

```
[UIHint("Product.Cost")]
public Double Cost { get; set; }
```

I am not a big fan of this particular method though; I think that it puts concerns in the wrong places (formatting code shouldn't be specified with your business objects). You could use this method on your `ViewModel` though, depending on where you specify it.

Using a partial view to segment view code

Oftentimes, you will encounter a scenario where your view starts to get a bit overwhelming. This might happen in the case of a shopping cart where you are displaying the items in a customer's cart, along with suggested products, products from their wish list, and various other items pertaining to a customer's order. In order to simplify a complex view of this nature, you might choose to put individual concerns of the larger view into separate partial views to keep the code of your view segments nice and small. You can then reassemble the partial views into one complex view.

How to do it...

1. Start by creating a new MVC application.
2. Then we will create a quick (simple) object model that will contain a `Cart`, `Address`, `Product`, `Account`, `OrderHeader`, and `LineItem`, which we will use to populate a cart display page.

Models/Cart.cs:

```
public class Cart
{
  public OrderHeader Header { get; set; }
  public List<LineItem> Items { get; set; }
  public double Total
  {
      get { return Items.Sum(i => i.SubTotal); }
  }
}
```

Models/Address.cs:

```
public class Address
{
  public string Street1 { get; set; }
  public string Street2 { get; set; }
  public string City { get; set; }
  public int Zip { get; set; }
  public string State { get; set; }
}
```

Models/Product.cs:

```
public class Product
{
  public double Price { get; set; }
  public string Name { get; set; }
  public double Tax { get; set; }
}
```

Models/Account.cs:

```
public class Account
{
  public string Username { get; set; }
  public string Email { get; set; }
  public string FirstName { get; set; }
  public string LastName { get; set; }
}
```

Models/OrderHeader.cs:

```
public class OrderHeader
{
  public Account Account { get; set; }
  public Address Billing { get; set; }
  public Address Shipping { get; set; }
}
```

Models/LineItem.cs:

```
public class LineItem
{
  public Product Product { get; set; }
  public int Quantity { get; set; }
  public double SubTotal
  {
    get
    {
      return ((Product.Price * Product.Tax) + Product.Price) *
        Quantity;
    }
  }
}
```

3. With this model created, we are now ready to create some fake data. We will do this by creating a `CartFactory` class, which we will use to generate the data and create a fully populated instance of our `Cart` object. We will create a `GetCart` method where we will create an instance of all the classes that we need to display in our cart.

Models/CartFactory.cs:

```
public Cart GetCart()
{
  Cart c = new Cart();
  c.Header = new OrderHeader();

  c.Header.Account = new Account()
  {
     Email = "asiemer@hotmail.com",
     FirstName = "Andrew",
     LastName = "Siemer",
     Username = "asiemer"
  };

  c.Header.Billing = new Address()
  {
     City = "Lancaster",
     State = "CA",
     Street1 = "Some Street",
     Street2 = "Apt 2",
     Zip = 93536
  };

  c.Header.Shipping = new Address()
  {
```

```
        City = "Fresno",
        State = "CA",
        Street1 = "This street",
        Street2 = "Front step",
        Zip = 93536
    };

    List<LineItem> items = new List<LineItem>();
    for (int i = 0; i < 10; i++)
    {
      Product p = new Product();
      p.Name = "Product " + i;
      p.Price = 2*i;
      p.Tax = .0875;

      LineItem li = new LineItem();
      li.Product = p;
      li.Quantity = i;

      items.Add(li);
    }

    c.Items = items;

    return c;
}
```

4. Now that we have our model and a factory class to generate the data that we need, we are ready to start creating the partial views we need. While we could manually create views for each of our objects, there is a much quicker way—we can create actions in our `HomeController` that returns an instance of an object from which we can generate a View. By doing this, we can quickly generate the markup that is required to display each of our `Cart` classes. To do this, open up the `HomeController` and add an `Address()` `ActionResult`. In this method, we will return a new instance of `Address`.

Controllers/HomeController.cs:

```
public ActionResult Address()
{
  return View(new Address());
}
```

5. Then we can generate a new partial `Address` details view that is strongly typed, based on the `Address` model.

Views/Home/Address.ascx:

```
<fieldset>
   <legend><%: ViewData["AddressType"] %></legend>

   <div class="display-label">Street1</div>
   <div class="display-field"><%: Model.Street1 %></div>

   <div class="display-label">Street2</div>
   <div class="display-field"><%: Model.Street2 %></div>

   <div class="display-label">City</div>
   <div class="display-field"><%: Model.City %></div>

   <div class="display-label">State</div>
   <div class="display-field"><%: Model.State %></div>

   <div class="display-label">Zip</div>
   <div class="display-field"><%: Model.Zip %></div>

</fieldset>
```

6. Now we can do the same thing for a list of `Cart` items. We will add an action called `Items` in the `HomeController` that returns a `List<LineItem>`.

Controllers/HomeController.cs:

```
public ActionResult Items()
{
   return View(new List<LineItem>());
}
```

7. Then we can generate another strongly typed partial view called `Items` that will be based on an enumerable list of `LineItem`. We will also add a couple of columns to the generated view to display the name and price.

Views/Home/Items.aspx:

```
<table style="width:600px;">
   <tr>
      <th></th>
      <th>
         Name
      </th>
      <th>
         Price
```

```
        </th>
        <th>
            Quantity
        </th>
        <th>
            Sub Total
        </th>
    </tr>

    <% foreach (var item in Model) { %>

    <tr>
      <td>
        Delete
      </td>
      <td>
         <%: item.Product.Name %>
      </td>
      <td>
         <%: String.Format("{0:C}", item.Product.Price) %>
      </td>
      <td>
         <%: item.Quantity %>
      </td>
      <td>
         <%: String.Format("{0:C}", item.SubTotal) %>
      </td>
    </tr>

    <% } %>
    </table>
```

8. With our partial views created and the ability to get a populated `Cart` class, we are now ready to display our shopping cart and all of its complexity. We will start by adding another `ActionResult` called `DisplayCart`. This result will return a new instance of a `Cart`, which we will get from our CartFactory class that we created earlier.

   Controllers/HomeController.cs:

```
public ActionResult DisplayCart()
{
  Cart c = new CartFactory().GetCart();

  return View(c);
}
```

9. Then we can generate a strongly typed empty view called `DisplayCart`. Inside of this view we will display the user's first and last name, as well as their e-mail address. We will then load the `Address` partial view and pass in the `billing` address. Next we will load the `Address` partial view and pass in the shipping address. The last view we will load is the `Items` partial view, which we will pass in the collection of `LineItems`. At the end of this view, we will display the total cost of the shopping cart.

Views/Home/DisplayCart.aspx:

```
<h2>Display Cart</h2>

<div>
  <%: Model.Header.Account.FirstName %>
  <%: Model.Header.Account.LastName %><br />
  <%: Model.Header.Account.Email %>
</div><br />
<table style="width:600px">
  <tr>
    <td>
      <% Html.RenderPartial("Address", Model.Header.Billing,
         new ViewDataDictionary() {new KeyValuePair<string,
         object>("AddressType", "Billing")}); %>
    </td>
    <td>
      <% Html.RenderPartial("Address", Model.Header.Shipping,
         new ViewDataDictionary() {new KeyValuePair<string,
         object>("AddressType", "Shipping")}); %>
    </td>
  </tr>
</table>

<% Html.RenderPartial("Items", Model.Items); %>

<br />
<div>
  <b>Total:</b> <%: String.Format("{0:C}", Model.Total ) %>
<div>
```

10. You are now ready to run the application. You can then navigate to the `/Home/DisplayCart` view, where you should see something of this nature:

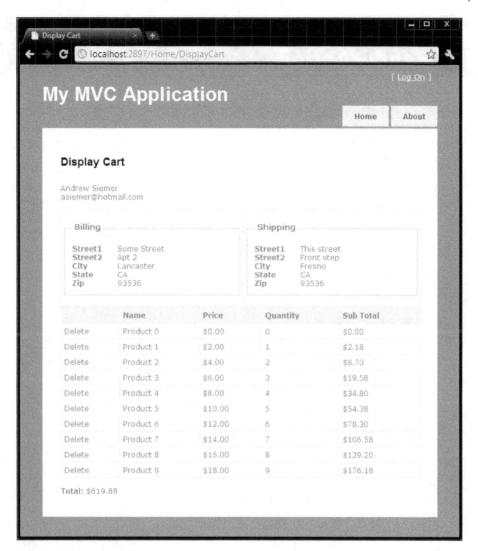

How it works...

While this recipe appears to be complex at first, it really isn't. I had to create some complexity to be able to appropriately demonstrate how and why we would use the RenderPartial method. As you can see, moving the complexity of our display logic into partial views not only allows us to reduce the amount of code we maintain in one file, but it also provides us with the opportunity to reuse our code (as seen by using the Address partial view for two different address instances).

Rendering a child view with Html.RenderAction

In the previous recipe, we took a look at how you can split up the view code into multiple partial views to make managing presentation code easier and more reusable. In most cases, this is exactly what you will need, as a view usually has a view model that is specially built just for it. In our previous recipe, we took pieces of the overall view's model and pushed bits of it off to the partial views.

In other cases though you may have totally separate models that are displayed by separate views. Sometimes they may even be handled by different actions in different controllers. In this case, you might try to render an action directly and put the result of that view into another view. In this way, we won't have to worry about cross-pollinating models and views from various controllers.

How to do it...

1. Create a new MVC application.
2. Then we will create a quick model to play with. We need two distinctly different models to be able to demonstrate why we would need to render one action from within another. We will create a `Post` class to represent some blog posts. And we will create a `Product` class to represent a list of suggested products, which we will display next to our blog posts.

Models/Post.cs:

```
public class Post
{
  public DateTime Created { get; set; }
  public string Title { get; set; }
  public string Body { get; set; }
}
```

Models/Product.cs:

```
public class Product
{
  public string Name { get; set; }
  public string Description { get; set; }
  public double Cost { get; set; }
}
```

3. Then we need to create a couple of service classes from which we will generate a list of our new object models. We will create a `ProductService` class and a `BlogService` class. Each of these classes will have `Get` methods on them to get a list of the specific objects we need.

Models/BlogService.cs:

```
public class BlogService
{
  public List<Post> GetPosts(int count)
  {
    List<Post> result = new List<Post>();

    for (int i = 0; i < count; i++)
    {
      Post p = new Post();
      p.Created = DateTime.Now;
      p.Title = "A really great post";
      p.Body = @"Lorem ipsum dolor sit amet, ...";

      result.Add(p);
    }

    return result;
  }
}
```

Models/ProductService.cs:

```
public class ProductService
{
  public List<Product> GetProducts(int count)
  {
    List<Product> result = new List<Product>();
    Random r = new Random();
    for (int i = 0; i < count; i++)
    {
      Product p = new Product();
      p.Cost = r.Next(5, 50);
      p.Name = "Really great product";
      p.Description = @"Lorem ipsum ...";

      result.Add(p);
    }

    return result;
  }
}
```

4. Now that we have the ability to generate a list of working data, we can next turn our attention to creating two controllers to handle views for each of our two object types. We will create a `BlogController` and a `ProductController`. The `BlogController` will expose an `Index` action to show a list of recent blog posts. The `ProductController` will have a `SuggestedProducts` action that will return a list of products.

Models/BlogController.cs:

```
public class BlogController : Controller
{
  public ActionResult Index()
  {
    return View(new BlogService().GetPosts(5));
  }
}
```

Models/ProductController.cs:

```
public class ProductController : Controller
{
  public ActionResult SuggestedProducts()
  {
    return View(new ProductService().GetProducts(7));
  }
}
```

5. The next thing for us to do is to generate a view for each of our controllers. We will start with the `ProductController`, as its view is the easiest. For this controller, we will generate a strongly typed partial view based on a `Product` using the details view. Once the view is generated, we have to change the model from a single instance of `Product` to a List of `Product`. Then we need to wrap the details view that was generated with a loop.

Views/Product/SuggestedProducts.aspx:

```
<%@ Page Title="" Language="C#" Inherits=
  "System.Web.Mvc.ViewPage<List<MvcApplication1.Models.Product>>"
%>
<%@ Import Namespace="MvcApplication1.Models" %>

<fieldset>
  <legend>Suggested Products</legend>
   <% foreach (Product p in Model) { %>
  <div class="display-field"><b><%: p.Name%></b></div>

  <div class="display-field">
    <i><%: String.Format("{0:C}", p.Cost)%></i>
  </div>
```

```
<div class="display-field"><%: p.Description%></div>

    <% } %>

</fieldset>
```

6. Now we need to generate our primary view, which will be responsible for showing a list of blog posts. In addition to displaying blog posts, we will also render the list of suggested products. Similar to our previous view, we will start by generating the view from the `Index` action of the `BlogController`. This will be a strongly typed details view based on the `Post` class. Once it is generated, we will need to wrap the generated view code with a table so that the list of blog posts can sit next to a list of suggested products. I also added a bit of styling to get things to line up a bit better.

Views/Blog/Index.aspx:

```
<h2>My Blog</h2>

<table style="width:800px;">
  <tr>
   <td style="width:200px;vertical-align:top;">
      <!-- Suggested products... -->
   </td>
   <td style="vertical-align:top;">
     <fieldset>
       <legend>Recent Posts</legend>
       <%
         foreach (Post p in Model)
         { %>

         <div class="display-field"><b><%: p.Title%></b></div>

         <div class="display-field"><i>
         <%: String.Format("{0:g}", p.Created)%></i></div>

         <div class="display-field"><%= p.Body%></div>
         <% } %>
     </fieldset>
   </td>
  </tr>
</table>
```

7. Now that we have our primary view created, we can turn our attention to rendering a list of suggested products. All that we need to do is add a call to `Html.RenderAction` where we currently have this comment `<!-- Suggested products...-->`. In order to make this call, we only need to specify the name of the action and the controller that we want to render.

 If, while rendering this recipe, you see two master pages, then the odds are that you didn't generate a partial view for your `SuggestedProducts` view!

Views/Blog/Index.aspx:

```
...
<td style="width:200px;vertical-align:top;">
    <% Html.RenderAction("SuggestedProducts", "Product"); %>
</td>
...
```

8. Now you can run the application. Navigate to `/Blog/Index` and you should see a list of blog posts. Next to that you should also see a list of suggested products. Notice that our blog controller didn't have to know anything about products in order for it to use the `SuggestedProducts` view. This is the power of the `RenderAction` helper method.

How it works...

In this recipe, we saw how we can separate the logic that views require into multiple controllers while still being able to use those views together. This functionality is built into the MVC framework and exposed through the `HtmlHelper` class.

There's more...

Be aware that using this method has one gotcha. If you want to use output caching on the rendered view—don't. It won't work (at the time of this writing). You can put an `OutputCache` attribute on the `SuggestedProducts` view, but when you render the `SuggestedProducts` partial view from within the product's Index, the `OutputCache` attribute is simply ignored from the parent view. Check out the chapter on caching and you will find a workaround to this issue!

Loading a view template from a database with NVelocity

In this recipe, we will take a look at a different view engine for the ASP.NET MVC framework called NVelocity. **NVelocity** is a very stable templating engine that has been around longer than the MVC framework has. It plugs into, and works quite nicely with, the ASP.NET MVC framework (as we will see). In this particular recipe, we will use NVelocity in a slightly different manner than just wiring in a different view engine. We will use NVelocity to render views directly from a database. This gives us templating abilities for rendering dynamic views, but this could also be used to render the contents of an e-mail, or any other template-driven blob of text.

Getting ready

As in the other recipes, we will start off with the `ViewModel` recipe, discussed earlier. Next, we need to grab a copy of the NVelocity library at `http://www.castleproject.org/castle/projects.html`. (I also put the library in the dependencies folder). You will need to have SQL Server Express installed to follow along with this recipe.

How to do it...

1. The first step to this project could be a number of things! Let's get started by adding a reference to the NVelocity library (`NVelocity.dll`) in the dependencies folder.

2. Next we need to set up a quick database to use in the steps ahead. Do this by right-clicking on the `App_Data` folder in your project and select **Add a new item**. Choose a SQL Server database. I named my database `Templates`.

3. Now in your Server Explorer window you should see under the **Data Connections** section a `Templates.mdf` entry. Expand that entry. Right-click on the `tables` folder and add a new table.

   ❑ Set the first column of this table, to be called `TemplateID`, with a data type of `int`. Set this column to be a primary key (by clicking on the key icon above). And then set the identity specification (**Is Identity**) to be **Yes**.

   ❑ Then add another column, called **TemplateContent**, with a data type of `VarChar(MAX)`.

   ❑ Add one more column called **ViewName**. This will be a `VarChar(100)` field. Save this table and call it `Templates`.

4. Then we will add LINQ to SQL to our project. Do this by right-clicking on the `Models` folder and select **Add new item**. Select the **LINQ to SQL Classes** entry and name it `Template.dbml`.

5. When the design surface opens, drag your `Template` table from the server explorer onto the design surface. Save that file and close it. Then build your project (this builds the `TemplateDataContext` class for you, which we will need in the following steps).

6. Right-click on the `Templates.mdf` entry in the server explorer and select **Properties**. In the **Properties** window, select and copy the entire connection string entry. It should look something like this:

```
Data Source=.\SQLEXPRESS;AttachDbFilename={driveLetter}:\
{pathToFile}\Templates.mdf;Integrated Security=True;User
Instance=True
```

7. Now create a new class in the `Models` directory called `TemplateRepository.cs`. In this class, we will create a method called `GetTemplateByViewName`, which will be responsible for getting a template from the database by the template's name.

Models/TemplateRepository.cs:

```
public class TemplateRepository
{
  public string GetTemplateByViewName(string ViewName)
  {
    string connectionString =
    @"Data Source=.\SQLEXPRESS;AttachDbFilename=
      {FilePathToDataBase}\Templates.mdf;Integrated Security=
        True;User Instance=True";

    string result = "";

    using(TemplateDataContext dc = new
      TemplateDataContext(connectionString))
    {
      Template template = (from t in dc.Templates
        where t.ViewName == ViewName select t).FirstOrDefault();
```

```
        result = template != null ? template.TemplateContent
             : "The requested template was not found for view " +
             ViewName;
    }

    return result;
  }
}
```

8. Now we can create a class that will work with NVelocity to parse our template. Right-click on the `Models` folder and add a new class called `TemplateService.cs`. This class will have a method called `ParseTemplateByViewName`. This method will be responsible for interacting with the NVelocity view engine to parse a passed in template.

    Models/TemplateService.cs:

```
public class TemplateService
{
  public string ParseTemplateByViewName(string template,
    Dictionary<string,object> viewParams)
  {
    VelocityContext vc = new VelocityContext();
    foreach (var v in viewParams)
    {
      vc.Put(v.Key, v.Value);
    }

    //create the engine
    VelocityEngine ve = new VelocityEngine();
    ve.Init();

    //the output stream
    StringBuilder sb = new StringBuilder();
    StringWriter sw = new StringWriter(sb);

    //merge the template
    ve.Evaluate(vc, sw, string.Empty, template);

    return sb.ToString();
  }
}
```

9. Now we need to add some code to our `HomeController`. Let's start by creating a new action called `AnotherProduct()`. Inside this action, we will still utilize the creation of a `Product` and a `Category`. And we will use our `ViewModel` as our transport object, which will carry the `Product` and `Category` instance for us. Then we need to create a dictionary that will take the variables we used in the parsing of our template. Lastly, we will call our `TemplateService` to parse out the template that the `TemplateRepository` locates for us.

Controllers/HomeController.cs:

```csharp
public ActionResult AnotherProduct()
{
    Product p = Builder<Product>
      .CreateNew()
      .Build();

    Category c = Builder<Category>
      .CreateNew()
      .Build();

    ProductView pv = new ProductView();
    pv.CurrentCategory = c;
    pv.CurrentProduct = p;

    //define the variable context
    Dictionary<string, object> variableParams = new
      Dictionary<string,object>();
    variableParams.Add("ProductView", pv);

    ViewData["content"] = new TemplateService()
      .ParseTemplateByViewName(new
      TemplateRepository().GetTemplateByViewName("AnotherProduct"),
      variableParams);

    return View();
}
```

10. Then you can create the `AnotherView` view. This will be an empty view that simply renders the content from within `ViewData`.

Views/Home/AnotherProduct.aspx:

```
<%@ Page Language="C#" Inherits="System.Web.Mvc.ViewPage" %>
<%= ViewData["content"] %>
```

11. Lastly, before anything will actually come together, we need to add an entry into our database. The `TemplateContent` entry will look like this:

```
<html><head><title>$ProductView.CurrentProduct.ProductName</
title></head><body><h2>$ProductView.CurrentProduct.ProductName</
h2>Hello world from an NVelocity template!</body></html>
```

The `ViewName` will be `AnotherProduct` to match our `AnotherProduct` action.

12. Now you can start debugging by hitting *F5* and see the results of our database-driven view.

How it works...

This is a simple modification to the way that NVelocity would normally work. In most cases, you would store your NVelocity templates on the file system or in the resource files. These are then read by a file-based template reader and parsed similarly to the fashion defined earlier. All that we did differently was grabbed our content from the database.

We have still piggybacked our implementation of NVelocity on top of the MVC framework and most importantly on top of the WebForms view engine. This means that we could use regular views for most of our pages, while templates from the database could be scattered about where we may want to have user-generated or easily administered content.

There's more...

Some people might complain about the choice to piggyback the NVelocity view engine on the back of the MVC framework and the WebForms view engine. However, think of the flexibility that you would have with this option when pulling your dynamic-view content from the database.

By using the WebForm's view engine on top of the MVC framework, you get all sorts of built-in features such as a master page, templated helpers, scaffolding support, and so on. Using the NVelocity engine you can then define the remainder of your content from the database. This means that rather than having a statically defined `Product` partial view that all of the products in your shopping cart catalog use, you could instead have a different `Product` layout for every product. Expand this thought a bit further so that you could call and parse many templates from the database for one view, allowing you to define NVelocity partial templates, such as a common `Product` header and footer, attributes layout, and so on. And now that all of this layout logic is persisted to the database, it can all be edited from the Web.

 What about performance? In a site with heavy load, the odds are that you would cache your database calls, page compilations, and so on. Only the output would ever actually be hit by every visitor of your site. No worries!

Replacing the default MVC view engine with NVelocity

If you are interested in replacing the default view engine (WebForms view engine) with NVelocity, have a look at the MVC Contrib (`codeplex.com/MVCContrib`) project. The guys at Headspring (`headspringsystems.com`) currently have various classes created that will allow you to override the MVC framework to use NVelocity as the primary view engine in the `MvcContrib.ViewEngines.NVelocity.dll` (currently).

Want to load templates in other ways?

While researching this particular recipe, I came across all sorts of ways to work with NVelocity. One demo went that extra step to show multiple ways to load templates in a very clean fashion. I put this demo in the code directory (included with the source of this book). You can find the original posting here: `http://mihkeltt.blogspot.com/2009/12/nvelocity-template-engine-sample.html`.

Want to use more than one view engine?

Javier Lozano has been putting together a product called **MVC Turbine**. One of its goals is to allow you to host content from many view engines at once (among many other cool things). Take a look here for more on that topic: `lozanotek.com/blog/archive/2009/10/05/Multiple_View_Engines_with_MVC_Turbine.aspx`.

Consuming a JSON with jQuery

In this recipe, we will see how to consume JSON using jQuery. We will continue to use our `Product` and `Category` concepts to be displayed in our view. We will still depend on our `ProductView` view model object to pass data to our view (we will just be using JavaScript to do it this time).

Getting ready

We will be starting from our `ViewModel` recipe discussed earlier. But before we get to coding, we need to go grab a copy of jQuery (you may have a copy in the `Scripts` folder already), which you can get from here: `http://docs.jquery.com/Downloading_jQuery`. Then we need to grab a copy of JSON.NET to help us quickly serialize our C# objects. You can get a copy of this here: `json.codeplex.com/releases/view/37810`.

> This recipe uses JSON.NET as it is a quick and easy way to generate JSON from your C# classes in any context. If for some reason you are not able to use JSON.NET, or prefer to stay away from open source, you can just as easily use the `JavaScriptSerializer` found in the .NET framework (`http://msdn.microsoft.com/en-us/library/system.web.script.serialization.javascriptserializer.aspx`) in an MVC project, you can simply use the `JsonResult` (covered in another recipe later) to serialize an instance of a class for you.

How to do it...

1. First, make sure you have a good copy of the JSON.NET libraries in the dependencies folder. Then add a reference to it from your project.

2. Then open up your `HomeController`. Add an action called `ProductJson`. This method will generate some JSON for you, using your existing `Product` and `Category` data. Then enter the following code (notice that this is almost identical to the previous recipes except for the highlighted `JsonConvert` call).

Controllers/HomeController.cs:

```
public ActionResult ProductJson()
{
  Product p = Builder<Product>
     .CreateNew()
     .Build();

  Category c = Builder<Category>
     .CreateNew()
     .Build();

  ProductView pv = new ProductView();
  pv.CurrentCategory = c;
  pv.CurrentProduct = p;

  ViewData["ProductView"] = JsonConvert.SerializeObject(pv);

  return View();
}
```

3. Now you need to add a new view in the `Views/Home` folder that this action will pass its data down to. Name this view `ProductJson.aspx` to correspond to the action that you just created.

4. Open up the new view and then add a call into the `ViewData` for the `ProductView` JSON that you just created.

Views/Home/ProductJson.aspx:

```
<%= ViewData["ProductView"] %>
```

5. Next you need to make sure that you have a reference to jQuery in your master page. Open the `Views/Site.Master` file. Then locate the `jquery script` file in the `Scripts` directory, and drag it into the head of your master page.

6. Now, focus on the rendering side of this problem. Open up the `Product.aspx` view—in there you will need to add a new `div` tag to output your JSON to. Then you will need to add some JavaScript to make a request for your `ProductView` JSON and output it to the `div` tag.

Views/Home/Product.aspx:

```
<asp:Content ID="Content2" ContentPlaceHolderID="MainContent"
    runat="server">
<div id="result"></div>
<script>
  $(document).ready(
    $.getJSON('http://localhost:6324/home/productjson',
            function (data) {
              $('#result').html('<p>' +
              data.CurrentProduct.ProductName + '</p>');
            }
        )
    );
</script>
</asp:Content>
```

7. Hit *F5* and see the result!

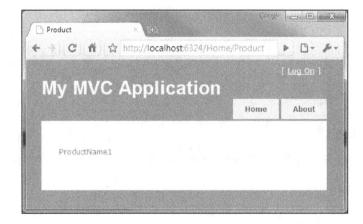

And if you navigate to /Home/ProductJson you should see the following.

{"CurrentProduct":{"Sku":"Sku1","ProductName":"ProductName1","Description":"Description1","Cost":1.0},"CurrentCategory":{"Name":"Name1","Id":1}}

How it works...

For the most part, the logic is the same as our other recipes, in that we used NBuilder to generate some fake data for us. Instead of passing that generated data directly down to our view though, we used some jQuery functions to request the data after the client's Product view page loaded. We used the getJSON method that takes the URL of the JSON and a callback method to perform operations on the result of the method call. In this case, our callback was defined directly in the initial function call.

We also used JSON.NET to help us with the serialization of our ProductView class. We will cover more of this when we discuss actions and controllers and how to expose JSON directly from the action itself.

There's more...

Obviously, this has quite a bit of power. The use of AJAX and jQuery in particular has reached out and touched just about every web application on the net in some way or the other. Using this method of data retrieval means that the pain of the post back and whole-page rendering doesn't need to be felt by the viewer nearly as often as before.

See Also

▶ Link to the _Taking Action in Your Controllers_ chapter for creating a JSON result

2
Taking Action in Your Controllers

In this chapter, we will cover:

- ▶ Exposing JSON using a JsonResult with Json.NET
- ▶ Creating custom action result to return an image
- ▶ Constraining an image's size from an ImageResult
- ▶ Creating a CAPTCHA system
- ▶ Generating a PDF order summary
- ▶ Implementing a controller factory for use with `StructureMap`

Introduction

This chapter is all about the **controller**—a very important ingredient to the Model View Controller recipe. In this chapter, we will take a look at a few things that can be done with actions and the controllers that host them. We will take a look at some flexibility that is now provided in .NET 4 with optional parameters. Next, we will create a custom action that exposes JSON. After that we will look at how to return image data from an action. With that under our belt, we will implement an action that not only returns an image, but is also able to constrain the sizes of that image. This will be followed by building an image-based CAPTCHA system. Next, we will implement an action that returns a PDF. And lastly, we will take a look at how to implement a controller factory for use with an **Inversion of Control (IoC)** product, such as `StructureMap`.

Exposing JSON using a JsonResult with Json.NET

In this recipe, we will take a look at the new `JsonResult` that comes with the MVC 2 framework.

Getting ready

We will use Json.NET (in the dependencies folder) to convert an object to JSON for us. And we will be using the `Product` class from the *Using magic strings and the ViewData dictionary* recipe of *Chapter 1*. We will also be using NBuilder (also in the dependencies folder) to hydrate a `Product` instance.

How to do it...

1. Start a new ASP.NET MVC application.

2. Add a reference to Json.NET.

3. Add a reference to NBuilder.

4. Create a new action named `GetJson` inside your HomeController. Instead of returning an `ActionResult`, we will specify that it will return a `JsonResult`.

   HomeController.cs:

   ```
   public JsonResult GetJson()
   {

   }
   ```

5. Add the `Product` class to your `Models` folder (or create a new `Product` class).

6. Make sure that the `Product` class is set to `[Serializable]`.

   Product.cs:

   ```
   using System;

   namespace ExposingJSONFromJsonResult.Models
   {
     [Serializable]
     public class Product
     {
       public string Sku { get; set; }
       public string ProductName { get; set; }
       public string Description { get; set; }
       public double Cost { get; set; }
     }
   }
   ```

7. Now we can specify our result by asking NBuilder to spit out an instance of `Product`. We can convert our `Product` object into JSON using a built-in method `Json`.

 When producing JSON in a `Get` method (as we are), you will also need to specify the `JsonRequestBehavior` to `AllowGet`. This is considered an XSS vulnerability though, so this is purely to render it in the browser as proof that it worked. Generally, you would want to use a `Post` method with something like jQuery to get your JSON payload off the server.

HomeController.cs:

```
public JsonResult GetJson()
{
    return Json(Builder<Product>.CreateNew().Build(),
        JsonRequestBehavior.AllowGet);
}
```

How it works...

Short of using NBuilder, we have utilized the power of the new MVC 2 framework to generate a JSON result for us. It even took care of the serialization for us.

There's more...

Be aware that exposing JSON via GET requests on your site potentially opens you up to cross-site scripting attacks. However, not allowing GET requests doesn't necessarily make you safe either—although it helps. Take a look at this discussion on **Stack Overflow** concerning this topic:`http://stackoverflow.com/questions/1625671/what-is-the-problem-with-a-get-json-request`.

See also

You might also be interested to know that there are the following other types of `ActionResult` classes:

- ► `ViewResult`
- ► `EmptyResult`
- ► `RedirectResult`
- ► `JavaScriptResult`
- ► `ContentResult`
- ► `FileContentResult`
- ► `FilePathResult`
- ► `FileStreamResult`

A custom ActionResult to return an image

I think the title pretty much sums this one up! In this recipe, we are going to implement our own custom `ActionResult`, whose sole purpose in life is to take a path to an image on the file system and render it to the web page directly. This is useful when you need to render images that are outside your website or when you want to control access to premium content that you would prefer not be leeched off your site.

There are many implementations to this recipe on the net. However, most of them involve a semi-messy approach requiring you to create a memory stream to your file, to determine the file's content type, and to access the code through some form of extension method. In this recipe, we will create a self-contained `ImageResult` that accepts the path to an image somewhere on the server, and then renders it directly.

Getting ready

To pull this recipe off you don't need anything special. It's all code!

How to do it...

1. To get started, we need to create a new ASP.NET MVC application.
2. In the `Models` folder, we create a new class named `ImageResult`.
3. Then we have our new `ImageResult` class inherit from `ActionResult`.
4. In order to implement `ActionResult`, we need to create a method named `ExecuteResult` that looks like this:

ImageResult.cs:

```
public override void ExecuteResult(ControllerContext context)
{

}
```

5. For our custom `ActionResult`, we need to be able to pass in the path to the image that we want to render. We will do this in the constructor of our class like this:

ImageResult.cs:

```
private string _path;

public ImageResult(string path)
{
  _path = path;
}
```

6. Now we are ready to create the guts of our `ImageResult`. To get started, we need to do some checking on some of our required bits. Because we expect to have an instance of the `ControllerContext` passed to us, we need to verify that it is not null. Also, we want to make sure that the path that was passed to us actually exists.

ImageResult.cs:

```csharp
public override void ExecuteResult(ControllerContext context)
{
  byte[] bytes;

  //no context? stop processing
  if (context == null)
     throw new ArgumentNullException("context");

  //check for file
  if(File.Exists(_path)) { bytes = File.ReadAllBytes(_path); }
  else { throw new FileNotFoundException(_path); }
```

7. Next, we need to determine the content type of the file that we intend to send down to the browser. We will do this in another method named `GetContentTypeFromFile`. In this method, we are simply getting the extension of the file that was passed in and then running it through a `switch` statement to make a best guess at the content type (supporting JPG and GIF at the moment).

ImageResult.cs:

```csharp
private string GetContentTypeFromFile()
{
  //get extension from path to determine contentType
  string[] parts = _path.Split('.');
  string extension = Path.GetExtension(_path).Substring(1);
  string contentType;

  switch (extension.ToLower())
  {
    case "jpeg":
    case "jpg":
    contentType = "image/jpeg";
    break;

    case "gif":
      contentType = "image/gif";
      break;
```

```
        default:
          throw new NotImplementedException(extension + "not handled");
      }

      return contentType;
    }
```

8. With this new method in place, we can then add an additional line to our
   `ExecuteResult` method where we set the result of `GetContentTypeFromFile`
   into a `String` variable.

   ImageResult.cs:

```
public override void ExecuteResult(ControllerContext context)
{
...
string contentType = GetContentTypeFromFile();
...
```

9. Next, we are going to set the `ContentType` of the response to the browser. We do
   this by getting a handle to the `HttpContext.Response` instance.

   ImageResult.cs:

```
public override void ExecuteResult(ControllerContext context)
{
    ...
    HttpResponseBase response = context.HttpContext.Response;
    response.ContentType = contentType;
```

10. Finally, we can wrap up this method by creating a `MemoryStream` from our file and
    then send it down to the client.

    ImageResult.cs:

```
MemoryStream imageStream = new MemoryStream(bytes);

    byte[] buffer = new byte[4096];

    while (true)
    {
        int read = imageStream.Read(buffer, 0, buffer.Length);

        if (read == 0)
            break;

        response.OutputStream.Write(buffer, 0, read);
    }
    response.End();
}
```

11. With our `ImageResult` completed, we can now turn our attention to the HomeController in our MVC application. Add a new `ActionResult` under the default "About action" of a new project (or wherever in your controller). This time, rather than specifying that the action will return an `ActionResult`, we want to specify that we plan to return an `ImageResult` and we will pass the path to our image to the constructor of our new `ImageResult`.

HomeController.cs:

```
public ImageResult GetImage()
{
    return new ImageResult(@"C:\{pathToImage}.jpg");
}
```

12. Hit *F5* and browse to your new action at `localhost:{port}/Home/GetImage`.

How it works...

We have basically used one of the many extensibility points in the MVC framework. In this case, we simply extended `ActionResult` to flush the contents of an image down to the client via the `Response` object.

The nice thing is that a good chunk of the code was guard code to ensure that items, as well as code to determine the content type of the image to load, existed. Pretty much all of the code is there to allow us to provide added functionality. Notice that there isn't any code to beat the framework into submission.

There's more...

There are many ways to implement this. Some examples will have many overloads to handle processing memory streams directly or via byte arrays. Others use various forms of extension methods dangled off of the controller itself.

An example of why you might want to keep this bit of complexity outside of the `ImageResult` is if you are pulling image data out of your database. In this case, you may want to create an overloaded constructor on the `ImageResult` class that will take a `MemoryStream` and the `ContentType` of the file. Then, inside the `ImageResult` class, you can bypass the loading of the image and just go straight to outputting the data in the response stream.

Specifying the size of an ImageResult

In this recipe, we will create another custom `ActionResult`. This one will also render an image, but in this case we will allow the user to set the size of the image.

Getting ready

Nothing is required to get this recipe running other than writing some quick code. Due to the changes of how this recipe works, we won't actually be building off of the last recipe.

How to do it...

1. Let's start by creating a new ASP.NET MVC project.

2. In the `models` folder, we create a new class and name it `ImageResizeResult`. Then, we set this new class to inherit from `ActionResult`.

   ImageResizeResult.cs:

   ```
   public class ImageResizeResult : ActionResult
   {
   ```

3. At the top of the class we are going to specify four `private` variables for use in our class. These variables will be populated via the constructor when this `ActionResult` is put to work.

   ImageResizeResult.cs:

   ```
   private string _path;
   private int _width;
   private int _maximumHeight;
   private bool _noZooming;
   ```

4. Remember that, if you want to pass data into the custom `ActionResult`, you will need to do it through the constructor. For that reason, we will define the constructor next. In our constructor, we will take in the name of the file that is requested (just the filename), which will allow us to hide the location of our files and (if we need to) move them too. We will also take in the height and width of the image that should be returned. We will also allow the requestor to specify whether or not the image can be zoomed (made bigger than the original). Notice that we are using a new .NET 4 optional parameter!

ImageResizeResult.cs:

```
public ImageResizeResult(string fileName, int width,
  int maximumHeight, bool noZooming = false)
{
  //put this path reference in a config file somewhere!
  _path = @"{path to files that can be loaded}\" + fileName;
  _width = width;
  _maximumHeight = maximumHeight;
  _noZooming = noZooming;
}
```

5. Next, we are going to reuse a snippet of code from the last recipe that will allow us to determine the content type (except that we are returning `ImageFormat` instead of String) of the image that we are playing with, so that it is rendered correctly on the client. This code interrogates the file extension of the file that was requested and uses a simple `switch` statement to determine the `ImageFormat`.

ImageResizeResult.cs:

```
private ImageFormat GetImageFormatFromFile()
{
  //get extension from path to determine contentType
  string[] parts = _path.Split('.');
  string extension = parts[parts.Length - 1];
  ImageFormat imageFormat;

  switch (extension.ToLower())
  {
    case "jpeg":
    case "jpg":
    imageFormat = ImageFormat.Jpeg;
    break;

    case "gif":
      imageFormat = ImageFormat.Gif;
      break;
```

```
        default:
          throw new NotImplementedException(extension + "not handled");
    }


    return imageFormat;
}
```

6. Now we can create a method to resize an image. In this case, we are expecting the users to pass in only the filename that they are interested in—which means that we need to do some checking to make sure that the image that was requested actually exists on the filesystem. If it does, then we load the image using the `Image.FromFile` helper method in the `Image` class.

ImageResizeResult.cs:

```
public Image ResizeImage(string imagePathToResize)
{
    Image fullsizeImage;

    //check for file
    if (File.Exists(_path))
    {
        fullsizeImage = Image.FromFile(_path);
    }
    else
    {
        throw new FileNotFoundException(_path);
    }

    //load the image from the file system
    fullsizeImage = Image.FromFile(_path);
```

7. Now we have to perform a little hackery to make sure that the image is loaded instead of the image's internal thumbnail.

ImageResizeResult.cs:

```
// hack to prevent the internal thumbnail from being used!
fullsizeImage.RotateFlip(RotateFlipType.Rotate180FlipNone);
fullsizeImage.RotateFlip(RotateFlipType.Rotate180FlipNone);
```

8. Next, we will implement a feature that allows the request to control whether we resize the image to larger than the original (zoom). In some cases, it might be inappropriate to enlarge an image. Enlargements frequently cause distortions (though the .NET graphics libraries have gotten much better at this).

ImageResizeResult.cs:

```
// can we zoom this image?
if (_noZooming)
{
```

```
if (fullsizeImage.Width <= _width)
{
    _width = fullsizeImage.Width;
}
}
```

9. Now we are going to make sure that we don't distort our image by setting the `width` and `zoom` to whatever was entered. Instead, we are going to maintain the aspect ratio of the image that we are working with. This means that if we have a square original image, we won't allow the request to turn it into a rectangle there by distorting the image.

    ImageResizeResult.cs:

```
// determine new height
int newHeight = fullsizeImage.Height * _width / fullsizeImage.
Width;
if (newHeight > _maximumHeight)
{
    // Resize with height instead
    _width = fullsizeImage.Width * _maximumHeight /
        fullsizeImage.Height;
    newHeight = _maximumHeight;
}
```

10. Now that we have all the information we need, we can create a new instance of `Image` by using another helper method—`GetThumbnailImage`. Then we will dispose of the instance of the original image. And finally, we will return the resized image.

    ImageResizeResult.cs:

```
Image newImage = fullsizeImage.GetThumbnailImage(_width,
    newHeight, null, IntPtr.Zero);

//dispose of the in memory original
fullsizeImage.Dispose();

return newImage;
}
```

11. Now we can build the `ExecuteResult` method, which is our hook into the MVC framework. In this method, we will perform all the orchestration that allows us to set the type of image we are returning in the response stream, resize the image, and then write the image down to the client (this part is very much like the last recipe). Pay close attention to where we dispose of the image that we created!

    ImageResizeResult.cs:

```
public override void ExecuteResult(ControllerContext context)
{
    byte[] buffer = new byte[4096];
```

```
        HttpResponseBase response = context.HttpContext.Response;

        //no context? stop processing
        if (context == null)
            throw new ArgumentNullException("context");

        //set files content type
        response.ContentType = "image/" +
          GetImageFormatFromFile().ToString();

        //get the resized image
        Image resizedImage = ResizeImage(_path);

        MemoryStream ms = new MemoryStream();
        resizedImage.Save(ms, GetImageFormatFromFile());
        MemoryStream imageStream = new MemoryStream(ms.ToArray());

        while (true)
        {
          int read = imageStream.Read(buffer, 0, buffer.Length);

          if (read == 0)
            break;

          response.OutputStream.Write(buffer, 0, read);
        }
        response.End();

        ms.Dispose();
        imageStream.Dispose();
    }
```

12. At this point, our `ActionResult` should be ready for use. For that reason, open up the HomeController and add a new `ActionResult` named `GetImage`. This `ActionResult` will return our new `ImageResizeResult`. In this action, we will allow the requester to pass in the requested image name, the width and height, and whether or not they want to allow zooming. However, we are going to use the new optional parameter functionality for the zooming option and give it a default value of `false`.

HomeController.cs:

```
public ImageResizeResult GetImage(string image, int width,
    int height, bool noZooming = false)
{
    return new ImageResizeResult(image, width, height, noZooming);
}
```

13. Now you can run your solution and browse directly to this action specifying all the appropriate `url` parameters, and you should get an image that you can resize till your heart is content!

14. With this working as expected, we can add some code to the Index view that exercises our resizing abilities. We will add three images to our `Index.aspx` view. The first one will show that we can take an image, which is normally 200x200, and blow it up to 250x250. The next example will show that we don't allow distortion of the image by trying to set the image's width to 75 and the height to 200. And the last example will show that we can control distortion in another way by not allowing zooming.

Index.aspx:

```
<p>
  <img src="/home/GetImage?image=me.jpg&width=250&height=250" />
  <img src="/home/GetImage?image=me.jpg&width=75&height=200" />
  <img src=
"/home/GetImage?image=me.jpg&width=1000&height=1000&noZooming=true
" />
</p>
```

How it works...

This example really isn't all that different from our last recipe, in that we created a class that implemented `ActionResult`. We did add a few additional parameters to allow the users to have more control over the process. And then we added some image resize code.

There's more...

The nice thing about this is that you have a generic image-resizing handler. Also, if all of your images go through either this or the previous recipe, you have a path that you can add to your image processing fairly easily. Something you might want to add down the road is that when an image is requested for the first time in a given size, you might save it to the file system. Then, when it is requested the next time, you might serve that file from the file system rather than attempting a resize every time. Or you might toss the resized file into a cache of some form and load it straight out of memory the next time. The key here is that you have control over how your images are served.

Creating a CAPTCHA system

We have been discussing the ability to return images directly from an action quite a bit. It wouldn't seem right if we had all these discussions and didn't quickly demonstrate how to implement a CAPTCHA system. **CAPTCHA** is defined as **Completely Automated Public Turing test to tell Computers and Humans Apart**. It is basically a simple challenge and response system to ensure that your system is not interacting with someone else's system when you are expected to be interacting with a human.

Getting ready

We are going to work off of the knowledge that we covered in the previous examples. No external requirements—just more code!

How to do it...

1. The first most important part to building anything CAPTCHA-related is to have something that generates an image with something easy for a human to parse but difficult for a computer to parse. You can find all sorts of code on the net to do this job. Just Google "C# CAPTCHA" and you will get lists of this sort of tutorial. I also included a class in the `Models` folder of this project that has the code I usually use. It generates an image like so:

2. With a working CAPTCHA class in hand we simply need to wire it up. The first thing for us to do is create a new class in the `Models` folder called `CaptchaResult`. This class will inherit from `ActionResult` like our other recipes.

CaptchaResult.cs:

```
public override void ExecuteResult(ControllerContext context)
{


}
```

3. We are going to need to specify to our CAPTCHA system the text that we want to use to verify the presence of a human. For that reason we need to have a way to pass in the text when we call on the services of our CAPTCHA generator. To do this, we need to add a `CaptchaResult` constructor like so:

CaptchaResult.cs:

```
public string _captchaText;
public CaptchaResult(string captchaText)
{
  _captchaText = captchaText;
}
```

4. Now we are ready to create the `ExecuteResult` method to fulfill our contract with the inherited `ActionResult`. This is a two-part process. First we need to create an instance of our `Captcha` class and define a few properties. Then we can save the generated image into the response stream to the browser.

CaptchaResult.cs:

```
public override void ExecuteResult(ControllerContext context)
{
  Captcha c = new Captcha();
  c.Text = _captchaText;
  c.Width = 200;
  c.Height = 50;
  c.FamilyName = "Century Schoobook";

  HttpContextBase cb = context.HttpContext;

  cb.Response.Clear();
  cb.Response.ContentType = "image/jpeg";
  c.Image.Save(cb.Response.OutputStream, ImageFormat.Jpeg);
  c.Dispose();
}
```

5. Now we can turn our attention to getting our home controller ready to spit out a CAPTCHA image. To do this, open the HomeController and add a new `CaptchaResult` action called `GetCaptcha`.

HomeController.cs:

```
public CaptchaResult GetCaptcha()
{
}
```

6. Then we need to make a call to our `Captcha` class to generate the challenge text. We can do this (in this case) with the handy-dandy `GenerateRandomCode` method that will give us a random number. You can tweak it to do as you like. Then we will stuff that code into a session variable for comparison later.

HomeController.cs:

```
public CaptchaResult GetCaptcha()
{
    string captchaText = Captcha.GenerateRandomCode();
    HttpContext.Session.Add("captcha", captchaText);
    return new CaptchaResult(captchaText);
}
```

7. Now that we have our `CaptchaResult` wired up as an action, we can call directly and wire up our view. Open the "Index" view for the `HomeController`. We first need to add a form to our view. Then we will add an image that loads the `GetCaptcha` method. We will also display a message prompting the user to enter what they see in the image. And we will provide them with a box to enter the text and a button to post their entry.

Index.aspx:

```
<% using (Html.BeginForm("index", "home")) { %>
<p><img src="/home/getcaptcha" /></p>
<p>Please enter the number above:</p>
<p><%=Html.TextBox("captcha")%></p>
<p><input type="submit" value="Submit" /></p>
<% } %>
```

8. This is far enough for you to preview your view. However, we don't have any code yet to handle the comparison aspect of our challenge. To create this, go back to the HomeController. Add a new `Index` action that expects a String named `captcha`. Then specify the `[HttpPost]` attribute to signify that this action will handle only form posts, not gets. Then we can do some simple comparison of what was entered versus what was displayed.

HomeController.cs:

```
[HttpPost]
public ActionResult Index(string captcha)
{
```

```
if (captcha == HttpContext.Session["captcha"].ToString())
   ViewData["Message"] = "CAPTCHA challenge was successful!";
else
   ViewData["Message"] = "CAPTCHA challenge failed - please try
      again!";

return View();
}
```

9. With all of this complete, you can hit _F5_ and see the recipe in action. You can enter
   the number that is displayed to test that it works. And you can enter something totally
   different from what you see to verify that the challenge system works the other
   way too.

How it works...

This recipe is a slight tweak on the previous ones. While we are still generating an image for display in the browser, this time we are generating some form of a text-based challenge for our user, which we store in the user's session. They are responsible for telling us what they see. We then compare what they say with the stored number that they see (which we generated initially).

While this is not an overly fancy code, having a CAPTCHA of this fashion is pretty flexible. You could put a CAPTCHA around your registration pages, on your commenting pages, wherever you need it. Anywhere that you would like to discourage spam is probably a good place for a CAPTCHA deterrent.

There's more...

The CAPTCHA code that I provided with this example is pretty old (I have used it for several years). It has quite a bit of flexibility options in it, in that you can easily adjust the background color, the background image, the color of the font, the color of the foreground and background specs, the font family, and so on. Feel free to poke about and tweak this to suit your needs.

Hatches and colors

You might not like the colors or hatch styles that I chose. No worries, there are quite a few options for you on this front. Take a look at this site to get started: `http://www.drewnoakes.com/snippets/GdiColorChart/`.

What is CAPTCHA?

You might also be interested in taking a look at Wikipedia for a broader explanation of what CAPTCHA is and the work surrounding that topic. It is quite interesting. `http://en.wikipedia.org/wiki/CAPTCHA`.

Other styles of CAPTCHA

CAPTCHA is a big area of study. CAPTCHA doesn't only come in the form of an image with distorted letters and numbers. There are projects such as reCAPTCHA (`http://recaptcha.net/`), SQUIGL-PIX, ESP-PIX, and a fancy drag-and-drop jQuery plug-in.

Generating a PDF order summary

We have spent quite a bit of time looking at all the various ways to render images and what we can do with those rendered images. It's time to turn away from image rendering and look at something perhaps equally useful. In this recipe, we will look at how we can generate a PDF from an action. We will specifically look at how to render an order summary. Obviously, you could take this in many directions!

Getting ready

There are a couple of things that we will need to do to get ready for this recipe. First of all, we are going to use the **iTextSharp library** (another project ported from the Java world). You can get this here: `http://sourceforge.net/projects/itextsharp/`. Make sure you download the 2.0 version. There is also a copy in the dependencies folder.

Then I am going to have you go fetch a helper class that will make working with iTextSharp way easier. The class we are going to use is called `HtmlToPdfBuilder` and was created by "Hugo Bonacci". You can find it here `http://somewebguy.wordpress.com/2009/05/08/itextsharp-simplify-your-html-to-pdf-creation/` or in the `Models` folder of this recipe's code.

How to do it...

1. Create a new ASP.NET MVC project.

2. Add a new class to the `Models` folder called `PdfResult`.

3. Set your new `PdfResult` class to inherit from `ActionResult`. Then create the `ExecuteResult`.

   PdfResult.cs:

   ```
   public class PdfResult : ActionResult
   {
     public override void ExecuteResult(ControllerContext context)
     {

     }
   }
   ```

4. Now we have somewhere to build a PDF. Inside the `ExecuteResult` method, we will piece together a PDF. First off, we need to create an instance of `HtmlToPdfBuilder`.

   ```
   HtmlToPdfBuilder builder = new HtmlToPdfBuilder(PageSize.LETTER);
   ```

5. Now we can create an instance of `HtmlPdfPage`, which we will use to create one page in our PDF.

```
HtmlPdfPage page1 = builder.AddPage();
```

6. Using the instance of `HtmlPdfPage`, we can create a page by feeding in chunks of HTML. You can programmatically do this either one chunk at a time, or you can feed in one big blob of HTML. Both methods work!

```
page1.AppendHtml("<h1>Order #19807</h1>");
page1.AppendHtml("<p>Andrew Siemer<br>");
page1.AppendHtml("4254 Some Street<br>");
page1.AppendHtml("Los Angeles, CA</p>");
page1.AppendHtml("<table><tr><td><b>Product</b></td><td><b>Price
</b></td></tr>");
page1.AppendHtml("<tr><td>ASP.NET MVC Cookbook</td>
   <td>$40.00</td></tr></table>");
```

7. From this point onwards, the code is very similar to rendering an image—in that we need to convert the PDF into an array of bytes to be pushed down to the browser. To convert the PDF into an array of bytes is a simple task though.

```
byte[] file = builder.RenderPdf();
```

8. Now we need to set our buffer size, declare the content type of our response stream, and create the stream we intend to send to the requester.

```
HttpResponseBase response = context.HttpContext.Response;
response.ContentType = "application/pdf";

MemoryStream pdfStream = new MemoryStream(file);
```

9. Once we are set up to send our stream down to the client, we can iterate through chunks of the stream, and write them out to the requester in the response's output stream.

```
while (true)
{
  int read = pdfStream.Read(buffer, 0, buffer.Length);

  if (read == 0)
     break;

  response.OutputStream.Write(buffer, 0, read);
}
response.End();
```

10. Now that our `PdfResult` is built, we can go to our HomeController. In our HomeController we will create a new method named `GetPdf`. This action will be a `PdfResult`. Because we coded our PDF generation directly in the `ActionResult`, all we need to do is declare the method.

HomeController.cs:

```
public PdfResult GetPdf()
{
   return new PdfResult();
}
```

11. With our new action declared, we can move out to our "Index" view. In the view, we will simply create a link to the action, which will generate a PDF for us.

Index.aspx:

```
Click <%= Html.ActionLink("here","GetPdf", "Home") %> to get your
order in PDF format!
```

12. Now you can hit *F5* and view your PDF.

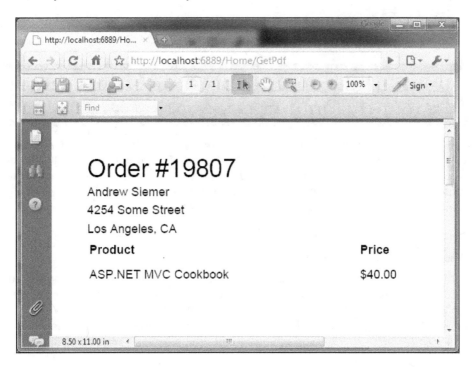

How it works...

In this recipe, we created a PDF using the `iTextSharp` product. We were able to do it so easily because we used the `HtmlToPdfBuilder` that Hugo Bonacci created. This class is an easy-to-use wrapper for a great but not so easy-to-use PDF generation tool.

Once we had the PDF, we converted it into an array of bytes. Once you have something converted into an array of bytes, streaming it down to the client that requested the resource is rather straightforward using the `HTTP` response.

There's more...

If you put what was discussed here to generate PDFs with the NVelocity recipe (which was discussed earlier) you will have a very powerful way of creating templates for generating HTML-based PDFs.

See also

> ▶ *Loading a view template from a database with NVelocity*

Implementing a controller factory for use with StructureMap

In this recipe, we will implement our own controller factory, which will allow us to utilize the structure map at the very top of the request cycle of the MVC framework. This will allow us to get rid of any object initialization that we might otherwise have to do directly in a controller. This in turn means that our controllers can conform to a dependency injection style of development, which will make them considerably easier to test.

Getting ready

The first thing we need to do to create a `StructureMap` controller factory is to download StructureMap here: `http://structuremap.sourceforge.net/Default.htm`. We will also use NBuilder to make our example a bit more of a real-world scenario. You can get NBuilder here: `http://nbuilder.org/`. Also, both of these tools are in the dependencies folder.

Next, I will list some code that we need in our solution prior to starting this recipe. We create a `ProductRepository` to get our products from the database, a `ProductService` to apply business logic to the list of products, and a `Product` definition to pass the data around. After that, we will need to wire up our HomeController to pass a list of products to our view. Here are those classes:

Product.cs:
```csharp
public class Product
{
  public int ProductID { get; set; }
  public string Name { get; set; }
  public double Cost { get; set; }
}
```

ProductRepository.cs:
```csharp
public class ProductRepository
{
  public List<Product> GetProducts()
  {
     return Builder<Product>.CreateListOfSize(50).Build().ToList();
  }
}
```

ProductService.cs:
```csharp
public class ProductService
{
  public List<Product> GetProducts()
  {
     return new ProductRepository().GetProducts();
  }
}
```

HomeController.cs:
```csharp
...
public ActionResult Index()
{
  ViewData["Message"] = "Welcome to ASP.NET MVC!";
  ViewData["Products"] = new ProductService().GetProducts();
  return View();
}
...
```

Index.aspx:
```aspx
...
<% foreach (var product in ((List<Product>)ViewData["Products"]))
{ %>
  <%= product.ProductID %> <%= product.Name %>
  <%= String.Format("{0:C}", product.Cost) %><br />
  <% } %>
...
```

With this code in place, we can run our project and we should see a list of products down the home page. We will also notice that our code is heavily coupled all over the place. Now let's turn to the recipe and refactor in our `StructureMap` controller factory and shed these dependencies.

How to do it...

1. Create a new ASP.NET MVC project.

2. Add a reference to NBuilder and StructureMap.

3. Then we need to extract an interface from our `ProductRepository`. You can use **ReSharper** to do this for you by clicking on the `ProductRepository` classname and pressing *Ctrl + Shift + R*, which will cause the refactor *this* menu to pop up, then choose **Extract Interface**. Or you can simply create a new interface file and define the interface for `ProductRepository`. Either way, you want to end up with an `IProductRepository` in your `Models` folder.

   IProductRepository.cs:

   ```
   public interface IProductRepository
   {
       List<Product> GetProducts();
   }
   ```

4. Next, we need to do the same thing for our `ProductService` and extract an interface named `IProductService`.

   IProductService.cs:

   ```
   public interface IProductService
   {
       List<Product> GetProducts();
   }
   ```

5. Once we have created our interfaces, we can then set our `ProductRepository` and `ProductService` to derive from those interfaces.

   ProductRepository.cs:

   ```
   public class ProductRepository : IProductRepository
   ```

   ProductService.cs:

   ```
   public class ProductService : IProductService
   ```

6. Now that we have classes that are defined by their interface, we can plug `StructureMap` into the flow of our program. We already added a reference to `StructureMap` to the project. Now we need to create a `Registry` class named `ProjectRegistry` to our project. This is where we tell `StructureMap` which types we want to use when we ask it to give us a class by interface.

ProjectRegistry.cs:

```
using StructureMap.Configuration.DSL;
...
public class ProjectRegistry : Registry
{
  public ProjectRegistry()
  {
    ForRequestedType<IProductRepository>().TheDefault.Is.
      OfConcreteType<ProductRepository>();
    ForRequestedType<IProductService>().TheDefault.Is.
      OfConcreteType<ProductService>();
  }
}
```

7. Then we need to create a bootstrapper class named `RegisterProject` that we will use to load our registry classes (we have only one...but we might have more as a project grows).

RegisterProject.cs:

```
using StructureMap;


...
public class RegisterProject
{
  public RegisterProject()
  {
    ObjectFactory.Initialize(x =>
    {
      x.AddRegistry(new ProjectRegistry());
      //add more registry classes here if you need too
      //x.AddRegistry(new DataRegistry());
    });
  }
}
```

8. Now that we have our registry and bootstrapper created, we can wire `StructureMap` the rest of the way into our application. We do this in the `Global.asax.cs` file in the `Application_Start` method.

Global.asax.cs:

```
protected void Application_Start()
{
  AreaRegistration.RegisterAllAreas();
  RegisterRoutes(RouteTable.Routes);

  new RegisterProject();
}
```

9. Now that `StructureMap` is wired in, you can build and run your project. We are not yet using `StructureMap`, but we want to make sure that everything works at this point. If you did something wrong you will quickly find out!

10. Assuming that all is good...we can now move on to refactoring our dependencies out of our application in favor of allowing `StructureMap` to handle them instead. We can start in our `ProductService`. We will move the instantiation of the `ProductRepository` up and out of the `ProductService` like this.

ProductService.cs:

```
public class ProductService : IProductService
{
    private IProductRepository _productRepository;
    public ProductService(IProductRepository productRepository)
    {
        _productRepository = productRepository;
    }
    public List<Product> GetProducts()
    {
        return _productRepository.GetProducts();
    }
}
```

11. Next, we need to push the usage of the `ProductService` up and out of the HomeController. Do that like this.

HomeController.cs:

```
public class HomeController : Controller
{
    private IProductService _productService;
    public HomeController(IProductService productService)
    {
        _productService = productService;
    }

    public ActionResult Index()
    {
        ViewData["Message"] = "Welcome to ASP.NET MVC!";
        ViewData["Products"] = _productService.GetProducts();
        return View();
    }
    ...
```

12. Now we can add a new class to our `Models` directory called `StructureMapController`. This class will be responsible for loading our dependencies into the constructor of each of our controllers.

StructureMapController.cs:

```
public class StructureMapControllerFactory :
   DefaultControllerFactory
```

```
{
    protected override IController  GetControllerInstance(
        RequestContext requestContext, Type controllerType)
    {
        if(controllerType == null)
            return base.GetControllerInstance(requestContext,
                controllerType);

            return ObjectFactory.GetInstance(controllerType) as
                Controller;
    }
}
```

13. In order for our `StructureMapController` to be used though, we will need to wire it into MVC. We will do this in the `Global.asax.cs` file as well.

Global.asax.cs:

```
protected void Application_Start()
{
    ControllerBuilder.Current.SetControllerFactory(
        new Models.StructureMapControllerFactory());

    AreaRegistration.RegisterAllAreas();
    RegisterRoutes(RouteTable.Routes);

    new RegisterProject();
}
```

14. Now you can hit *F5* and see `StructureMap` do its magic.

How it works...

In order to make this work, we have created a custom controller factory that is derived from `DefaultControllerFactory`. This requires that we have a `GetControllerInstance` method that returns an instance of `IController`. Inside this method, we are checking to see if we know the requested `ControllerType` or not. If we don't know what was requested, then we return control to MVC. If we do know the `Controller Type` though, then we ask `StructureMap` to go get a configured instance of the requested controller. The benefit here is that when `StructureMap` gets an instance of something, it will also inject appropriate instances of other classes into the constructor of the requested controller. This is what allows us to push our dependencies up and out of our code and request that the dependencies be provided to us via the constructor of our classes.

3
Routing

In this chapter, we will cover:

▶ Creating a route to support a reporting engine

▶ Making hackable routes for a product catalog

▶ Filtering your matches with routing constraints

▶ Using wildcard parameters to support slug URLs

▶ Creating a 404 page with routing

▶ Moving routes out of `Global.asax`

▶ Supporting pagination in your URLs

▶ Supporting content hierarchies with a custom `RouteHandler`

▶ Creating a blacklist route constraint

Introduction

In this chapter, we are going to take a look at the very powerful routing engine that first came into being with MVC. With the release of .NET 4.0 though, this chapter now applies to both MVC and web form applications. We will take a look at how to create both, the simple route as well as some more advanced features such as wildcard parameters for slug support and action filters for route translations.

Creating a route to support a reporting engine

In this recipe, we will take a look at how to create a route to support a reporting engine. In this case, we want to be able to capture a report name as well as the start and ending date of the report. We will attempt to support a route that looks something like this:

SalesReport/From/2010/01/01/To/2010/05/01

How to do it...

1. Create a new MVC application.

2. Open up the `global.asax` file.

3. Now we can add a couple of new routes after the `IgnoreRoute` to support the `url` format we discussed: **SalesReport/From/2010/01/01/To/2010/05/01**. Notice that each of these routes is going to be mapped to two different actions, named `ReportPartial` and `ReportComplete`.

   Global.asax:
   ```
   routes.MapRoute("ReportPartial",
     "Report/{reportName}/from/{fromYear}/{fromMonth}/{fromDay}",
     new {controller = "Home", action = "ReportPartial"});

   routes.MapRoute("ReportComplete",
     "Report/{reportName}/from/{fromYear}/{fromMonth}/{fromDay}/to/
     {toYear}/{toMonth}/{toDay}",
     new { controller = "Home", action = "ReportComplete" });
   ```

4. With our routing in place, we now need to stand up some actions to handle the requests. Open up the `HomeController` file. Then add two new actions—one called `ReportPartial` and the other called `ReportComplete`. Both of these actions will return a view that does not map to their name. Specifically, we will set each of these actions to return a Report view.

   Controllers/HomeController.cs:
   ```
   public ActionResult ReportPartial(string reportName, int fromYear,
     int fromMonth, int fromDay)
   {
     return View("Report");
   }

   public ActionResult ReportComplete(string reportName,
     int fromYear, int fromMonth, int fromDay, int toYear,
     int toMonth, int toDay)
   {
     return View("Report");
   }
   ```

5. Now you can add the new report action to support the Report view that our other actions will be returning.

Controllers/HomeController.cs:

```
public ActionResult Report()
{
  return View();
}
```

6. With our actions set up to handle the routes that we created, we can add some super simple logic to pretend that we are actually building a report with the specified data. We will do this by creating a helper method that will build a report for us. This method will take in all the parameters that are passed into the reporting routes we created.

Controllers/HomeController.cs:

```
public string GenerateReport(string reportName,
  int fromYear, int fromMonth, int fromDay, int toYear,
  int toMonth, int toDay)
{
  string result = "";
  if (toYear == 0)
    result = "The " + reportName +
      " shows great financial figures from " +
      fromMonth + "/" + fromDay + "/" + fromYear + " to present!";
  else
    result = "The " + reportName +
      " shows great financial figures from " +
      fromMonth + "/" + fromDay + "/" + fromYear +
      " to " + toMonth + "/" + toDay + "/" +  toYear + "!";

  return result;
}
```

7. With our helper function in place, we can now plug it into our ReportPartial and ReportComplete actions. We will put the result of our GenerateReport method into ViewData to be passed down to our Report action.

Controllers/HomeController.cs:

```
public ActionResult ReportPartial(string reportName,
  int fromYear, int fromMonth, int fromDay)
{
  ViewData["report"] = GenerateReport(reportName,
    fromYear, fromMonth, fromDay, 0, 0, 0);
  return View("Report");
}
```

```
public ActionResult ReportComplete(string reportName,
  int fromYear, int fromMonth, int fromDay, int toYear,
  int toMonth, int toDay)
{
  ViewData["report"] = GenerateReport(reportName,
    fromYear, fromMonth, fromDay, toYear, toMonth, toDay);
  return View("Report");
}
```

8. All that is left is to update our Report view to show the results of our generated report.

   Views/Home/Report.aspx:

```
<asp:Content ID="Content2" ContentPlaceHolderID="MainContent"
  runat="server">
<h2>Report</h2>
<%: ViewData["report"] %>
</asp:Content>
```

9. Now you can build the application. Navigate to: `http://localhost:{yourPort}/Report/salesReport/from/2010/1/1/to/2010/5/1`. You should see the report view with the appropriate output.

How it works...

In this recipe, we created two routes—one to support the specification of just the start of the report and the other route to capture the start and end date of the report. To make sure that we don't end up writing the same code over and over again, we moved the report generation into a helper method (in reality this would probably go into your business layer). We then passed the output of the helper method down to the report view, where we actually show the results of the report.

Making hackable URLs for a product catalog

When designing your URL scheme you might consider trying to make hackable URLs. By this I mean to say that your URLs should be able to support user manipulation. A URL such as `Product/Details/2` is fine for displaying a product, but it doesn't show any information for Google to slurp up when ranking your site; it also doesn't provide any additional navigational abilities to your viewing customer, it just shows a product. Now take the following URL: `Catalog/Computers/Laptops/Toshiba/Satellite-650`. With this sort of URL, you are providing your customers with the ability to remove the specific laptop `Satellite-650` and display all of the laptops that Toshiba makes. You could further remove the `Toshiba` from the URL and see a list of all the `Laptops` that the site offers. And you could remove `Laptops` and see all the computers, and so on.

One thing to keep in mind when creating these types of URLs is that you do have to do additional work. Each of these URLs become additional routes with corresponding actions in a controller, which ultimately map to a view that displays the appropriate data. If you provide hackable routes for one area of your site, your customers are inevitably going to try to hack other areas of your site's URLs. Be consistent in the implementation of hackable URLs on your site.

Also, you may have noticed in the preceding URL examples that we had some data separated by slashes, while other data was separated by dashes. The general idea is that data separated by slashes can be removed to view additional results. Data separated by dashes can't be modified for additional results.

Getting ready

In order to demonstrate how hackable URLs work, we first need to create an application, which is capable of showing data for each state of the URL. In this case, we will create a product catalog that allows you to navigate from a category to a subcategory, to manufacturers, to products, to a product—and back again.

I will describe the tasks for setting up the routing in detail, but I will point to the other sections of code only as needed. To see the full example code, feel free to take a look at the source code included with the book.

How to do it...

1. We still start by first creating a new MVC project.
2. Now open `Global.asax.cs` and take a look at the `RegisterRoutes` method. We will start by creating a new route. This first route will handle displaying all of the categories in our product catalog. As that is a simple task, we will end up with a simple route—this route will be called `Categories`. We will start all of these product catalog routes with the word `Catalog` to keep this set of routes separate from any other routes we might create for this application. Also, all of these routes will map to the Home Controller regardless of what is stated in the URL. The last thing for us to be concerned with is the action we want to use for this route. We will specify the `ShowAllCategories` action (which we will need to create). As you can see, this is a parameterless route.

    Global.asax.cs:

    ```
    routes.MapRoute("Categories", "Catalog",
      new {controller = "Home", action = "ShowAllCategories"});
    ```

3. Add a new action to our Home Controller called `ShowAllCategories`. This action will make a call into the `ProductCatalogFactory` to get the appropriate instance of a view-specific model object called `AllCategoriesModel`. The `ProductCatalogFactory` makes a call into a non-specific `Repository` class that generates instances of various classes as we need them using NBuilder. The action then returns the properly hydrated instance of the `AllCategoriesModel` to the view.

Global.asax.cs:

```
public ActionResult AllCategories()
{
   AllCategoriesModel model =
      ProductCatalogFactory.AllCategoriesModelFactory();

   return View(model);
}
```

Models/ViewModels/AllCategoriesModel.cs:

```
public class AllCategoriesModel
{
   public List<Category> Categories { get; set; }
}
```

Models/Services/ProductCatalogFactory.cs:

```
public static AllCategoriesModel AllCategoriesModelFactory()
{
   AllCategoriesModel result = new AllCategoriesModel();
   result.Categories = new Repository().GetCategories();
   return result;
}
```

Models/Repositories/Repository.cs:

```
public List<Category> GetCategories()
{
   return Builder<Category>
      .CreateListOfSize(10)
      .Build()
      .ToList();
}
```

Models/Domain/Category.cs:

```
public class Category
{
   public Guid CategoryId { get; set; }
   public string Name { get; set; }
}
```

Views/Home/AllCategories.aspx:

```
...
<h2>Catalog</h2>

<fieldset>
  <legend>Categories</legend>
  <% foreach(Category category in Model.Categories) { %>
  <div class="display-label">
      <%:Html.Label(category.Name) %>
  </div>
  <div class="display-field">

  <%:Html.ActionLink(category.Name,"AllSubCategoriesForCategory",
   new {categoryName = category.Name}) %>
  </div>
    <% } %>
</fieldset>
...
```

4. With our Catalog view showing all the categories in our fake system, we can now move on to the next route. If a person was to select a category from our catalog, then we would expect it to show perhaps subcategories or related products. In this case, we are building a pretty specific system that requires a subcategory to be selected next. For that reason, we will now build a route to capture the selected category, so that we can display its subcategories.

   Global.asax:

```
routes.MapRoute("Category", "Catalog/{categoryName}",
  new {controller = "Home",
  action = "AllSubCategoriesForCategory"});
```

5. Next, we can build a route to additionally capture the selected subcategory. With the subcategory known, we can then grab all the manufacturers for display.

   Global.asax:

```
routes.MapRoute("SubCategory",
  "Catalog/{categoryName}/{subcategoryName}",
  new { controller = "Home",
    action = "AllManufacturersForSubCategory" });
```

6. You may be seeing the bigger picture here—in that we can continue to drill down as deep as we like by simply adding a new route to our route dictionary. The next route will allow us to show a list of products for a selected manufacturer.

   Global.asax:

```
routes.MapRoute("Manufacturer",
  "Catalog/{categoryName}/{subcategoryName}/{manufacturerName}",
  new { controller = "Home",
   action = "AllProductsForManufacturer" });
```

7. With the products displaying for the selected manufacturer, we are finally ready to show the product details. We will need to add one more route to capture the selected product.

Global.asax:

```
routes.MapRoute("Product", "Catalog/{categoryName}/" +
    "{subcategoryName}/{manufacturerName}/" + "{productName}",
    new { controller = "Home", action = "ProductDetails" });
```

8. From here you are now ready to run the program and drill through the product catalog. Keep in mind that we are using NBuilder to generate some data for us, so that the data may look a bit odd but it is indeed working as you would expect it to.

How it works...

When a request comes in, it is matched to routes in the **route** dictionary. The collection of routes are interrogated from the top down, or from the first item added to the list. The thing to keep in mind here is that the order is very important. If you have a very general route specification at the top of the list that matches every request, then none of your other routes will be acted on. You usually want to have the more specific routes at the top of the list and the less specific routes towards the bottom.

There's more...

You could have done this in a slightly different manner. Had you been willing to put all of your display logic into one view, you could have also consolidated all of your routes into one specification. This would ultimately give you less code to manage but it would also yield less overall flexibility. In this case, we can use different views for each route, which may be good or bad depending on what you are building.

Filter your matches with routing constraints

You may have noticed how easy it is to set up a new route. It took us no time at all to create several rules to match various features for our product catalog in the previous recipe. The thing that you have probably noticed though is that our routes are fairly unprotected from any user input. While it is true that we can control our data entry with the parameter types in our action signatures, it would be even better if we could do some validation further up the chain.

If you expect a number in a certain format, a date, or an e-mail address, you can supply a regular expression as part of your route definition to ensure that the match occurs only when the data is appropriate. In this way, if no routes are appropriately matched, down to the actual signature of the supplied data, your 404 page or some other page can handle the missing route.

Getting ready

In this recipe, we will take a look at how to create a phone directory. We want the ability to have phone numbers as part of our route so that Google can find the information and so that our URLs are clean. But if we are going to have phone numbers as data, which is possibly entered by the users, we want to make sure that the data is appropriately formatted.

How to do it...

1. Start by creating a new MVC application.

2. Then open up `HomeController.cs`. We will add two new actions—one to handle appropriate phone number input and the other to handle everything else.

   Controllers/HomeController.cs:

   ```
   public ActionResult GetPhoneDetails(string phoneNumber)
   {
     ViewData["phoneNumber"] = phoneNumber;
     return View();
   }


   public ActionResult InputNotSupported(string phoneNumber)
   {
     ViewData["phoneNumber"] = phoneNumber;
     return View();
   }
   ```

3. Next, we need to open up the `Global.asax` to add our new routes. We will have one route to capture all appropriate phone number entries. This route will use a **regex pattern** to determine if the phone number is appropriate or not. It will allow (123)123-4567 and 123-123-4567 as valid forms of phone numbers. The other route will be a pass through to capture any input that didn't match our filter.

   Global.asax:

   ```
   routes.MapRoute("PhoneLookup", //capture appropriate matches
     "Directory/{phoneNumber}",
     new {controller = "Home", action = "GetPhoneDetails"},
     new {phoneNumber = @"^(\()?([0-9]{3})(\)|-)?([0-9]{3})(-)?
       ([0-9]{4}|[0-9]{4})$"});


   routes.MapRoute("PhoneLookupFailed", //capture anything else that
       matches this signature but not the filter
       "Directory/{phoneNumber}",
       new { controller = "Home", action = "InputNotSupported" });
   ```

4. You can now run your application. Browse to `/Directory/123-456-7890`, or `/Directory/(123)456-7890`, or `/Directory/1234567890` and you should see the `GetPhoneDetails` view. If you browse to `/Directory/12345678901` or `/Directory/HelloWorld` you will see the `InputNotSupported` view.

How it works...

Routing constraints are built into the routing system. You can supply any regex required to create a specific route for a set pattern of data. This not only gives you control to keep certain data out, but it also gives you control to match different patterns of data and handle those matches with different controllers and actions. In our previous example, you may want to handle the lookup for US phone numbers in one database and European phone numbers by another controller and action. This could be handled by specifying different routes with different constraints.

Using wildcard parameters to support slug URLs

Every now and then you may find yourself in a situation where you need to put a bunch of stuff in the URL for SEO purposes, but you may not need the information much beyond that. Or you might have all sorts of data in the URL to uniquely describe an article or blog post, that unique string is actually stored with your content as a **SLUG** or **permalink**. In either scenario, we need to be able to get a chunk of the URL rather than the individual pieces.

In this recipe, we will build a simple routing structure that allows us to determine the controller, action, and a slug of information to determine an article. We will create two routes— one for News articles and one for Political articles. We will allow the action to be identified by the URL and will allow the slug to be provided as the remainder of the URL.

How to do it...

1. Create a new MVC application.
2. Open up the `HomeController.cs` file. We need to add two new actions to handle our News and Politics reviews. The `id` of the article will be passed in as a slug, which we will pass down to the view so that we can see what I mean by SLUG.

Controllers/HomeController.cs:

```
public ActionResult News(string id)
{
  ViewData["articleid"] = id;
  return View();
}
```

```
public ActionResult Politics(string id)
{
  ViewData["articleid"] = id;
  return View();
}
```

3. With our actions created, we are ready to generate our views. Do this by right-clicking on the action and selecting **Add View**. Add one empty view per action.

4. Then open up the `Global.asax` file so that we can add a new route to handle our two new views. Notice that we are putting an asterisk in front of our `id` parameter to specify that we want to capture all of the URL past the action and work with it in the `id` variable.

   Global.asax:

   ```
   routes.MapRoute("CmsSlug", "Article/{action}/{*id}",
       new { controller = "Home"});
   ```

5. Now you can run the application. Navigate to `/Article/News/Here/Is-My/Favorite/News-Article` (specify what you like after `/Article/News/`) and you should see a page that displays a SLUG value of `Here/Is-My/Favorite/News-Article`. This can be stored along with your article as a permanent link to your content.

How it works...

This is another feature that is built into the MVC framework (and now the .NET 4 framework) to allow us to get a bit more control over our URLs. When a request is made to our application, the routing module takes a look at the various aspects of the request and tries to map this to a route in the route dictionary.

Creating a 404 page via routing

In this recipe, we will take a look at a way to easily handle that pesky **Page cannot be found** error. Specifically, we will handle the `404` error by providing a very loose route at the bottom of our route dictionary. This route will catch any request that doesn't match any of our routes. Then, we will take a look at a few other scenarios where a `404` might be encountered.

How to do it...

1. Create a new MVC application.

2. Then open up the `Global.asax`, so that we can add a very open route.

3. Add this wildcard route to your route table.

   Global.asax:

   ```
   routes.MapRoute("NothingMatched", "{*url}",
       new { controller = "Error", action = "Http404"});
   ```

4. Next, we need to create an **Error controller** in the `Controllers` directory.

5. Then add a new action named `Http404`.

   Controllers/ErrorController.cs:

   ```
   public ActionResult Http404()
   {
       return View();
   }
   ```

6. Then right-click on your new action and choose to add a new empty view. Add a little message to your new view stating that the user has attempted to navigate to a page that doesn't exist.

7. Now in one of the content areas of your view, add the following code to set the `StatusCode` of the view to a `404` error number (otherwise search engines might index your error page).

   Views/Error/Http404.aspx:

   ```
   <% HttpContext.Current.Response.StatusCode =
       (int)HttpStatusCode.NotFound; %>
   ```

8. At this point, you can run your application. When navigating to `/RandomController/RandomAction/RandomID` you might expect to see a `404` error page. Instead you will see an error page. This is due to the default route that comes with the MVC application and how it grabs almost any request that comes into the system.

9. To deal with this, we are going to create a `ControllerFactory` class to handle our requests using an inversion of control container called `StructureMap`. This class will be responsible for catching errors when requests don't match the controllers in the system. To do this, let's start by adding a `MyControllerFactory` class to the `Models` directory.

10. This class will override `GetControllerInstance` from the `DefaultControllerFactory` class. In our new implementation of `GetControllerInstance`, we will add a `try`/`catch` statement to wrap the call to the base `GetControllerInstance`. If we catch an error, we will test what type of exception we have and either throw an error or return our new error page.

Models/MyControllerFactory.cs:

```
protected override IController GetControllerInstance(
    System.Web.Routing.RequestContext requestContext,
    Type controllerType)
{
    try
    {
        return base.GetControllerInstance(requestContext,
            controllerType);
    }

    catch (HttpException ex)
    {
        int httpCode = ex.GetHttpCode();
        if(httpCode == (int)HttpStatusCode.NotFound)
        {
            IController controller = new ErrorController();
            ((ErrorController)controller).Http404();
            return controller;
        }
        else
        {
            throw ex;
        }
    }
}
```

11. In order for our new controller factory to see the light of day, we will need to wire it into our application. We can do this in the `Global.asax` in the `Application_Start` method.

Global.asax:

```
protected void Application_Start()
{
    ControllerBuilder.Current.SetControllerFactory(
     new MyControllerFactory());

    AreaRegistration.RegisterAllAreas();
    RegisterRoutes(RouteTable.Routes);
}
```

12. With this in place, you can now run the application again. Navigating to `/RandomController/RandomAction/RandomId` should now redirect you to the `404` page. But try to navigate to `/Home/ActionThatDoesntExist/RandomId` and you will not get your `404` page!

13. To fix this last problem, we need to override the `HandleUnknownAction` method exposed by the `Controller` class. To do this, we need to create a base controller class called `BaseController` in the `Models` directory and set it to inherit from the `Controller`. Then we will override the `HandleUnknownAction` method to catch when a controller is found but the requested action is not.

Models/BaseController.cs:

```
public class BaseController : Controller
{
  protected override void HandleUnknownAction(string actionName)
  {

  }
}
```

14. Next, we need to add a method that allows us to programmatically build up and execute a route to our `404` page. This method will be called `RouteTo404`. Then we will call this new method from our implementation of `HandleUnknownAction`.

Models/BaseController.cs:

```
public class BaseController : Controller
{
  protected override void HandleUnknownAction(string actionName)
  {
     RouteTo404(HttpContext);
  }

  public ActionResult RouteTo404(HttpContextBase context)
  {
    IController errorController = new ErrorController();
    RouteData rd = new RouteData();
    rd.Values.Add("controller", "Error");
    rd.Values.Add("action", "Http404");
    errorController.Execute(new RequestContext(context, rd));

    return new EmptyResult();
  }
}
```

15. For our base class to work, we need to set all of our existing controllers to inherit from our `BaseController` class instead of the default `Controller` class.

16. Now you can run your application again, this time all forms of missing resources should get the `404` view that you created.

 Also, because you have the `RouteTo404` method in your `BaseController` class, you can now call the `404` view when legitimate controllers and actions are called with bogus data. For example, when someone calls `/ProductCatalog/GetProduct/999` and there is no product with an ID of 999, you could return the `404` page appropriately.

How it works...

We have used some of the exposed hooks in the MVC framework for catching the various forms of missing resources. We used an anything goes route to catch unmapped routes. We used a controller factory to catch missing controller requests. We used a method in the `Controller` class to handle missing actions on valid controllers. We even created a way to show our `404` page when inappropriate, or no longer appropriate data is requested from our application in an appropriate (correct controller/action combinations) manner.

There's more...

The absolute best coverage I have found on this topic, and indeed what inspired me to write more than just an `Application_Error` method in Global (an approach that works but is very lacking in its flexibility), was this very thorough post on `StackOverflow`: `http://stackoverflow.com/questions/619895/how-can-i-properly-handle-404s-in-asp-net-mvc/2577095#2577095`.

Moving routes out of Global.asax

Having all of your routes defined in `Global.asax` is initially quite convenient. However, after a while you might find that your application has grown so large that the long list of route definitions might need to be moved out of `Global.asax`. Technically, this is a good habit to get into when you first create your application. But many argue that having your routes in an editable file is convenient. However, I would suggest to you that if your routes are changing, odds are that something else has probably caused this change and that the change is probably larger than just a simple routing change!

How to do it...

1. Start by creating a new MVC application.

2. Then create a new class in the `Models` folder called `RouteLibrary.cs`.

3. Then copy out the entire `RegisterRoutes` method in `Global.asax` and paste it into your new `RouteLibrary` class.

   Models/RouteLibrary.cs:

```
public class RouteLibrary
{
    public static void RegisterRoutes(RouteCollection routes)
    {
        routes.IgnoreRoute("{resource}.axd/{*pathInfo}");

        routes.MapRoute("Default", // Route name
          "{controller}/{action}/{id}", // URL with parameters
          new { controller = "Home", action = "Index",
          id = UrlParameter.Optional } // Parameter defaults);

    }
}
```

4. Then in the `Global.asax` file, make a call to the new `RegisterRoutes` method.

   Global.asax:

```
protected void Application_Start()
{
    AreaRegistration.RegisterAllAreas();

    RouteLibrary.RegisterRoutes(RouteTable.Routes);
}
```

5. Now you are ready to run your application.

How it works...

You will probably notice that not much has changed here. However, with the route definitions moved into the `RouteLibrary` you are now able to manage them a bit better. You could even go so far as to create separate methods for each major area of your application, with each method containing all the appropriate routes for that area. In the end, you have more flexibility with routes in the `RouteLibrary` and you have reduced the number of concerns that your `Global.asax` file is responsible for.

There's more...

Because there are several people who would suggest that moving your routing into a class of its own removes the convenience of having the route definitions in Global.asax, I will leave you with this bit of advice—consider putting your routing into its own class library. This way, if your routes really do change that often, you can deploy your routing library separate from the rest of your code. Though I don't think your routes will change that often in such a manner, than only the route that needs to be redeployed!

Supporting pagination in your URLs

This recipe is sort of a mix of routing and tomfoolery. While the routing aspect of this is pretty simple, the underlying bits that populate the URL can be a bit more complex. For that reason, we will cover both the routing aspect and a reusable control for managing pagination in any data set.

How to do it...

1. Create a new MVC application.
2. Add a reference to NBuilder (in the dependencies folder), so that we can create some data to play with.
3. Then open up your Global.asax, so that we can add a new route to handle paging. We will create a route that will allow us to use our HomeController without the customer knowing it, and that will expose a page variable instead of the id variable. Also, instead of making the page variable optional, we will set the default value to page 1.

   Global.asax:

   ```
   routes.MapRoute(
     "Products", // Route name
     "ProductCatalog/Products/{page}", // URL with parameters
     new { controller = "Home", action = "Products", page = 1 }
       // Parameter defaults
   );
   ```

4. Now that we have a route that accepts page numbers, we need to create a Products action to catch the page number in the HomeController.

   Controllers/HomeController.cs:

   ```
   public ActionResult Products(int page)
   {
     return View();
   }
   ```

5. Before we get into the details of our new action, we need to discuss the model that we are going to create and use. As you may have guessed, we are going to build a products catalog, inside of which we will display products. For that reason we need to create a `Product` class.

Models/Products.cs:

```
public class Product
{
  public string ProductName { get; set; }
  public double Price { get; set; }
  public string Description { get; set; }
}
```

6. Next, we need to create a couple of data transfer objects or view models, depending on the school of thought you subscribe too. The first one will be the `Pager`, which we will use to keep track of our pagination data such as what page we are on, how many pages we have in the set of data we are working with, whether there is a next or previous page, and so on. This is a simple class with a collection of properties. The constructor is used to set the data that this class will require.

Models/Pager.cs:

```
public class Pager
{
  public Pager (int currentPage, int numberOfPages, string action,
    string controller)
  {
    CurrentPage = currentPage;
    NumberOfPages = numberOfPages;
    Action = action;
    Controller = controller;
  }

  public bool ShowPrevious {
    get
    {
      if (CurrentPage == 1)
        return false;
      else
          return true;
    }
  }

  public bool ShowNext {
    get
    {
        if (CurrentPage < (NumberOfPages-1))
```

```
                return true;
            else
                return false;
        }
    }

    public int PreviousPage
    {
      get
      {
        if (CurrentPage - 1 > 0)
            return CurrentPage - 1;
        else
            return 1;
      }
    }

    public int NextPage
    {
      get
      {
          if (CurrentPage + 1 <= NumberOfPages)
              return CurrentPage + 1;
          else
              return NumberOfPages;
      }
    }

    public int CurrentPage { get; set; }
    public int NumberOfPages { get; set; }
    public string Controller { get; set; }
    public string Action { get; set; }
}
```

7. Next, we need to create a `ProductsModel` class, which we will use to transfer our collection of product data as well as the `Pager` instance. We will use these two bits of data to build the list of products data and to control how our paging control displays.

Models/ProductsModel.cs:

```
public class ProductsModel
{
  public List<Product> Products { get; set; }
  public Pager Pager { get; set; }
}
```

8. Now that we have our `Product`, `Pager`, and `ProductsModel` created, we can move on to the implementation of our `Products` action. In this action, we will create a list of products using NBuilder. Then we will set the properties of our `Pager` class (current page, total number of pages, the action to process the next page, and the controller that the action lives in). We will then take the list of products and our configured pager and stick them into our `ProductsModel`. With the `ProductsModel` created and hydrated with our data, we will then pass that down to our view.

Controllers/HomeController.cs:

```
public ActionResult Products(int page)
{
    ProductsModel pm = new ProductsModel();

    List<Product> products = Builder<Product>
        .CreateListOfSize(pageCount * pageCount)
        .Build().ToList();

    Pager pager = new Pager(page, (products.Count/pageCount),
        "Products", "Home");

    pm.Products = products.Skip(page * pageCount)
        .Take(pageCount).ToList();

    pm.Pager = pager;

    return View(pm);
}
```

9. Now we can create our view. Right-click on the action and add a view. Set this view to be a list of `Product`. When the view opens up, you will need to change the type that the page inherits from `IEnumerable<Product>` to `ProductsModel`. Then update the `foreach` statement to iterate over a collection of `Model.Products`. (I removed some of the fluff that the wizard adds.)

Views/Home/Products.aspx:

```
<table>
  <tr>
    <th>
      ProductName
    </th>
    <th>
      Price
    </th>
    <th>
```

```
            Description
        </th>
    </tr>

<% foreach (var item in Model.Products) { %>

    <tr>
        <td>
            <%: item.ProductName %>
        </td>
        <td>
            <%: String.Format("{0:C}", item.Price) %>
        </td>
        <td>
            <%: item.Description %>
        </td>
    </tr>

<% } %>

</table>
```

10. Now we can create our pagination control (a partial view). Start by creating a new partial view in the `Views/Shared` directory called `PagerView`. This view will be strongly-typed, based on the `Pager` class that we created earlier. Then we will use the properties we created on the `Pager` class to show the next and previous `ActionLinks`. We will also perform some logic to determine what page we are on, so that we can highlight the appropriate page link. We will also determine how many pages there are in the set of data, so that we can show a link for each page. (I added some CSS classes to the output to help control the look and feel.)

Views/Shared/PagerView.ascx:

```
<%@ Control Language="C#"
  Inherits="System.Web.Mvc.ViewUserControl<
    MvcApplication1.Models.Pager>" %>

<div class="Pager">
  <% if(Model.ShowPrevious) { %>
    <div class="PagerPreviousPage">
    <%= Html.ActionLink("<< Previous",Model.Action,
      Model.Controller, new { page = Model.PreviousPage }, null)
      %></div>
  <% } %>

  <div class="PagerPageNavigation">
    <% for (int i = 1; i < Model.NumberOfPages;i++) { %>
```

```
<%
   string className = "PagerPageNavItem";
   string activeClassName = "PagerActivePageNavItem";
   string currentClassName = "";

   if (i == Model.CurrentPage)
       currentClassName = activeClassName;
   else
       currentClassName = className;
%>
<div class="<%= currentClassName %>">
<%= Html.ActionLink(i.ToString(),Model.Action, Model.Controller,
   new { @page = i}, null) %></div>
      <% } %>
</div>

<% if(Model.ShowNext) { %>
  <div class="PagerNextPage">
  <%= Html.ActionLink("Next >>",Model.Action, Model.Controller,
     new { @page = Model.NextPage }, null) %></div>
<% } %>
</div>
```

11. Finally, we are ready to drop in our new page control. Go back to the
    `Products.aspx` view. Add a call to `Html.RenderPartial` above the
    table you created earlier. Specify the name of our new `PagerView`. Also, pass
    in the instance of the `Pager` class that we instantiated and hydrated earlier.

    Views/Shared/Products.aspx:

    ```
    . . .
    <% Html.RenderPartial("PagerView", Model.Pager); %>
    <div style="display:block;clear:both;" />
    . . .
    ```

12. You are now ready to build the site. Navigate to the `/ProductsCatalog/Products`
    URL. This will use the default Page value of one and should display ten product
    records. You can click on **Next** to get the next set of data. Then you can click on
    Previous. You can also click on the page number you want to see, or you can edit
    the URL page number directly.

How it works...

The route we created in the first part of the recipe catches all of the URLs that begin with `ProductCatalog`. It also expects the `Products` action to be called and sets the initial page to one. The majority of the magic was then handled by the `Pager` class that we created, which manages all the paging data, such as what page we are currently viewing, how many pages there are, and so on. The other important part of the magic came in the form of our query structure—in that we controlled how many records to show and which set of data we were on.

Some of this logic could have probably been moved into the `Pager` class, but it seemed more appropriate, and efficient to keep it with the query for this example. You could probably create a generic `Pager` class that takes in a type to operate on. You could also extend the `Pager` a bit to take in a repository class according to an interface with a standard method to call, that takes the current page number and the number of records to show. That is a bit bigger topic than this book is prepared to cover though.

Supporting content hierarchies with a custom RouteHandler

In this recipe, we will take a look at a great use of the wildcard route. We will show how to make a single route that handles multiple URLs from `/Sports/Football/Padding/ Rawlings/ShoulderPads` to `/Aquariums/100-Gallon/Stands/Marineland/ Monterey-Stand`. We will also take this concept one step further by supporting additional commands other than just a `Get content` type scenario. We will also add support `Delete`, `Post`, and `Edit`, so that our single route can support an inline style content management solution.

How to do it...

1. Start by creating a new MVC application.

2. Then open up the `Global.asax` file. In the routing section, add a new route definition to the bottom of the list. This route will not specify a controller, an action, or any other parameters. Instead it will have only a wildcard option to catch all requests that make it to the bottom of our route dictionary. This route will use the Home Controller and a `Catalog` action that we will create shortly. Also, this route will use a custom `RouteHandler` called `CatalogRouteHandler`.

   Global.asax:

   ```
   routes.MapRoute("DbContent", "{*path}",
     new {controller = "Home", action = "Catalog"})
       .RouteHandler = new CatalogRouteHandler();
   ```

3. Next, we need to create our `Catalog` action. This action should technically not be reached by this style of request, but it can be used as an entry page to your catalog.

Controllers/HomeController.cs:

```
public ActionResult Catalog()
{
    return View();
}
```

4. Then we need to create our `CatalogRouteHandler`. This class will implement the `IRouteHandler`, which requires that a `GetHttpHandler` method be specified.

Models/CatalogRouteHandler.cs:

```
public class CatalogRouteHandler : IRouteHandler
{
    public IHttpHandler GetHttpHandler(RequestContext
      requestContext)
    {
        . . .
    }
}
```

5. With our method in place, we now need to add the guts. This method will be responsible for catching the path requested and parsing it in the best manner possible. You could use the entire path value as the unique ID in your system to identify a piece of content. Or you could use just the last part of the path as the unique identifier. I will leave that up to you! In our implementation we will parse for the entire path. We will also check to see if there is an additional command at the end of the path, so that we can support different types of commands (which will translate to different actions) for pretty much the same URL.

Models/CatalogRouteHandler.cs:

```
string path = requestContext.RouteData.Values["path"] as string;

//remove trailing slash if there is one
if (path.EndsWith("/"))
  path = path.Substring(0, path.Length - 1);

if(path != null && path.Contains("/")) //valid path parameter
{
    int lastIndex = path.LastIndexOf('/');
    if(lastIndex >= 0)
    {
        string commandName = path.Substring(lastIndex + 1);

            . . .

    }
}
```

6. Once we have the path in hand and have parsed for the command that may or may not be there, we can then try to route to the appropriate action for the given request. We will use a simple `switch` statement to achieve this. Once we locate the type of command we are going to use, we will then modify our current route definition to have the appropriate action as well as the cleaned and adjusted path.

Models/CatalogRouteHandler.cs:

```
switch(commandName.ToUpper())
{
  case "GET": //get the catalog item
    requestContext.RouteData.Values["action"] = "Get";
    //add the path minus the command back in
    requestContext.RouteData.Values["path"] =
      path.Substring(0, lastIndex);
    break;

  case "DELETE": //delete catalog item
    requestContext.RouteData.Values["action"] = "Delete";
    //add the path minus the command back in
    requestContext.RouteData.Values["path"] =
      path.Substring(0, lastIndex);
    break;

  case "EDIT": //edit catalog item
    requestContext.RouteData.Values["action"] = "Edit";
    //add the path minus the command back in
    requestContext.RouteData.Values["path"] =
        path.Substring(0, lastIndex);
    break;

  case "POST": //save catalog item (insert/update)
    requestContext.RouteData.Values["action"] = "Post";
    //add the path minus the command back in
    requestContext.RouteData.Values["path"] =
      path.Substring(0, lastIndex);
    break;

  default: //we will allow nothing to act as a GET
    requestContext.RouteData.Values["action"] = "Get";
    //add the path minus the command back in
    requestContext.RouteData.Values["path"] = path;
   break;
}
```

7. Once the appropriate route has been picked, we are ready to return the modified route.

   Models/CatalogRouteHandler.cs:

   ```
   . . .
   }
     return new MvcHandler(requestContext);
   }
   ```

8. Now that we have a dynamic routing engine that is capable of determining all sorts of different actions based on the passed in URL, we need to actually create the actions and views to capture the requests.

   Controllers/HomeController.cs:

   ```
   [HandleError]
   public class HomeController : Controller
   {
       . . .

       public ActionResult Get(string path)
       {
           return View();
       }

       public ActionResult Delete(string path)
       {
           return View();
       }

       public ActionResult Post(string path)
       {
           return View();
       }

       public ActionResult Edit(string path)
       {
           return View();
       }
   }
   ```

9. Next we need to create the views for each action. These will just be empty views as our recipe is about routing rather than data access and application. (I am not showing empty views as that is boring!)

10. Now you can build and run the application. You can browse to just about anything and you will be routed to one of our new actions, as long as you don't navigate to /Home/About or /Home/Index or /Account/LogOn, and so on!

How it works...

As with most other recipes of this type, we have hooked into yet another extension point of the MVC framework. We have defined a catch all route at the bottom of our route dictionary. When this route is picked for a request, we shell out to a custom route handler, which doctors the route to suit its needs and returns the appropriate route definition.

There's more...

When researching a CMS system that I was building, I needed a recipe of this nature. While this post doesn't quite do all that I would have liked, it got me pretty close to what I was trying to achieve. Credit where credit is due! Thanks chris166. `http://stackoverflow.com/questions/1023252/asp-net-mvc-complex-routing-for-tree-path`.

Creating a blacklist route constraint

Sometimes you want to take control over all of your requests prior to them getting too deep into your application. While you could do this with an `HttpHandler` or an `HttpModule`, that wouldn't be very MVC-like. Instead, we will implement this sort of logic in the next step of the pipeline by way of a custom `RouteConstraint`.

In our example, we will take a look at implementing a blacklist filter, using a wide open wildcard route and a `RouteConstraint` that checks all requests against a few different types of blacklists. If the user is on the blacklist, we will have the option to route them off our site or to a page in our site specifically for blacklisted folks.

How to do it...

1. Create a new MVC application.
2. Open up the `Global.asax` file. In the routing section, at the top of the list of routes, we need to create a new route. This route will be named `BlacklistFilter` and will have only a wildcard entry for its path pattern matching, essentially funneling all requests through this route for a check. Then comes the magic in that we will specify a custom `RouteHandler` called `BlacklistConstraint`.

Global.asax:

```
routes.MapRoute("BlacklistFilter", "{*path}",
    new { controller = "Blacklist", action = "Index", },
    new {isBlacklisted = new BlacklistConstraint()}
);
```

3. Then we can create a new controller called `BlacklistController` in the `Controllers` folder. This controller will have one action on it named `Index` and will take in a parameter named reason which we will use to capture the reason the user is on the blacklist.

Controllers/BlacklistController.cs:

```
public class BlacklistController : Controller
{
  public ActionResult Index(string reason)
  {
    ViewData["Reason"] = reason;
    return View();
  }
}
```

4. From this new action, we can generate a new `Index` view, which will be an empty view. In the view, we will display a simple message to the user telling them that they have been blacklisted. We will also say why we think they have been blacklisted.

Views/Blacklist/Index.aspx:

```
<asp:Content ID="Content1" ContentPlaceHolderID="TitleContent"
    runat="server">
  Blacklisted!
</asp:Content>

<asp:Content ID="Content2" ContentPlaceHolderID="MainContent"
    runat="server">

  <h2>Uh oh!</h2>
   <div>
     It looks like you have been blacklisted.  If you feel that
    you are seeing this mistakenly please contact us at...
   </div>
   <fieldset>
      <legend>Why was I blacklisted?</legend>
      <%= ViewData["reason"] %>
   </fieldset>
</asp:Content>
```

5. Lastly, we will need to create our custom `RouteConstraint`. Create a new class in the `Models` folder named `RouteConstraint`. Set this new class to implement `IRouteConstraint` and then create the one required method, `Match()`.

Models/BlacklistConstraint.cs:

```
public class BlacklistConstraint : IRouteConstraint
{
```

```
public bool Match(HttpContextBase httpContext, Route route,
    string parameterName, RouteValueDictionary values,
    RouteDirection routeDirection)
{


}
}
```

6. All that this method needs to do is return a `Boolean` result. Whatever method you use to determine if a user is on your blacklist is up to you. If you locate the user on the blacklist, return true, which will route them to your blacklisted page. If you don't find them, return false, and the processing will continue. You may also want to drop a cookie or set a session variable so that the check is not repeated over and over—unless you want to. For our recipe, we will define some blacklists directly in the class, for example purposes only. We will also create a simple variable to track if this user is flagged or not.

Models/BlacklistConstraint.cs:

```
bool blacklisted = false;

//you could get your blacklist data from a database
//and cache it when the app starts

//ip address list
List<string> _ipBlacklist = new List<string>()
    {
        "127.0.0.1",
        "192.168.1.100",
        "192.168.1.101",
        "192.168.1.102",
        "192.168.1.103",
        "192.168.1.104",
        "192.168.1.105",
        "192.168.1.106",
        "192.168.1.107",
        "192.168.1.108",
        "192.168.1.109",
        "192.168.1.110"
    };

//username list
List<string> _usernameBlacklist = new List<string>()
    {
        "asiemer",
        "anonymous"
    };
```

```
//email list
List<string> _emailBlacklist = new List<string>()
  {
    "asmith@hotmail.com",
    "jsmith@hotmail.com"
  };
```

7. Once you have the mechanism in place to keep track of who is blacklisted, you can add the actual checking implementation. For us, this will be a few checks to see if the user exists on any of our lists. If we find that the user is on the list, then we will set our flag to true, signifying that they match the constraint and can be processed by this route. We will also set a `reason` variable in our route data that can be displayed in our blacklist index view.

Models/BlacklistConstraint.cs:

```
//check ip addresses
if (_ipBlacklist.Contains(httpContext.Request.UserHostAddress))
{
  values.Add("Reason", "You were blacklisted because of your IP
    address: " + httpContext.Request.UserHostAddress);
  blacklisted = true;
}


//check usernames
if (httpContext.Profile != null && _usernameBlacklist.Contains(
  httpContext.Profile.UserName.ToLower()))
{
  values.Add("Reason", "You were blacklisted because of your
    username: " + httpContext.Profile.UserName.ToLower());
  blacklisted = true;
}


//check email addresses
if (_emailBlacklist.Contains("values['email'].ToString()"))
{
  values.Add("Reason", "You were blacklisted because of your email
    address: values['email'].ToString()");
  blacklisted = true;
}
```

8. Once we have processed all of our lists, we can then handle the fact that the user is indeed blacklisted. In our case, we could redirect the user to `PeopleOfWalmart.com` or we could send them to our blacklist page, where they can see that they are blacklisted as well as the reason for which they are blacklisted. We will also set the `HttpStatusCode` of our response to access denied (403).

Be aware that telling your blacklisted user that they are actually blacklisted, as well as why they are blacklisted, may not be the best way to handle such a user. If it is to be a temporary blacklist due to abuse of a site feature, telling the user might be appropriate. Telling a malicious user that they are blacklisted due to their IP address might get them to go through a proxy server prior to coming to your site. Just think about what you do here.

Models/BlacklistConstraint.cs:

```
//do some stuff before booting the user
if (blacklisted)
{
  //of, if you don't want to keep them around...
  //httpContext.Response
    .Redirect("http://www.peopleofwalmart.com");

  //set the status code to access denied
  httpContext.Response.StatusCode = (int)HttpStatusCode.Forbidden;
}

//return the result
return blacklisted;
```

9. From here, you should be able to run your application. The sheer act of attempting to view the home page from your local computer should get you blacklisted from your site, as most likely you are browsing from 127.0.0.1. If for some reason you are not blacklisted by IP address, you can run ipconfig at the command prompt to get your current IP. Or you can create an account in the site and add your username to the username list.

How it works...

This recipe takes advantage of an extension point of the MVC framework. Specifically, we used a custom RouteConstraint to add to our route definition. The nice bit about the RouteConstraint is that anything goes here, as it is just a standard class from which we can do pretty much anything. The combination of the route definition and this added bit of Boolean logic makes your routing capabilities very powerful.

4

Master Pages

In this chapter, we will cover:

- ► How to create a master page
- ► Determining the master page in the `ActionResult`
- ► Controlling which master page is used with a view base class
- ► Setting the master page from a controller base class
- ► Passing data to the master page
- ► Rendering data in a master page from another view
- ► Creating nested master pages

Introduction

Master pages are a very important part of any large-scale site. They allow you to easily manage the boilerplate code that every page in your site uses. This might encompass features such as navigational items, header and footer layout, basic layout, and so on.

In this chapter, we will discuss how to create and use master pages to control application-wide formatting. We will also take a look at how to employ a base page, to control which master page is used. Then we will see how to pass data from the view to the master page.

How to create a master page

In this recipe, we will take a look at how to create a master page and associate it with our view. Part of creating a master page is defining placeholders for use in the view. We will then see how to utilize the content placeholders that we defined in the master page.

How to do it...

1. Start by creating a new ASP.NET MVC application.

2. Then add a new master page to your solution called `Custom.Master`. Place it in the `Views/Shared` directory.

3. Notice that there is a placeholder already placed in the middle of our page. Let's wrap that placeholder with a table. We will put a column to the left and the right of the existing placeholder. Then we will rename the placeholder to `MainContent`.

   Views/Shared/Custom.Master:

```
<table>
  <tr>
    <td>

    </td>
    <td>
      <asp:ContentPlaceHolder ID="ContentPlaceHolder1"
          runat="server"></asp:ContentPlaceHolder>
    </td>
    <td>

    </td>
  </tr>
</table>
```

4. Next, we will copy the placeholder into the first and the third columns.

   Views/Shared/Custom.Master:

```
<table>
  <tr>
    <td>
      <asp:ContentPlaceHolder ID="ContentPlaceHolder1"
          runat="server"></asp:ContentPlaceHolder>
    </td>
    <td>
      <asp:ContentPlaceHolder ID="MainContent"
          runat="server"></asp:ContentPlaceHolder>
    </td>
    <td>
      <asp:ContentPlaceHolder ID="ContentPlaceHolder2"
          runat="server"></asp:ContentPlaceHolder>
    </td>
  </tr>
</table>
```

5. Next, we need to add a new action to the `HomeController.cs` file, from which we will create a new view. Do this by opening the `HomeController.cs` file, then add a new action named `CustomMasterDemo`.

Controllers/HomeController.cs:

```
public ActionResult CustomMasterDemo()
{
  return View();
}
```

6. Then right-click on the `CustomerMasterDemo` and choose `AddView`, and select the new `Custom.Master` page that we created. Next, you need to change the `ContentPlaceHolderID` box to show the center placeholder name **ContentPlaceHolder2**. Then hit **Add** and you should see a new view with four placeholders.

Views/Home/CustomMasterDemo.aspx:

```
<asp:Content ID="Content1" ContentPlaceHolderID="MainContent"
    runat="server">
  <h2>Custom Master Demo</h2>
</asp:Content>

<asp:Content ID="Content2" ContentPlaceHolderID="head"
    runat="server">
```

```
      <meta name="description" content="Here are some keywords for our
        page description.">
    </asp:Content>

    <asp:Content ID="Content3"
      ContentPlaceHolderID="ContentPlaceHolder1" runat="server">
      <div style="width:200px;height:200px;border:1px solid #ff0000;">
        <ul>
          <li>Home</li>
          <li>Contact Us</li>
          <li>About Us</li>
        </ul>
      </div>
    </asp:Content>

    <asp:Content ID="Content"
      ContentPlaceHolderID="ContentPlaceHolder2" runat="server">
      <div style="width:200px;height:200px;border:1px solid #000000;">
        <b>News</b><br/>
          Here is a blurb of text on the right!
      </div>
    </asp:Content>
```

7. You should now see a page similar to this:

How it works...

This particular feature is a server-side carry over from web forms. It works just as it always has. Before being sent down to the client, the view is merged into the master file and processed according to the matching placeholder IDs.

Determining the master page in the ActionResult

In the previous recipe, we took a look at how to build a master page. In this recipe, we are going to take a look at how to control what master page to use programmatically. There are all sorts of reasons for using different master pages. For example, you might want to use different master pages based on the time of day, if a user is logged in or not, for different areas of your site (blog, shopping, forum, and so on).

How to do it...

1. We will get started by first creating a new MVC web application.

2. Next, we need to create a second master page. We can do this quickly by making a copy of the default master page that is provided. Name it `Site2.Master`.

3. Next, we need to make sure we can tell these two master pages apart. The easiest way to do this is to change the contents of the `H1` tag to say `Master 1` and `Master 2` in each of the master pages.

4. Now we can take a look at the `HomeController`. We will check if we are in an even or odd second and based on that we can return an even or odd master page. We do this by specifying the master page name that we want to use when we return the view.

   Controllers/HomeController.cs:

   ```
   public ActionResult Index()
   {
     ViewData["Message"] = "Welcome to ASP.NET MVC!";

     string masterName = "";

     if (DateTime.Now.Second % 2 == 0)
         masterName = "Site2";
     else
         masterName = "Site";

     return View("Index", masterName);
   }
   ```

5. Now you can run the application. Refreshing the home page should alternate between the two master pages now and then. (Remember that this is based on the second and is now just a pure alternating page scheme.)

How it works...

This method of controlling which master page is used by the view is built into the MVC framework and is the easiest way of performing this type of control. However, having to dictate this type of logic in every single action would create quite a bit of fluff code in our controller. This option might be appropriate for certain needs though!

Controlling which master page is used with a view base class

In this recipe, we are going to take a look at another approach for setting which master page is used by the view. Specifically, we are going to create a base class that can be inherited by our view pages. In the base class we can then override the `OnPreInit` method, inside of which we can easily control the master page that is used by the view.

How to do it...

1. Start by creating a new MVC project.

2. Next, create a copy of the existing master page and call it `Site2.Master`.

3. Change the `H1` text to show `Master 1` and `Master 2`, so that we can easily tell which master page is being used.

4. Then we need to create a new class in our `Models` folder called `BaseViewPage.cs`.

5. In the new base class that we are creating, we need to inherit from `System.Web.Mvc.Viewpage`. Then we need to define a method that overrides the framework's `OnPreInit` method. Inside of our method, we will build up some logic to check if we are in an even or odd second when the page loads. Based on the result of our test, we will load the `Site2.master` file or `Site.master` file.

   Models/BaseViewPage.cs:

```
public class BaseViewPage : System.Web.Mvc.ViewPage
{
  protected override void OnPreInit(EventArgs e)
  {
    if(DateTime.Now.Second%2==0)
        Page.MasterPageFile = "~/Views/Shared/Site2.Master";
    else
        Page.MasterPageFile = "~/Views/Shared/Site.Master";

    base.OnPreInit(e);
  }
}
```

6. For this logic to get executed, we need to set our Index view to inherit from our new base class instead of inheriting from `System.Web.Mvc.ViewPage`.

   Views/Home/Index.aspx:

   ```
   <%@ Page Language="C#" MasterPageFile="~/Views/Shared/Site.Master"
     Inherits="MvcApplication1.Models.BaseViewPage" %>
   ...
   ```

7. Now you can run your application. Refreshing the home page should show the master pages being switched now and then, based on the second that the page is being loaded.

How it works...

Because our view was set to inherit from our custom base class and our base class catches the `OnPreInit` event, we are able to set the master page prior to the page being built. This is important as you can toggle the master page that a view uses after it has started being rendered! Now all we need to do is use our base class for all of our views (a good idea even if you don't yet need it, as it will provide you with an added point of extensibility).

Setting the master page from a controller base class

In this recipe, we will take a look at how to control our master pages at a higher level. We will create a controller base class. In the controller base class, we will then take control of which master page is used by the views that are controlled by controllers that inherit from our shiny new base class.

How to do it...

1. The first step is to create a new MVC application.

2. Then copy the existing master page and create a new master page called `Site2.master`.

3. Next, change the `H1` text for each of the master pages to `Master 1` and `Master 2` accordingly.

4. Now, we can create a `BaseController` class in the `Models` folder. This class will inherit from `Controller`. Then we will set the `BaseController` to override the `OnActionExecuted` method. In this method, we will get an instance of the current `ViewResult` from the passed-in context. We need to check to make sure that the instance is not null. Then we will perform some logic to check if we are in an even or odd second, and set the corresponding master page based on the results of that test. Then we return the context to the pipeline.

Models/BaseController.cs:

```
public class BaseController : Controller
{
  protected override void OnActionExecuted(
    ActionExecutedContext filterContext)
  {
    var action = filterContext.Result as ViewResult;
    if (action != null)
    {
      if (DateTime.Now.Second % 2 == 0)
        action.MasterName = "Site2";
      else
        action.MasterName = "Site";
    }

    base.OnActionExecuted(filterContext);
  }
}
```

5. With our `BaseController` created we can wire it up to our `HomeController` by having our `HomeController` inherit the new `BaseController`.

Controllers/HomeController.cs:

```
public class HomeController : BaseController
```

6. Now you can run the application and refresh the home page. You should see the Site and Site2 master pages being used now and then.

How it works...

This is just another example of a hook that we can attach to affect how the MVC application works. In this case, we are hooking into the `OnActionExecuted` event. This event is raised prior to the view being rendered and after the `action` method is executed—which means we still have time to alter the master page that is used by the current view.

Passing data to the master page

In this recipe, we are going to take a look at how to pass data down to the master page. While we could pass data from a normal `ActionResult` to the view via the `ViewData` dictionary and then have the `MasterPage` use that data, we won't as that creates a lot of redundant code spread out over multiple actions in the controller. We could alleviate some of this action code and move it up to the `OnActionExecuted` method in our controller. However, if our master page is shared across multiple controllers, then this too wouldn't be a good solution. For that reason, we will instead create a controller base class and use that for creating the data for our master page.

How to do it...

1. The first step is to create a new MVC application.

2. Next, we will create a controller base class called `BaseController`. In this base controller, we will initiate a list of data for navigational purposes.

    Models/BaseController.cs:

    ```
    public class BaseController : Controller
    {
      public BaseController()
      {
        List<string> manufacturers = new List<string>();
        manufacturers.Add("Ford");
        manufacturers.Add("Toyota");
        manufacturers.Add("Chevy");
        manufacturers.Add("Dodge");
        manufacturers.Add("Nissan");
        manufacturers.Add("Mazda");
        manufacturers.Add("Audi");

        ViewData["manufacturers"] = manufacturers;
      }
    }
    ```

3. Next, we will alter our `HomeController` to inherit from our new `BaseController`.

    Controllers/HomeController.cs:

    ```
    public class HomeController : BaseController
    ```

4. Now that our data is being created and passed down to every view that is created from this controller, we need to update our master page to take advantage of this data.

Views/Shared/Site.Master:

```
. . .
<div id="main">
  <%string menu = "";
    if (ViewData["manufacturers"] != null)
    {
      StringBuilder sbMenu = new StringBuilder();
      List<string> manufacturers = ViewData["manufacturers"] as
        List<string>;
      foreach (string item in manufacturers)
      {
        sbMenu.Append(item + " - ");
      }

      menu = sbMenu.ToString().Substring(0,
        sbMenu.ToString().Length - 3);
    }
  %>
  <%: menu %>
    . . .
</div>
. . .
```

5. Now you can browse to your Index and About views and you should see a new listing of auto manufacturers, which represents a navigation menu, without links. If you browse to the login or registration views, which use the Account controller, the navigation menu will disappear.

How it works...

To achieve this, we have essentially injected data that is required by our master page into the controller pipeline by inserting a controller base class. As long as our controller inherits from the base class, the ViewData will contain the navigation data. This helps us to centralize such logic and can obviously be taken in many different directions.

Rendering data in a master page from another view

In this recipe, we are going to take a look at how to render views directly within a master page. Really, this technique can be used in any view. The nice bit about this is that we don't have to concern ourselves with what data and other dependencies the other view requires to be rendered, such as rendering partial views. This allows us to easily call this view from anywhere without having to concern ourselves with the guts of the view.

How to do it...

1. We first need to create a new MVC application.

2. Next, we need to create a new `ActionResult` and view in our `HomeController`. We will call this new method `_Categories`. (I usually use the underscore prefix for partial views and views that can only be rendered as a child using `[ChildActionOnly]`.)

3. In the `_Categories` action, we will create a quick list of common e-commerce categories. This list will then be returned to the view by way of the `ViewData` dictionary. We will also mark the action with the `[ChildActionOnly]` attribute to ensure that this view can't be rendered by just anyone.

   Controllers/HomeController.cs:

   ```
   [ChildActionOnly]
   public ActionResult _Categories()
   {
     List<string> navigation = new List<string>();
     navigation.Add("Books");
     navigation.Add("Cars");
     navigation.Add("Clothes");
     navigation.Add("Computers");

     ViewData["navigation"] = navigation;

     return View();
   }
   ```

4. Next, we will create the view that goes with our new `_Categories` action.

   Views/Home/_Categories.ascx:

   ```
   <%
     List<string> navigation = ViewData["navigation"]
       as List<string>;
     StringBuilder output = new StringBuilder();
   ```

```
    foreach (string s in navigation)
    {
        output.Append(s + " - ");
    }
    string nav = output.ToString().Substring(0,
        output.ToString().Length - 3);
%>


<%: nav %>
```

5. With our new action and the view to go with it, we can now turn our attention to rendering our view inside of our master page. This can be quickly achieved using the `Html.Action` method, which requires the view and controller to be passed in. The rest of what is needed to render the view is hidden away from us!

    Views/Shared/Site.Master:

```
...
<div id="main">

    <%= Html.Action("_Categories", "Home") %>

    <asp:ContentPlaceHolder ID="MainContent" runat="server" />

    <div id="footer">
    </div>
</div>
...
```

6. Now that everything is plugged in, you can view the new master page. Make sure that you also try to navigate to `/Home/_Categories` to see that the view can't be viewed directly.

How it works...

This method of rendering a partial view in line with another view is part of the MVC framework. Some people like this method of rendering data view within a view, others do not. By using this method you are allowing a view to be in charge of what it renders rather than only rendering what the controller says it can.

This method of rendering data has its upside though. As you are rendering the two views—the calling view and the partial view—separately, you can control the caching, security, and so on, separately too.

Creating nested master pages

If you are a really heavy user of master pages, then the odds are that you have reached the extent of their usefulness in a single master page environment. This is where having nested master pages may come in to help you. Nested master pages are specifically useful when you want to have a generic master page to specify the site's header, standard navigation, and footer. Then you can have a nested master page to control the specific area of your application. An example of this would be a nested master page for forums, blogs, product catalog, and so on.

How to do it...

1. Let's start by creating a new MVC application.
2. Then we will add a new nested master page file called `NestedMasterPage1.master` (you could just as easily add a view master page—both will work).
3. Part of creating a new nested master page is picking the master page you want to use for your nested master page—choose the default `Site.Master`.
4. Once the nested master page is created, you will see that the two content areas are implemented in the `Site.Master`. In order for any views to be able to use our nested master page, we need to create some instances of `ContentPlaceHolder` inside some of the defined content areas.

    Views/Shared/NestedMasterPage1.master:

    ```
    <asp:Content ID="Content1" ContentPlaceHolderID="TitleContent"
        runat="server">
      <asp:ContentPlaceHolder ID="TitleContent" runat="server">
      </asp:ContentPlaceHolder>
    </asp:Content>

    <asp:Content ID="Content2" ContentPlaceHolderID="MainContent"
        runat="server">
      Content provided by the nested master page...
      <asp:ContentPlaceHolder ID="MainContent" runat="server">

      </asp:ContentPlaceHolder>
    </asp:Content>
    ```

5. Now we can swap out the master page that our home page uses.

    Views/Home/Index.aspx:

    ```
    <%@ Page Language="C#"
    MasterPageFile="~/Views/Shared/NestedMasterPage1.Master"
    Inherits="System.Web.Mvc.ViewPage" %>
    ```

6. The application is now ready to run. You should see the customer message as well as the normal page on the home page.

How it works...

This recipe is similar to the nested master page days of standard ASP.NET web forms. The one nice improvement is that you have some added wizard support for picking the master page that it plans to extend. The basic idea behind how this works is that when a view is loaded, its master page (nested in this case) is loaded, and if there is another master page to load, it loads that too.

Working with Data in the View

5

In this chapter, we will cover:

- ► Reintroducing `for` and `foreach`
- ► Handling an array of checkboxes
- ► Handling an array of radio buttons
- ► Working with a pageable set of data
- ► How to navigate sortable data
- ► Delete a record with an intermediary "Are you sure?" page
- ► Add a jQuery delete link with confirmation
- ► Creating a master/detail page with inline details via jQuery
- ► Adding a master/detail page with modal details window using JSON

Introduction

In this chapter, we are going to look at all sorts of different recipes that pertain to playing with data in the view. We will try to cover as many of the standard day-to-day topics, which every ASP.NET developer might need to know. This will take us through a bunch of quick recipes that demonstrate simple concepts, such as iterating through a collection to more complex scenarios like how to handle the creation of master/detail pages with Ajax modal pop-ups.

Reintroducing for and foreach

In this recipe, we will take a look at how to iterate over a collection of data using `for` and `foreach`. In this recipe, we will use NBuilder to create a list of `Product` classes for us to work with. Then we will build three views that will iterate over the collection in different ways. We will show how to iterate over a collection of products pulled from `ViewData` using `foreach`. Then we will see how we can iterate over the `Model` property of a strongly typed view. And finally, we will create another strongly typed view and use a `for` statement to iterate over the collection.

How to do it...

Initial bits...

1. The first thing that we need to do is create a new ASP.NET MVC project. Then we will add a reference to NBuilder (in the dependencies folder of the download).

2. Next, we will create a new class in the `Models` folder of our application called `Product`. This class will be used for creating a collection of data for our iteration examples.

   Models/Product.cs:

   ```
   public class Product
   {
     public int ProductId { get; set; }
     public string Name { get; set; }
     public double Price { get; set; }
     public string Description { get; set;}
     public DateTime CreateDate { get; set; }
   }
   ```

3. As we are going to have three examples in this recipe, we will need to centralize the code that we will use to generate the list of products. We will do this by creating a `ProductRepository` class in the `Models` folder. This class will use NBuilder to do the generation work for us.

   Models/ProductRepository.cs:

   ```
   public class ProductRepository
   {
     public List<Product> GetProducts()
     {
       List<Product> result = Builder<Product>
         .CreateListOfSize(30)
         .WhereAll()
   ```

```
        .Have(x => x.Description =
            @"...long lorem ipsum string...")
        .Build()
        .ToList();

    return result;
  }
}
```

foreach over ViewData collection

1. Now that we have a working repository to get a list of data from, we can create our
    first example of a `foreach` loop. Start by opening the home controller. In the existing
    Index view, we will add a line of code passing a collection of `Products` into the
    `ViewData` dictionary.

    Controllers/HomeController.cs:

    ```
    ViewData["Products"] = new ProductRepository().GetProducts();
    ```

2. Then we need to open up the Index view corresponding to the `Index` action we just
    added the code to. Then remove all of the fluff that the template adds for us. Now we
    will add a line of code to grab the list of products out of the `ViewData` collection.

    Views/Home/Index.aspx:

    ```
    <% List<Product> products = ViewData["Products"] as List<Product>;
    %>
    ```

3. With reference to our collection of products, we can work on the iteration aspect of
    our recipe. Iteration code is pretty quick and to the point.

    Views/Home/Index.aspx:

    ```
    <% foreach (Product p in products) { %>
    ...
    <% } %>
    ```

4. To finish off this portion, we will need to add our formatting code and the output of
    our data.

> There is a new shorthand syntax in MVC 2 that allows us to perform
> an `Html.Encode`. There is the previous syntax `<%=` that allows
> us to write data as if we had used `Response.Write`. Then there
> is the new `<%:` syntax. This `<%:` variant encodes the data prior
> to spitting it out, allowing us to remove all the `<% Html.Encode`
> statements that we would have to use. But as Visual Studio's code
> generator still uses `<%= Html.Encode`, we will leave it as it is.

Views/Home/Index.aspx:

```
<div class="display-label">ProductId</div>
<div class="display-field"><%= Html.Encode(p.ProductId) %></div>

<div class="display-label">Name</div>
<div class="display-field"><%= Html.Encode(p.Name) %></div>

<div class="display-label">Price</div>
<div class="display-field">
  <%= Html.Encode(String.Format("{0:c}", p.Price)) %></div>

<div class="display-label">Description</div>
<div class="display-field"><%= Html.Encode(p.Description) %></div>

<div class="display-label">CreateDate</div>
<div class="display-field">
  <%= Html.Encode(String.Format("{0:g}", p.CreateDate)) %></div>

<hr />
```

foreach over strongly typed view model

1. With the iteration over `ViewData` completed, we can now take a look at how things differ when using a strongly typed view instead. To start this portion of the recipe, open the home controller. Then we will add a new `ActionResult` called `ForEach`. In this method, we will again get a list of products from our repository and return that collection to our view. This time though, we will not use the `ViewData` dictionary to pass out the data. Instead, we will pass it directly to the view.

Controllers/HomeController.cs:

```
public ActionResult ForEach()
{
  List<Product> products = new ProductRepository().GetProducts();
  return View(products);
}
```

2. Next, we will look at the code generation that Visual Studio can do for us. Right-click on the method and choose **Add View**. This will open the **Add View** dialog.

3. In the **Add View** dialog you have lots of options. We will leave the view name as it is (the view that will be generated). Then we will check the **Create a strongly typed view** box. Next, we will choose the type that we want the view to be typed to (MvcApplication1.Models.Product in this case). In the **View content:** drop-down list, there are all sorts of good options...we will choose to generate a **Details** view. Then you can choose to use a master page for your view. Click on **Add**.

4. You may have noticed that we chose to add a **Product** but we returned a product list in our action definition. To fix this mismatch, we will need to edit the declaration of our generated view from expecting one product to instead expect a collection of products.

```
Inherits="System.Web.Mvc.ViewPage
    <MvcApplication1.Models.Product>"
```

to

```
Inherits="System.Web.Mvc.ViewPage<List
    <MvcApplication1.Models.Product>>".
```

5. Now we will need to create our `foreach` statement wrapped around our generated details view.

   Views/Home/ForEach.aspx:

   ```
   <% foreach (Product p in Model) { %>
   ...
   <% } %>
   ```

6. Then we need to edit the details view code to use the `p` reference in place of the `Model` object. Change:

   ```
   <%= Html.Encode(Model.ProductId) %>
   ```
   to
   ```
   <%= Html.Encode(p.ProductId) %>
   ```

   (The same for all other `Model` references.)

for over strongly typed view model

1. With the example of `ViewData` and strongly typed view `Model` iterations using the `foreach` statement, we can now look at a strongly typed view `Model` example using the `for` statement. To start this example, we need to create another new action called `For`. This method will also return a list of products from our `ProductRepository`.

   Controllers/HomeController.cs:

   ```
   public ActionResult For()
   {
     List<Product> products = new ProductRepository().GetProducts();
     return View(products);
   }
   ```

2. As in the last example, we will generate a view by right-clicking on the method and choosing **Add View**. Name this view **For**. All the other options will be the same as before.

3. We will need to change the inherited type for this view as we did in the last example by changing:

   ```
   Inherits="System.Web.Mvc.ViewPage
      <MvcApplication1.Models.Product>"
   ```
   to
   ```
   Inherits="System.Web.Mvc.ViewPage<List
     <MvcApplication1.Models.Product>>".
   ```

4. Then we need to create our `for` statements.

   Views/Home/For.aspx:

   ```
   <% for (int i = 0; i < Model.Count; i++) { %>
   ...
   <% } %>
   ```

5. With our `for` declaration in place, we then need to update the generated details view to reference an index in the collection of products, rather than referencing properties of a single product model. We will have to change all references of

   ```
   <%= Html.Encode(Model.ProductId) %>
   ```

   to

   ```
   <%= Html.Encode(Model[i].ProductId) %>
   ```

6. Now you can hit *F5* and view all three different manners of model iteration!

How it works...

The iteration over a collection is pretty standard to all languages. The syntax of each iteration style was the focus of this recipe. More importantly, how to reference the collection is what varies the most. For a quick recap:

▶ In a non-strongly typed view we have to reference the collection in the `ViewData` dictionary and cast it out as the type we expect.

   ```
   List<Product> products = ViewData["Products"] as List<Product>;
   foreach (Product p in products)
   p.ProductId
   ```

▶ For a strongly typed view there is no casting required. However, you need to know that the collection is contained in the `Model` rather than in the `ViewData`.

   ```
   foreach (Product p in Model)
   p.ProductId
   ```

▶ And finally, the syntax for a strongly typed view using the `for` syntax is also different.

   ```
   for (int i = 0; i < Model.Count; i++)
   Model[i].ProductId
   ```

There's more...

Now there is the question of which method of iteration you use, `for`, or `foreach`? This is not the place to address that. Understand that the `for` syntax is the most efficient, but the `foreach` syntax is considerably more readable! Take a look at Jon Skeet's post on the performance implications between the two (`http://msmvps.com/blogs/jon_skeet/archive/2009/01/29/for-vs-foreach-on-arrays-and-lists.aspx`).

Handling an array of checkboxes

In this recipe, we will display a view with a list of checkboxes. We will then look at how to catch that collection when it is posted back to the handling controller.

Getting ready

We will be using our `Product` and `ProductRepository` classes from the previous recipe. This means that we will also be using the NBuilder tool to generate a list of product data for us.

How to do it...

1. First we will create a new MVC 2 application. Then we need to add a reference to the NBuilder assembly in the dependencies folder.

2. Now we need to create a `Product` and `ProductRepository` class (copied over from the first recipe).

3. Then we can get to work by passing a collection of data down to the default view for the home controller.

   Controllers/HomeController.cs:

   ```
   public ActionResult Index()
   {
     ViewData["Products"] = new ProductRepository().GetProducts();
     return View();
   }
   ```

4. Then we need to create a form and iterate through our product list to spit out some checkboxes. Notice that we are using a standard HTML input. Also notice that the value of our checkbox contains the `ProductId` integer, which is important for the next step.

   Views/Home/Index.aspx:

   ```
   <% using (Html.BeginForm()) { %>
     <% List<Product> products = ViewData["Products"]
        as List<Product>;%>
     <% foreach (Product p in products) { %>
   ```

```
<div><input type="checkbox" name="products"
    value="<%= p.ProductId %>" /> <%= p.Name %></div>
<% } %>
<input type="submit" value="Submit" />
<% } %>
```

 There are a couple ways to display checkboxes and radio buttons. Both are included in the code download. I will present the first method in this recipe and the second method in the next recipe.

5. Now that we have checkboxes showing on our view, we need to create an action to capture the posted selections. To do this, we will add an additional index action that accepts only posts. It will expect an array of integers, that is of the ProductId from the last step.

Controllers/HomeController.cs:

```
[HttpPost]
public ActionResult Index(Int32[] products)
{
    //do some work with the selected products

    ViewData["Products"] = new ProductRepository().GetProducts();

    return View();
}
```

How it works...

In this recipe, we took a look at how to use a traditional HTML input checkbox. This included creating a form. We then iterated over our collection of products and output a checkbox in its place. In order to capture the selected checkboxes, we created a new post—the only action that expected an array of integers.

There's more...

You may have noticed that a traditional HTML input field was used in this example. There is, of course, an Html.CheckBox included in the MVC framework. An example of how this works is included in the code download. In the next recipe, we will see a version of this around the concept of radio buttons.

See also

▶   *Handling an array of radio buttons*

Handling an array of radio buttons

This recipe is very similar to the previous recipe—we will be outputting a list of input controls based on a collection of products. The difference is in the implementation that we will be using. In this case, we will use the `Html.RadioButton`, which works in a manner similar to `Html.CheckBox`.

Getting ready

Like our previous recipes, we will be using a `Product` class and a `ProductRepository` class. In addition to that, we will use the NBuilder tool.

How to do it...

1. Start by creating a new MVC web application. Then add a reference to the NBuilder assembly. Next, create a `Product` and `ProductRepository` class in the `Models` folder (or copy them from the `Models` folder of the previous recipe).

2. Then in the home controller we will add a new action called `Index2`. This action will pass a list of products down to the view.

    Controllers/HomeController.cs:

    ```
    public ActionResult Index2()
    {
      ViewData["Products"] = new ProductRepository().GetProducts();

      return View();
    }
    ```

3. Now we can create a new view called `Index2` in the `Views/Home/` directory. This view will iterate through the list of products and display a radio button for each one, using the `Html.RadioButton` method.

    Views/Home/Index2.aspx:

    ```
    <% using (Html.BeginForm()) { %>
      <% List<Product> products = ViewData["Products"]
          as List<Product>;%>
      <% foreach (Product p in products) { %>
        <div>
    ```

```
<%= Html.RadioButton("product_" + p.ProductId.ToString(),
    false) %> <%= p.Name %>
</div>
<% } %>
<input type="submit" value="Submit" />
<% } %>
```

4. Once this is complete, we have a page that lists the products. Now we need to create a new action to catch the form post, like we did in the last recipe. However, this action will work with the `FormCollection` rather than expecting a specific key (this is also covered in the checkbox recipe code).

Controllers/HomeController.cs:

```
[HttpPost]
public ActionResult Index2(FormCollection collection)
{
    ViewData["Products"] = new ProductRepository().GetProducts();

    foreach (var key in collection.Keys)
    {
        if (key.ToString().StartsWith("product_"))
        {
            int productId = int.Parse(key.ToString().Replace(
                "product_", ""));

            //do some work with the selected product
        }
    }

    return View();
}
```

How it works...

This recipe is not overly complex in what it achieves. However, it does show you how to work with the `FormCollection` that is posted to this action. The `FormCollection` gives us access to any HTML bits that are posted by a form. This is useful for radio buttons, checkboxes, and any other input that is not directly bound to our model.

See also

▶ _Handling an array of checkboxes_

Working with a pageable set of data

In this recipe, we will take a look at how you can create and display a pageable set of data. We will also see how we can navigate to the next and previous pages of data.

Getting ready

Because this recipe is not so much about how to run queries as it is about how to display a page of data and navigate to the next and previous pages, we will use NBuilder to mock our data access. We will also continue to use our `Product` and `ProductRepository` classes as the data to work with.

How to do it...

1. To get started we need to create a new MVC project. As we will be using NBuilder to mock our data access, we will need to add a reference to the NBuilder assembly (in the dependencies directory). You will also want to copy over the `Product` and `ProductRepository` classes from the previous recipes.

2. Next, we will update our `ProductRepository` to add the pagination functionality. First, we need to add two parameters to our `GetProducts` method. We will need a `Page` parameter to tell us what page of data we need to display, and we will need a `RecordCount` to tell us how much data to return for each page.

   Models/ProductRepository.cs:

   ```
   public List<Product> GetProducts(int page, int recordCount)
   {
       . . .
   ```

3. Then we need to add a guard clause to the top of the method to make sure that we are operating on at least page 1, working on page 0 would return nothing!

   Models/ProductRepository.cs:

   ```
   public List<Product> GetProducts(int page, int recordCount)
   {
       if (Page < 1)
           Page = 1;
   ```

4. Now we are at the point where we can update the query that we are performing (or mocked query) to return only a set of paged data of the size that we request. This method call will be added just after the `Build()` method and before the `ToList()` call.

   Models/ProductRepository.cs:

   ```
   . . .
   .Build()
   ```

```
//skip the appropriate amount of records
.Skip((page - 1) * recordCount)
.ToList();
...
```

5. With our `ProductRepository` updated, we can now update our controller to work with the new `GetProducts` signature. We will also specify the default record count to be used by our `ProductRepository`. We will also pass the page ID down to our view to play with later.

Controllers/HomeController.cs:

```
private int RecordCount = 20;
public ActionResult Index(int id = 1)
{

  ViewData["Products"] = new ProductRepository().GetProducts(
    id, RecordCount);
  ViewData["id"] = id;
  return View();
}
```

6. With our repository and controller updated, we can now update our view a little. Technically, the display is just another example of iterating through a collection of products, which has been covered to death in this chapter! All that is needed to complete this recipe is to show how we determine the previous page and the next page of data, and how to create the links to get us to the previous and next page of data.

Views/Home/Index.aspx:

```
<fieldset>
  <legend>Products</legend>

  <% int id = (int) ViewData["id"];
     int PreviousId = (id - 1) < 1 ? 1 : id - 1;
     int NextId = id + 1;
  %>

  <%= Html.ActionLink("Previous","Index",new {@id=PreviousId}) %>
  -

  <%= Html.ActionLink("Next","Index",new {@id=NextId}) %>
```

How it works...

The key to this recipe is knowing how big the set of data is you want to work with, and which page you are currently on. Tracking this, as people navigate from one page of data to the next, is all that is really required. Once you have tracked where you are and how big the page set is, you then need a way for your users to go forward and backward within that set of data. Other than that, you need to be able to communicate these needs with your data, be it XML, files, objects, or relational data in a database.

How to navigate sortable data

In this recipe, we will take a look at all the workings of getting a view in MVC to sort data. The focus will not be so much on the data side of the implementation, as any data source is applicable. Instead, we will look at all of the various places that must be touched to get the plumbing working as required to sort by various fields of data. This recipe will take a look at what is needed to get the routing, view, and controller, as well as a bit of fancy LINQ over a collection of objects.

Getting ready

Having sortable data without data that pages seems incomplete to me. For that reason, we will start with the code from the previous recipe to get us started. This will include the `Product` and `ProductRepository` classes. It will also include the use of NBuilder.

How to do it...

1. In order to be able to sort data, we need to specify the field that we want to sort by, as well as the direction that we want our data sorted in. To do this, we will need to modify our `ProductRepository.GetProducts()` method. We will add a new `string` parameter of `sortField`. We will also add a Boolean parameter of `reverseSort`.

    Models/ProductRepository.cs:

    ```
    public List<Product> GetProducts(int page, int recordCount,
      string sortField, bool reverseSort)
    {
    ```

2. Once we have our additional inputs, we need to modify our original NBuilder query. We need to move the skip logic to the last part of the query (because we are primarily using NBuilder to generate a collection for us). Then we will add a call to `SortBy`—an extension method that we will build shortly. Finally, we will check the `reverseSort` property to see if we need a descending order or not. Here is what we had:

Models/ProductRepository.cs:

```
List<Product> result = Builder<Product>
  .CreateListOfSize(Page * RecordCount)
  .WhereAll()
    .Have(x => x.Description = @"...").Build()
      //skip the appropriate amount of records
    .Skip((Page - 1) * RecordCount)
    .ToList();
```

Here is what our `ProductRepository` looks like now.

Models/ProductRepository.cs:

```
//build the collection of data
List<Product> result = Builder<Product>
    .CreateListOfSize(page*recordCount).WhereAll()
      .Have(x => x.Description = @"...").Build()
    .SortBy(sortField)
    .ToList();

//reverse the sort?
if (reverseSort)
  result.Reverse();

//do the paging
return result.Skip((page - 1) * recordCount).ToList();
```

3. The `SortBy` extension method is what allows us to sort by a dynamic string. In our case, we need to have the ability to accept a property name as a string from our UI, and convert that string to the actual property, for the query to work as expected. In order to do this, we will use a bit of reflection to get the property by name in our `GetPropertyValue` method.

Models/RepositoryHelpers.cs:

```
private static object GetPropertyValue(object obj,
  string property)
{
  System.Reflection.PropertyInfo propertyInfo =
    obj.GetType().GetProperty(property);
  return propertyInfo.GetValue(obj, null);
}
```

4. With the `GetPropertyValue` method defined, we can then create a generic `SortBy` extension method (allowing us to reuse this for any `IList` collection). This method will use standard LINQ syntax to sort our collection using the `orderby` clause. We specify that we want to order by the result of our new `GetPropertyValue` method.

Models/RepositoryHelpers.cs:

```
public static IList<T> SortBy<T>(this IList<T> list,
   string property)
{
   //order the results
   if (!String.IsNullOrEmpty(property))
      list = (from item in list.AsEnumerable()
      orderby GetPropertyValue(item, property)
      select item).ToList();
   return list;
}
```

5. Now that our `ProductRepository` works as expected, we can move up to the presentation layer. We could start anywhere—the view, the controller, or the routing. We will look at the routing first as it sets the basis of understanding for the requirements in the other two sections. In the `Global.asax.cs` file, we will add a new route to the top of our route specification. This route will allow us to have a URL that specifies the page, the property we are sorting by, and the direction we are sorting: `Home/Index/Page/2/Property/Name/Reverse/True`. Notice that each property has a default specified.

Global.asax.cs:

```
routes.MapRoute("Products", "{controller}/{action}/Page/{page}/
    Property/{property}/Reverse/{reverse}",
   new { controller = "Home", action = "Index", page = 1,
      property = "Name", reverse = false }
);
```

6. Now we can move to the logic in our controller. We need to be able to accept the page number that is requested, the property that we are going to sort by, and whether or not we are going to reverse our sort or not. This data will also need to be fed into our `ProductRepository`, so that we create the appropriate set of data. We will then pass our properties to the view, so that we can build the appropriate links in the view.

Controllers/HomeController.cs:

```
private int RecordCount = 20;
public ActionResult Index(int page = 1,
string property = "Name", bool reverse = false)
{
   if (page < 1)
```

```
    page = 1;

ViewData["Products"] = new ProductRepository().GetProducts(
    page, RecordCount,
  "Price", reverse);

ViewData["page"] = page;
ViewData["property"] = property;
ViewData["reverse"] = reverse;

return View();
}
```

 Keep in mind that you are dealing with string data that is passed into your application. You will most certainly want to add some guard clauses to your app to make sure that only what is expected is passed in—otherwise use a default sort property.

7. Now that all the logic for our sorting has been created, we can move to the view for the actual implementation. The first thing we need to do is receive the properties from the controller from the `ViewData` collection.

Index.aspx:

```
int page = (int) ViewData["page"];
string property = ViewData["property"].ToString();
bool reverse = (bool) ViewData["reverse"];
```

8. With this data accessible, we can then determine the page number for our next and previous links, and ensure that we don't go below the first page of data (it would be hard to display the −1 page of data).

Index.aspx:

```
int PreviousPage = (page - 1) < 1 ? 1 : page - 1;
int NextPage = page + 1;
```

9. Now that all of our data is defined, we can update our next and previous page links (from the previous recipe).

Index.aspx:

```
<%= Html.ActionLink("Previous", "Index", new { @page =
    PreviousPage, @property = property, @reverse = reverse })%> -
<%= Html.ActionLink("Next", "Index", new { @page = NextPage,
    @property = property, @reverse = reverse })%>
```

10. Now we can define the three links that will communicate our need for sorting by various properties (`Name`, `Price`, and `CreateDate`) in our collection of data. This looks mostly like our next and previous links, with the exception that we need to pay attention to the toggling of our reverse property based on whether or not the links property is the current property and the current state of the reverse property.

Index.aspx:

```
<%= Html.ActionLink("Sort By Name", "Index", new { @page = page,
@property = "Name", @reverse = property == "Name" && reverse ?
false : true })%> |

<%= Html.ActionLink("Sort By Price", "Index", new { @page = page,
@property = "Price", @reverse = property == "Price" && reverse ?
false : true })%> |

<%= Html.ActionLink("Sort By Date", "Index", new { @page = page, @
property = "CreateDate", @reverse = property == "CreateDate" &&
reverse ? false : true })%>
```

11. That's it! Hit *F5* and see how you can sort the data.

> Do be aware that you might see some oddities in the sorting, NBuilder is generating only one page of data for you. You will always be seeing the last page of the current set of data! Whether it is the first page or the 100th page.

How it works...

The key ingredient for this recipe is the handy `extension` methods that we have access to with the addition of LINQ. We are easily able to order a collection by a property. We are also able to reverse that order just as easily. Where we have problems with the native implementation of LINQ is that a lambda expression is expected in the `OrderBy` method, and all we have is a string that represents the property that we want to sort by.

No worries, we were easily able to overcome this shortcoming with a little help from reflection. With reflection we were able to get the property name by the passed-in string. The rest of this recipe was largely plumbing-related code.

There's more...

Credit where credit is due! I picked up this nugget for sorting from one of my favorite sites: **StackOverflow**. Specifically, it was listed here (along with loads of other great and more complex ways to accomplish this goal): `http://stackoverflow.com/questions/41244/dynamic-linq-orderby#41262`. Thank you to Kjetil Watnedal for making this recipe easier!

Deleting a record with an intermediary "Are you sure?" page

In this recipe, we are going to present a list of data with an option to delete one of the records. When the user clicks on the link to delete a record, they will be taken to a page confirming that they actually want to delete the record. From there, the user can post the ID to the controller and actually perform the delete on the record they selected.

Getting ready

This recipe will build from the first recipe. By that I mean to say that we will be using the `Product` class and `ProductRepository` along with NBuilder to generate our data for us.

How to do it...

1. To start off we need to make sure that we have the `Product` and `ProductRepository` class in our `Models` folder (you can get this from any of the previous recipes).

2. Then we need to open up our `ProductRepository` and add a method called `GetProduct` in addition to the existing `GetProducts` method.

   ProductRepository.cs:

   ```
   public Product GetProduct(int productId)
   {
     Product product =
       Builder<Product>.CreateNew().With(x=>x.ProductId =
         productId).Build();
     return product;
   }
   ```

3. Next, we need to ensure that we are passing a collection of data out to our index view.

   Controllers/HomeController.cs:

   ```
   public ActionResult Index()
   {
   ```

```
ViewData["Message"] = "Welcome to ASP.NET MVC!";

ViewData["Products"] = new ProductRepository().GetProducts();

return View();
}
```

4. With our controller passing out the appropriate collection of data, we need to update our view to show a list of product details. At the top of each record, we will add a link that will allow us to delete the records.

Views/Home/Index.aspx:

```
<fieldset>
  <legend>Products</legend>
  <% List<Product> products = ViewData["Products"]
     as List<Product>; %>

  <% foreach (Product p in products) { %>
    <div class="display-label">
      <%= Html.ActionLink("Delete", "ConfirmDelete",
      new {@id=p.ProductId}) %>
    </div>

        . . .

    <hr />
  <% } %>
</fieldset>
```

5. Notice that this link points to the ConfirmDelete action. Let's add that now. In the home controller we will add a new action called ConfirmDelete. This action will instantiate the appropriate Product and pass it down to the view to prompt the user to be sure that they want to delete that record or not.

Controllers/HomeController.cs:

```
public ActionResult ConfirmDelete(int id)
{
  Product product = new ProductRepository().GetProduct(id);
  return View(product);
}
```

6. Now right-click on the `ConfirmDelete` method name and choose to add a new view. Make this view strongly typed to the `Product` class and select the details view. Then open up the new view and add this form to the top of the page, which will allow the user to post their request to delete the appropriate record.

    Views/Home/ConfirmDelete.aspx:

    ```
    <% using(Html.BeginForm("Delete", "Home",
      new {@id=Model.ProductId})) {%>
    <div>
      Are you sure you want to delete this record?<br/>
      <%= Html.HiddenFor(m=>m.ProductId) %>
      <input type="submit" value="Delete Record!" />
    </div>

    . . .

    }
    ```

7. This form posts the appropriate `Product ID` to the delete action where the appropriate data deletion logic can be placed. Let's add that new action now. Notice that we are enforcing this action to accept posted data only with the `[HttpPost]` attribute.

    Controllers/HomeController.cs:

    ```
    [HttpPost]
    public ActionResult Delete(int id)
    {
      //perform delete logic on your data

      return View();
    }
    ```

8. Right-click on the new `Delete` action and select **Add View**. This view can either be strongly typed or not...that is up to you. Add a message in your view letting your user know that you have to delete the record as they requested. I also provided a link back to the home page.

    Views/Home/Delete.aspx:

    ```
    <h2>Record Deleted</h2>

    <%= Html.ActionLink("Home", "Index") %>
    ```

9. Done! Hit *F5* and walk through a record deletion simulation.

How it works...

This recipe is more of a lesson in workflow rather than complex cutting edge technology! In this recipe we listed some data. Each piece of data is linked to a deletion confirmation page, where we asked the user in a very Windows manner if they were sure they wanted to delete the specified bits of data. If they clicked the button to delete the data, we deleted it and told the user that we did so.

It is important to note however that we did not perform the deletion on a GET request (standard HTML link requesting a page). You should stay away from GET requests that perform any action on your application other than reading data. Instead, use a post to do actions such as deletes. Think of it this way...if Google were to spider your site and crawl a bunch of links that requested your delete links by way of a GET request, you might wake up and find all your data deleted! There are of course other ways to stop this from happening but this is a quick and easy rule to remember, just in case things don't go as planned.

Adding a jQuery delete link with confirmation

In this recipe, we will take a look at how we can safely delete a record using a link. We will use jQuery to override the normal GET functionality of a link and replace it with a POST action. We will add a JavaScript confirmation to make sure they don't accidentally delete data. Also, because we can't guarantee that everyone is able to utilize JavaScript, we will provide an intermediary delete confirmation step.

Getting ready

In this recipe, we will build from the previous recipe where we created an intermediate delete confirmation page. The delete to intermediate "Are you sure?" page is great for folks who don't have JavaScript capabilities. However, why make those with JavaScript suffer? For that reason we will now make that initial **Delete** link take action.

We want to make sure that we don't use a GET request to delete data though, as any spider crawling your site could delete your content (solved by adding security to your site). Also, we don't want our users to click **Delete** and have no chance to change their mind. To solve these two issues, we will use jQuery to override the GET aspect of our **Delete** link and exchange it for a post direct to our delete logic. We will also add a confirmation pop-up to our link asking the user if they are sure they want to delete the specified resource.

How to do it...

1. By starting off with the last recipe, we have an index page that lists a bunch of products. Each product's details are displayed and on top of that is a delete link. On the backend, we have a `ConfirmDelete` and `Delete` view that do exactly what their names describe. All we need to do is jazz up the UI a bit. Let's start by adding a reference to jQuery in our master page.

   Views/Shared/Site.Master:

   ```
   <script src="/Scripts/jquery-1.3.2.js"
       type="text/javascript"></script>
   ```

2. Then in our index page, we can start to modify our HTML a little bit to make it more friendly for scripting. We are going to wrap our product details display with a parent `div`. We will give this parent `div` a unique ID for the product that it is displaying by adding the `ProductId` to its `class` property. This will allow us to remove it from the display. Then we need to make the `div`—that houses our delete link—easier to find in the same way, so that we can swap in a **Deleting...** message. We will also need to add a class to our delete links called `delete` to make them easier to differentiate from other links on the page.

   Views/Home/Index.aspx:

   ```
   <div class="container<%= p.ProductId %>">
     <div class="busy<%= p.ProductId %>">
   <%= Html.ActionLink("Delete", "ConfirmDelete", new {@id=p.
   ProductId}, new {@class="delete"}) %></div>

     //details for the product...

   </div>
   ```

3. Now we can turn to some jQuery. We will now spotweld or ajaxify our current functionality. Inside our `indexContent` content area, we can add our `<script>` tags. Then the first part that we want to add is our opening line of jQuery waiting for the page to load.

   Views/Home/Index.aspx:

   ```
   <asp:Content ID="indexContent" ContentPlaceHolderID="MainContent"
       runat="server">

   <script>
       $(document).ready(...)
   ```

4. Once our `ready` function fires, we want to wire up a new function that will iterate through all of our delete links (using the link dot class name selector: `a.delete`) to override our `OnClick` event.

Views/Home/Index.aspx:

```
<script>
    $(document).ready(function () {
        $('a.delete').click(...)
```

5. When users click on the delete link, we want to ask them if they are really sure they want to delete the resource or not. We will do this with a simple confirmation window. We will then store the result of that question in a `doDelete` variable for later use, where we can see if they want to delete the resource or not. Obviously, if they don't want to delete the resource we won't!

Views/Home/Index.aspx:

```
$('a.delete').click(function () {
    var doDelete = confirm('Are you sure you want to delete this
        record?');
    if (doDelete) { ... }
    else { return false; } }); });
```

6. Now that we are able to capture a "yes...please delete this" response from the user, we have our workspace to begin doing other magic. The first thing we need to do is capture some data from the link being operated on for the processing needs coming up. We need to get the current URL, that the delete link is wired to, to use and replace the `ConfirmDelete` action name with `Delete` (allowing us to bypass the confirmation view). Then we can split the URL into an array of strings on the forward slash character—at the end of which is the `ProductId` that we are going to be working with. All of these values will be stuffed into conveniently named variables— `url`, `arr`, and `id`.

Views/Home/Index.aspx:

```
if (doDelete) {
    var url = this.href.replace('Confirm', '');
    var arr = url.split('/');
    var id = arr[arr.length - 1];
```

7. Now that we have our data collected, we can update our display by replacing the delete link with a message to the user telling them that we are **Deleting...** the record.

Views/Home/Index.aspx:

```
$('div.busy' + id).html("Deleting...");
```

8. Now comes the real work. We are going to perform a post using the jQuery `.post()` method using our altered URL and passing in the `ProductId` of the record we are deleting. We will also pass in a callback function, allowing us to capture when the record is actually deleted.

Views/Home/Index.aspx:

```
$.post(url, '',
    function () {...}
```

9. Once the record is deleted, we can do a few things. We could simply refresh the page, which would update the display to show that the record is missing. However, we could just as easily remove the record from the display directly. So we will use the last option. We could also just call `hide()` on the `div` containing our record, but that is generally too abrupt on the user experience. Instead, we will animate the record into oblivion using the `animate()` method from the `div` selector. Once the `div` has been animated away, we will hide it for good measure.

Views/Home/Index.aspx:

```
$.post(url, '',
    function () {
        $('div.container' + id).animate({
            opacity: 0.25,
            left: 'toggle',
            height: 'toggle'
        }, 1000, function () {
            $('div.' + id).hide(); }); });
```

10. Lastly, we need to make sure that our link doesn't call its `href` after doing all this work. For that reason, we will add one more line returning `false` to the link, stopping its execution entirely.

Views/Home/Index.aspx:

```
return false; }
```

11. Here is the entire script:

Views/Home/Index.aspx:

```
<script>
  $(document).ready(function () {
    $('a.delete').click(function () {
      var doDelete = confirm('Are you sure you want to delete this
        record?');

      if (doDelete) {
        var url = this.href.replace('Confirm', '');
        var arr = url.split('/');
        var id = arr[arr.length - 1];
```

```
            $('div.busy' + id).html("Deleting...");

            $.post(url, '',
              function () {
                  $('div.container' + id).animate({
                      opacity: 0.25,
                      left: 'toggle',
                      height: 'toggle'
                  }, 1000, function () {
                  $('div.' + id).hide(); }); });
                  return false; }
          else { return false; } }); });
      </script>
```

12. You can now hit *F5* and run this.

How it works...

In this example, we are simply adding functionality with Ajax rather than being totally reliant on it. This means that whether the user has JavaScript or not won't matter. If they have it, their experience will be enhanced. But more importantly, if they don't have it they won't lose any functionality.

This is primarily done by using jQuery selectors and overriding existing events. Once we have our hooks into the HTML elements that we need, the sky is the limit as to what we can do.

There's more...

This recipe was originally inspired by Phil Haack's awesome blog—`haacked.com`. Check it out here for more details as to why you might want to post to instead of get a `delete` method:

`http://haacked.com/archive/2009/01/30/simple-jquery-delete-link-for-asp.net-mvc.aspx`.

One of the most important reasons for posting a form to perform a delete is that when a spider comes through your site performing gets on every link it finds, your data doesn't accidentally get deleted each time a crawl is performed!

Master/detail page with inline details via jQuery and a partial view

In this recipe, we are going to look at a method for creating a master/detail page scenario. We will use a partial view to provide us with the formatting of the details. Then we will use a bit of jQuery to do the fetching of that partial view, as well as placing it into the page for us.

Getting ready

This recipe will follow the other recipes in this chapter, in that it will be using the `Product` and `ProductRepository` classes to provide us with some data to work with, using NBuilder to generate some data for us. You can grab the `Product` and `ProductRepository` class as well as NBuilder from the previous recipes in this chapter.

How to do it...

1. The first thing we want to do is create a new ASP.NET MVC project.

2. Next, we can add the `Product` and `ProductRepository` classes to the `Models` folder in our project (which you can get from the previous recipe). Also, drag over the previous, home controller, which has the action code that we need for this recipe to get and show products.

3. Then we need to add a reference to NBuilder, which is in the dependencies folder.

4. Now we need to add a reference to jQuery, so that it is present when we go to use it. You can do this by opening the master page in the `Views/Shared` folder. Then expand the `Scripts` folder and drag the `jquery-1.4.2.js` file (the version that is shipped with Visual Studio) into the header declaration of the master page. Or you can reference the latest version of jQuery by adding this line:

   Views/Shared/Site.Master:

   ```
   <script src= http://code.jquery.com/jquery-1.4.2.min.js
       type="text/javascript"></script>
   ```

5. Then we need to create our `Products` display page. To do this, create a new view in the `Views/Home` folder called `Products.aspx`. Open it up and add a quick reference to `Products` in the `ViewData` dictionary (we will put the products collection in there shortly). Then add a `foreach` loop to iterate through the products to display them. We will display the product's price and name. Notice that I pass the ID of the product into the ID used to communicate with our controller, as well as in the `ID` attribute of our link.

   Views/Home/Products.aspx:

   ```
   <h2>Products</h2>
   <p>
     <%
        List<Product> products = ViewData["Products"] as
         List<Product>;
        foreach (Product product in products)
        {
     %>
      <div class="display-field">
      <%: String.Format("{0:c}", product.Price)%>
   ```

```
<%= Html.ActionLink(product.Name, "ProductDetail",
  new {@id=product.ProductId}, new {@id=product.ProductId,
  @class="list-item"}) %></div>
<%
    }
%>
</p>
```

6. Now that we have a `Products` display page, we need to add a `ProductDetail` page. This page will be a standard page that our users can see in case they don't have JavaScript enabled or, more importantly, in case they are viewing your site from a device that doesn't support JavaScript. To do this, we will create a new page called `ProductDetail.aspx`. This page will load a partial view called `GetProductDetail`, which will house our product details formatting.

Views/Home/ProductDetail.aspx:

```
<h2>Product Detail</h2>

<% Html.RenderPartial("GetProductDetail"); %>
```

7. Next, we can create the `GetProductDetail` partial view (also in the `Views/Home` folder called `GetProductDetail.ascx`). This view will expect that a product exists in the `ViewData` dictionary, as that is where it will load its details from.

Views/Home/GetProductDetail.ascx:

```
<%
    Product p = ViewData["Product"] as Product;
%>

<div class="display-label">Id: </div>
<div class="display-field"><%: p.ProductId %></div>

. . .

<div class="display-label">Desc: </div>
<div class="display-field"><%: p.Description %></div>
<hr />
```

8. At this point, you should have a working Master/Detail page set up that will show a list of products. Clicking on a product should take you to the details page. Now we need to spotweld some JavaScript into these pages, to remove some of the unnecessary full page refreshing that is going on, and instead display the details of the product on the same page. Before we start putting together some JavaScript, we need to prepare the page a little bit by adding a `div` tag to display our product details in. Add this just under the page header before the products display.

Views/Home/Products.aspx:

```
<h2>Products</h2>
<div id="detail"></div>
<p>
```

9. Now we can add our JavaScript. Do this by adding a script block to the `head` section of our products page. Then we will add a snippet of jQuery that will select all of the links that have the class list item assigned to them. We will then have jQuery clear the HTML of the `div` tag with the ID of `detail` (which we just added).

Views/Home/Products.aspx:

```
<script>
  $(function () {
      $('a.list-item').click(function () {
          $("#detail").html('');
      });
  });
</script>
```

10. Next is the real meat and potatoes. We will have jQuery load the HTML that is generated by our `GetProductDetail` partial view into the HTML of the `detail` div. Then we will cancel out the `links` event by returning false. Here is the full script:

Views/Home/Products.aspx:

```
<script>
  $(function () {
      $('a.list-item').click(function () {
          $("#detail").html('');
          $('#detail').load('<%: Url.Action("GetProductDetail") %>',
              { id: this.id });
          return false;
      });
  });
</script>
```

11. Now you can hit *F5* and see the page load the details into the page above the product listing. To prove that this page still works for clients that don't have JavaScript support, simply remove the JavaScript from your page and run your web page again!

How it works...

This recipe is probably the easiest way to control the formatting of snippets of HTML that you want to inject into your page to create an Ajax site for your users. You simply add a link to your page that sends the user to a details view page. You then take all the display code that you would normally put into your details page and put it into a partial view instead. The partial view is then loaded into the details page, but because it just renders raw HTML, it can also be loaded directly by JavaScript. This makes your site much more flexible with regards to serving clients!

There's more...

While this is the easiest way to get Ajax into your application, it is by no means the most efficient manner to add Ajax capabilities to your site. We are requesting a rather large blob over the wire when having the server do the rendering for us. Another option would be to request only the data and then format it on the client-side, which we will cover in the next recipe.

See also

▶ *Creating a master/detail page with modal pop-up and JSON*

Creating a master/detail page with modal pop-up and JSON

This recipe is going to be a slight twist on the previous one. Rather than force-feeding our details into the top of our page using a partial view, we will instead display the details in a modal pop-up using JSON and a jQuery plug-in called `nyroModal`. You will find that two things occur with this method, which are a bit different from our last task. First, the time it takes to display the details after clicking on them is considerably less, as the package of data that is passed is much smaller. Also, there is less processing to be performed on the server-side as the formatting of the data occurs on the client-side, which also adds to the improved performance. Second, the user experience is greatly improved as the list of product data doesn't get pushed and pulled all over the place, this is because the details are cleared from and displayed in the page.

Getting ready

As with the other recipes in this chapter, we need to have some data to work with in order to be able to implement this recipe. We will be using our `Product` and `ProductRepository` classes as well as NBuilder. In addition to this, we will also be using the `nyroModal` jQuery plug-in, which can be downloaded from `http://nyromodal.googlecode.com/files/nyroModal-1.6.2.zip` (I am using 1.6.2 in this recipe).

How to do it...

1. The first thing that we need to do is to bring in our `Product` and `ProductRepository` classes from the previous recipe.
2. Then we need to add a reference to NBuilder in the dependencies folder.
3. Then we need to add the downloaded `nyroModal javascript` file to our `Scripts` directory. Also, we have to add the `nyroModal.css` file to our `Content` directory.

4. Now we need to open up the `Views/Shared/Site.Master` file, so that we can add some script references in. I am adding a reference to the latest jQuery, you might choose to use the jQuery that comes with the MVC template. Then we need to add a reference to `jquery.nyroModal-1.6.2.js` (the latest version of `nyroModal` at the time of writing). We also need to add a reference to `nyroModal.css`.

Views/Shared/Site.Master:

```
<head runat="server">
  <title><asp:ContentPlaceHolder ID="TitleContent"
    runat="server" /></title>
  <script src=http://code.jquery.com/jquery-1.4.2.min.js
    type="text/javascript"></script>
  <script src="../../Scripts/jquery.nyroModal-1.6.2.js"
     type="text/javascript"></script>
  <link href="../../Content/nyroModal.css" rel="stylesheet"
    type="text/css" />
  <link href="../../Content/Site.css" rel="stylesheet"
    type="text/css" />
  <asp:ContentPlaceHolder ID="head" runat="server" />
</head>
```

5. If you started off with a copy of the previous recipe, then you should already have a `Product` and `ProductRepository` class. You should also have a `Products.aspx` page that iterates over a collection of products for display on the page (if not, grab a copy of those files). In the `Products.aspx` page, remove the existing JavaScript that writes the product details into the top of the `Products` page.

6. We should also have the `ProductDetail.aspx` and `GetProductDetail.ascx` files. With these in place and the previous JavaScript removed, you should have a working products page that shows the details on another page.

7. Now we can start to build up some JavaScript to show our modal window. This script will hide the details `div` that we used previously, so that when we load data into it in the page, they will not show inline with the rest of the page. It will then set the position to be absolute on the details `div`, so that when we load data into the details `div`, hidden or not, it won't shift the contents of the rest of the page.

Views/Home/Products.aspx

```
<script>
    $(function () {
        $("#detail").css('visibility', 'hidden');
        $("#detail").css('position', 'absolute');
    });
</script>
```

8. Next, we will spotweld a bit of JavaScript onto all of our product links. We are going to use a jQuery selector to iterate over all of the links with a class of `list-item`. For each link we find, we will override the `click` event of the link.

Views/Home/Products.aspx:

```
$('a.list-item')
    .click(function () {
        ...
    });
```

9. Now we can add the real functionality inside of our new click event handler. We need to always make sure that the details `div` is empty before we try to add something to it. We can do this by selecting the details `div` by its ID, `detail`. Then we will access the `html` property of that `div` and clear it out.

Views/Home/Products.aspx:

```
$("#detail").html('');
```

10. Now that our details `div` is empty, we can focus on adding the appropriate product details into it. We will do this by posting a request to our `GetProductDetail` action in the home controller. However, instead of using the `GetProductDetail.ascx` partial view, we want to return some JSON directly to the calling JavaScript. To do this, we will need to add a new action to our home controller. This action will simply load the appropriate product and serialize it to JSON using a JsonResult. Because we already have an action named `GetProductDetail` that takes in a product ID, we have two options—we can either add an unused parameter to our action or we can alter the name of the action, allowing us to create a new method signature. I am opting for a slightly different name by prepending an underscore.

Controllers/HomeController.cs:

```
[HttpPost]
public JsonResult _GetProductDetail(int id)
{
    Product p = new ProductRepository().GetProductByID(id);
    return Json(p);
}
```

11. With this new action in place, we can write some JavaScript to communicate with our new `_GetProductDetail` action. In this case, we will use jQuery to post a request to our `_GetProductDetail` action passing along the product ID. This action will then serialize a `Product` object and pass it back to us. To do something with this data, we will also write a callback function that takes in a `data` parameter.

Views/Home/Products.aspx:

```
.click(function () {
    $("#detail").html('');
    $.post('_GetProductDetail', { id: this.id },
```

```
            function(data) {


                });
    });
```

12. The next thing for us to do is handle the callback and process the data that is passed back to us. For this, we will write a couple of new functions to handle formatting and showing our data. We need one function to handle the pushing formatted data into the details `div`. We will need another one to handle the formatting of each of the properties of the `Product` class.

Views/Home/Products.aspx:

```
$(function () {
    ...


            .click(function () {
                $("#detail").html('');
                $.post('_GetProductDetail', { id: this.id },
                function (data) {
                    showProduct(data);
                });

                return false;
            });
    });

function showProduct(data) {
    $("#detail").html(
        formatLine('Id',data.ProductId) +
        formatLine('Name',data.Name) +
        formatLine('Price',data.Price) +
        formatLine('SKU',data.Sku) +
        formatLine('Created',data.CreateDate) +
        formatLine('In Stock',data.InStock) +
        formatLine('Desc',data.Description)
    );
}

function formatLine(label, value) {
    return '<div class="display-label">' + label + ':</div><div>'
        + value + '</div>';
}
```

13. With all of this completed, we can now run our `Products` page. You will see a listing of products, all of which you can click on. Clicking on a link will make a request to get the appropriate product. That product will then be serialized and returned to the client. The product will then be formatted and pushed into our details `div`, but nothing will show on the page! In order to get our product details to show on the page, we need to hook up the `nyroModal` window. This is one line of code calling the `nyroModalManual` function with some display settings right after we call the `showProduct` function that we just created.

Views/Home/Products.aspx:

```
$.nyroModalManual({ url: '#detail', minHeight: 150, minWidth: 300,
    width: 300, height: 150 });
```

14. To finish off this recipe, we need to cancel the navigation request that clicking the link causes to happen. If we don't do this, then we will click on the link, get the details, display the modal window, and then refresh the page as we navigate to the `ProductDetails` page!

View/Home/Products.aspx:

```
.click(function () {
    $("#detail").html('');
    $.post('_GetProductDetail', { id: this.id }, function (data) {
        showProduct(data);
        $.nyroModalManual({ url: '#detail', minHeight: 150,
            minWidth: 300, width: 300, height: 150 });
    });
    return false;
});
```

15. Now you can hit *F5* and run the site. Clicking on a product should show the product details in a modal pop-up. By commenting out the JavaScript, you can simulate what a client with their JavaScript disabled might see. Specifically, you should be able to click on a product and navigate to the `Product Details` page.

How it works...

Describing how this process works outside of code is much easier to understand. When the page has loaded, a JavaScript (jQuery) runs and overrides the `OnClick` event of the appropriate links on the page. In the new click event handler, we then make a request to get some serialized data from our home controller by calling the `_GetProductDetail` action. Once this data has been returned to the client, we format it and store it in a `div`. We then call our `nyroModal` pop-up and tell it to display the data stored in the details `div`.

See also

▶ *Master/detail page with inline details via jQuery and a partial view*

6

Working with Forms

In this chapter, we will cover:

- ► Using HTML helpers to create forms
- ► Building a custom HTML helper to display a WYSIWYG
- ► Centralizing create and edit forms for reuse
- ► Adding custom attributes to form elements
- ► Defining a default button using jQuery
- ► Hijaxing a form with jQuery
- ► Performing an auto postback with a select list
- ► Autocomplete with jQuery UI

Introduction

One of the big advantages that ASP.NET MVC has over web forms is the ease with which you can work with forms. In this chapter, I'll take you from the basics of setting up a form using HTML helpers to more advanced concepts such as autocomplete.

I'd suggest looking at the first recipe before jumping further into the chapter, as I'll be using the project created there as a baseline for all of the other recipes.

The majority of the recipes in this chapter will need a model to work with. To make life easier, I have created a simple `Article` class, which will help demonstrate the different ways in which ASP.NET MVC deals with data types.

Models/Article.cs:
```
public class Article {
    public Guid ID { get; set; }
```

```csharp
public string Title { get; set; }
public string Subject { get; set; }
public string Description { get; set; }
public DateTime CreateDate { get; set; }
public bool IsPublished { get; set; }
public int TimesViewed { get; set; }

public string FormattedCreateDate
{
  get
  {
    if(CreateDate != DateTime.MinValue)
        return string.Format("{0:d/M/yyyy HH:mm:ss}", CreateDate);

    return "";
  }
}
}
```

Using HTML helpers to create forms

In this recipe, we will take a look at how to create a form manually using HTML helpers. This will include creating the form, checkboxes, textboxes, and so on. We will work with a strongly typed view based on an `Article` object that we will quickly put together.

How to do it...

1. The first step of this recipe is to create a new ASP.NET MVC 2 empty web application.

2. Once created, add a new class to the `Models` folder called `Article`. Drop in the preceding code snippet.

3. Because we've elected to use an empty project, we'll need to create our home controller from scratch. Right-click on the `Controllers` folder and add a controller called `HomeController`.

4. We will also need a master page; right-click on the `Shared` folder (in `Views`) and add an MVC 2 View Master called `Site.Master`.

5. Now let's go into the `Controllers/HomeController.cs` file that we created a second ago and right-click on the `Index` action. Add a view—the specifics aren't important—just make sure our newly created `Site.Master` is the master page.

6. Okay, we've got a basic MVC project setup now, let's create a form. Underneath the `Index` action, create a new action called `Article`. We'll pass in a new `Article` object as the view model.

Controllers/HomeController.cs:

```
public ActionResult Article() {
  return View(new Article());
}
```

7. Now build the project. Our next step is easier if Visual Studio can see the `Article` class that we created in the `Models` folder.

8. Right-click on the newly created action and select **Add View**. Make sure **Create a strongly-typed view** is checked and choose the `Article` class in the drop-down. The drop-down will list any models detected in the last build.

9. In the **View content** drop-down, you have several options. As we are interested in working with forms in this recipe, let's choose to create an **Edit** view. Additionally, make sure our master page is selected.

10. Click on **OK**.

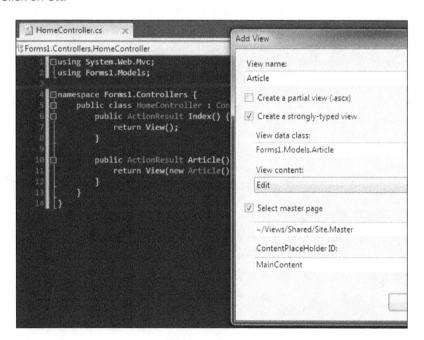

If Visual Studio has not already done so, make sure you are looking at `Article.aspx`. You should have a basic form laid out before you, listing each property of the `Article`. Each property should have a corresponding label, textbox, and validation message (in the form of a HTML helper).

11. Let's make some changes. The ID field is of no use to the end user, but future editing to the `Article` depends on the field being there. We will change the `Html.TextBoxFor` method to an `Html.HiddenFor` method. Then remove all the markup (including the label, and validation) surrounding that field.

```
<!-- Old Html -->
<div class="editor-label">
    <%: Html.LabelFor(model => model.ID) %>
</div>
<div class="editor-field">
    <%: Html.TextBoxFor(model => model.ID) %>
    <%: Html.ValidationMessageFor(model => model.ID) %>
</div>

<!-- New Html -->
<%: Html.HiddenFor(model => model.ID) %>
```

 We'll see later on that ASP.NET MVC can digest form data and produce a strongly typed model. By retaining the ID field as a hidden input, we get a more complete model to work with on the server.

12. We will remove the `CreateDate` field entirely as that would never be set by the user in the view.

13. Rather than displaying the `Description` property in a `TextBox`, we might instead want to show it in a `TextArea`. To do this, change the call `TextBoxFor` to `TextAreaFor`.

14. Next, we will change the `IsPublished` property to show in a checkbox. Do this by replacing the call to `Html.TextBoxFor` to an `Html.CheckBoxFor` call.

15. The `TimesViewed` field would also not be set in by the user, so we can safely remove that as well.

16. If you run the form (*F5*), we should now have a form that more appropriately represents what we would expect for an Article editing form.

How it works...

You have now seen how easy it is to not only generate a form but, more importantly, how to quickly tweak it so that it displays appropriately. This works based on a series of extension methods off of the `HtmlHelper`. The nice thing about this setup is that you can quickly and easily add your own `HtmlHelper` methods, too. This means that if you generate a view for an object and find that there are no methods of the `HtmlHelper` class that suit your needs, you can quickly set up a new extension method (covered in the next recipe actually).

Building a custom HTML helper to display a WYSIWYG

In this recipe, we are going to take a look at how you can create your own HTML helpers by using extension methods. This will allow you to quickly add all sorts of functionality that will be right at your fingertips when knocking together forms. We will specifically build an HTML helper to display a **What You See Is What You Get** (**WYSIWYG**) editor.

Getting started

In order for us to see how an HTML helper is created to display a WYSIWYG, we first need to go grab a WYSIWYG editor to be displayed. I will be working with the **CKEditor**—you can probably get just about any WYSIWYG to work. Go to `http://ckeditor.com/download` to download the CKEditor. There is also a copy in the `dependencies` directory!

We're going to carry on where we left off with the first chapter, so if you've not already done so, please create the project as described or load it up from the source code.

How to do it...

1. Extract the downloaded CKEditor files into a folder called `ckeditor`, and place that folder in the root of your MVC application.

2. Go into the `ckeditor` folder and open the `_samples` directory. Locate the `index.html` file and browse to the file to verify that your installation is working (right-click on the `index.html` file and "View in browser"). Click on one of the examples to be sure that your WYSIWYG editor is working.

3. Next, we will add the CKEditor script to our master page so that things will magically work later. Open the `Site.Master` file (in the `Views/Shared` directory) and drag the `ckeditor/ckeditor.js` file into the head of your master page (this should create the script include we need).

   Views/Shared/Site.Master:
   ```
   <script src="../../ckeditor/ckeditor.js" type="text/javascript">
   </script>
   ```

    You have probably already come across this, but the tooling support for ASP.NET MVC is a bit patchy in places. Dragging a script of style reference into your page will often result in something like `../..` being prepended to the file path. The file reference will work just fine until you start messing around with routing. You're far better off making every static file reference begin at the root of the site.

4. Now we can add a new class called `Extensions` into a new directory called `Helpers`. This class will hold our HTML helper extension method and some functions to make building extension methods easier for future use. Whatever the name of the folder you put the class in, if it's newly created, you'll have to reference it in `Web.config`.

   ```
   <system.web>
     ...
     <pages>
   ```

```
  <namespaces>
    <add namespace="System.Web.Mvc" />
    <add namespace="System.Web.Mvc.Ajax" />
    <add namespace="System.Web.Mvc.Html" />
    <add namespace="System.Web.Routing" />
    <add namespace="Forms.Helpers"/>
  </namespaces>
</pages>
    ...
</system.web>
```

5. In the `Extensions` class, we will define a new extension method called `WysiwygFor` to allow us to display the CKEditor easily. For the sake of consistency, we will make this a generic method that accepts a *lambda* expression.

Our method will return a `MvcHtmlString`, which is essentially an indication that the resulting string will be HTML and should not be encoded again. `MvcHtmlString` was built specifically for ASP.NET MVC, but was replaced in .NET 4 with `HtmlString`. We will continue using `MvcHtmlString` to ensure backward compatibility with .NET 3.5, but I'd recommend using `HtmlString` in .NET 4 projects.

Models/Extensions.cs:

```
public static class Extensions {
   public static MvcHtmlString WysiwygFor<TModel, TProperty>(
      this HtmlHelper<TModel> htmlHelper,
      Expression<Func<TModel, TProperty>> expression) {

         ...

      }
```

6. With the method signature out of the way, we then need to look towards the body of the method. There are a few ways with which we can render HTML. We could use a string, a `StringBuilder`, or in our case a `TagBuilder`. With the `TagBuilder` we can quickly knock up our text area with the appropriate classname (for CKEditor to just work), column specification, and tag name. We will then return the tag builder through the creation of an `MvcHtmlString`.

```
var builder = new TagBuilder("textarea");
builder.AddCssClass("ckeditor");
builder.MergeAttribute("cols", "80");

return MvcHtmlString.Create(builder.ToString());
```

7. We are missing two important pieces at this point though. We need to be able to map the property name that is passed into our helper to the ID of the textarea. We also need to be able to populate the WYSIWYG editor with the content of the property that is passed in. To get the property name we will create a new helper method called `MemberName` that will extend our expression. We will then grab the body of the expression, from which we can get the property name.

```
private static string MemberName<T, V>(
    this Expression<Func<T, V>> expression)
{
    var memberExpression = expression.Body as MemberExpression;
    if (memberExpression == null)
        throw new NullReferenceException("Expression must be a member
            expression");

    return memberExpression.Member.Name;
}
```

8. Now we can add the ID and name to our text area by making a call to our new `MemberName` method.

```
var builder = new TagBuilder("textarea");
builder.GenerateId(expression.MemberName());
builder.AddCssClass("ckeditor");
builder.MergeAttribute("cols", "80");
builder.MergeAttribute("name", expression.MemberName());
```

9. All that is left is for us to do is to grab the data out of the passed-in property and push it into our new WYSIWYG editor. We can do this using the `ModelMetadata.FromLambdaExpression()`.

Models/Extensions.cs:

```
var meta = ModelMetadata.FromLambdaExpression(expression,
    htmlHelper.ViewData);
var value = meta.Model;
if (value != null)
    builder.SetInnerText(value.ToString());
```

10. With the value in hand, we can then push it into our `TagBuilder`. Here is the complete listing.

```
public static MvcHtmlString WysiwygFor<TModel, TProperty>(
    this HtmlHelper<TModel> htmlHelper,
    Expression<Func<TModel, TProperty>> expression)
{
    var builder = new TagBuilder("textarea");
    builder.GenerateId(expression.MemberName());
```

```
builder.AddCssClass("ckeditor");
builder.MergeAttribute("cols", "80");
builder.MergeAttribute("name", expression.MemberName());

var meta = ModelMetadata.FromLambdaExpression(expression,
  htmlHelper.ViewData);
var value = meta.Model;
if (value != null)
  builder.SetInnerText(value.ToString());

return MvcHtmlString.Create(builder.ToString());
}
```

```
namespace Forms.Helpers {
    public static class Extensions {
        private static string MemberName<T, V>(this Expression<Func<T, V>> expression)
            var memberExpression = expression.Body as MemberExpression;
            if (memberExpression == null)
                throw new NullReferenceException("Expression must be a member expression");

            return memberExpression.Member.Name;
        }

        public static MvcHtmlString WysiwygFor<TModel, TProperty>(this HtmlHelper<TModel> htmlHelper,
            Expression<Func<TModel, TProperty>> expression) {
            var builder = new TagBuilder("textarea");
            builder.GenerateId(expression.MemberName());
            builder.AddCssClass("ckeditor");
            builder.MergeAttribute("cols", "80");
            builder.MergeAttribute("name", expression.MemberName());

            var meta = ModelMetadata.FromLambdaExpression(expression, htmlHelper.ViewData);
            var value = meta.Model;
            if (value != null)
                builder.SetInnerText(value.ToString());

            return MvcHtmlString.Create(builder.ToString());
        }
    }
}
```

11. Now that we have our `HtmlHelper` extension method working, we can plug this into the view. Open up `Article.aspx` and change the `Html.TextBoxFor` to a `Html.WysiwygFor` method call.

Views/Home/Article.aspx:

```
<div class="editor-label">
   <%: Html.LabelFor(model => model.Description) %>
</div>
<div class="editor-field">
  <%: Html.WysiwygFor(model => model.Description) %>
   <%: Html.ValidationMessageFor(model => model.Description) %>
</div>
```

12. Now you can hit *F5*, browse to `home/article`, and you should see the CKEditor!

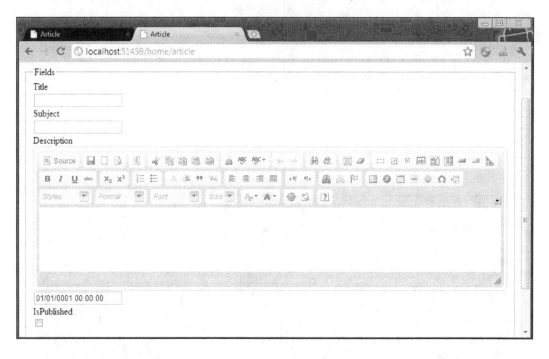

13. Click on the **Submit** button though; you'll see we're not looking so hot. By default, ASP.NET checks every form post for the existence of potentially harmful script. Make the following changes to the home controller and `Web.config` to allow the code to succeed.

```
// Controller
[ValidateInput(false)]
public ActionResult Article() {
...
```

```
<!-- Web.config -->
<system.web>
    ...
<httpRuntime requestValidationMode="2.0" />
</system.web>
```

The changes mentioned in the previous step switch off the default safeguards for our `Article` action. If you're building a form that will be freely accessible on the Internet, you're potentially leaving yourself open to *script injection attacks*. So you'll need to put in your own safeguards for dealing with malicious scripts.

How it works...

Apart from creating a reusable way to add a WYSIWYG editor to our forms, this recipe demonstrated the use of lambda expressions in method signatures.

In order for us to populate the ID for our WYSIWYG element, we needed to get the property name from the passed-in lambda expression. To do this, we cast the expression body to a `MemberExpression`, which then gives us access to the `Name` property.

We were able to get the property value by using the `ModelMetadata.FromLambdaExpression()` method, which takes the lambda expression, as well as the `ViewData` that comes along with the HTML helper that we are extending. This method essentially whittles down the full model of the page to just the property that is captured by the expression. This value is then exposed by the `Model` property, which is now the property that is passed in via the expression.

There's more...

If you take a look at the code download inside the `Extensions` class, you will notice that there are a few other helper methods in there, which are not discussed here in the text. While researching bits for this recipe, I came across several helpful functions for building helper extensions that I thought would be useful for any MVC developer's toolbox. Thanks to Chris Patterson for these found here: `http://stackoverflow.com/questions/1559800/get-custom-attributes-from-lambda-property-expression#1560950`.

The solution I initially worked up for this recipe used some not-so-fancy reflection of the `helper.ViewData.Model` to determine the value of the property that was being passed in. This would be appropriate in MVC 1 (as `ModelMetadata` came about with MVC 2). I thought there might be a better solution though, which prompted me to post a query to `StackOverflow` to get some added insight. Darin Dimitrov provided me with a better way to get at this data (using the new `ModelMetadata`). Thanks Darin! See my query here: `http://stackoverflow.com/questions/2846778/what-is-the-easiest-way-to-get-the-property-value-from-a-passed-lambda-expression#2847712`.

With regards to CKEditor itself, like a lot of similar editors, CKEditor is packed with lots of features, of which we've scratched only the surface. Another good WYSIWYG editor worth taking a look at is **TinyMCE** (`http://tinymce.moxiecode.com/`).

Centralizing create and edit forms for reuse

Views and Partial Views rely a great deal on View Context; they're not so much bothered about their physical location, as they're about the action that called them. We can leverage this to make our form reusable.

How to do it...

1. Starting from where we left off on either of the last two recipes, open the `HomeController.cs` file and add a new `CreateArticle` action. Then set your action to return a new instance of `Article`.

   Controllers/HomeController.cs:

   ```
   public ActionResult CreateArticle() {
      return View(new Article());
   }
   ```

2. As we have done previously with the `Article` action, right-click on the action and add a new view. Make sure that the view is strongly typed to `Article` and that our master page is selected.

3. `CreateArticle.aspx` will look very similar to `Article.aspx` before we made any updates. We want `CreateArticle.aspx` to benefit from the changes made to `Article.aspx` without having to repeat ourselves. Select the form in `Article.aspx` (including the `using` statement) and copy it to your clipboard.

4. Then go to the `Views/Home` directory in your **Solution Explorer**. Right-click on the `Home` directory and add a new empty partial view that is strongly typed based on an `Article`. Name this partial view `_ArticleFormFields`. Paste your code into the body of the partial view that you just created.

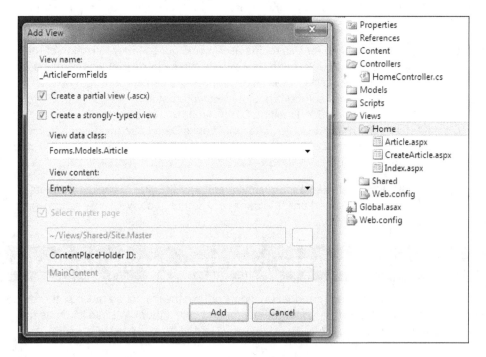

5. Open up the `Article` and `CreateArticle` views and replace your form declarations with a call to `RenderPartial` with the name of your new partial view.

   ```
   <% Html.RenderPartial("_ArticleFormFields"); %>
   ```

6. Now you can build and run your application. Navigate to `Home/CreateArticle` and to `Home/Article`. You should see that your view code is now centralized for both of those views.

How it works...

One of the keys to using ASP.NET MVC is that it gets you closer to the HTML of your application. As you can see, the views that are generated for you are just plain old HTML and some HTML helper methods (which also render plain HTML). Because of this, it is very easy to relocate that HTML into a centralized view and include that view (by way of the `RenderPartial` method) in a fashion very similar to Classic ASP and the `includes` of the old days.

Adding custom attributes to form elements

Having the ability to quickly generate forms based on the type that the view is tethered to makes creating management screens quick and painless. But what happens when you need to add more information to the forms? Perhaps you need to add a CSS class for formatting or jQuery for selection purposes? This recipe will show you how you can add custom attributes to your form elements.

How to do it...

1. Jump in from anyone of the last three recipes and navigate to `Article.aspx` in `Views/Home`. Let's disable the `Title` field. We do this by adding a new object to the end of the `Html.TextBoxFor()` method.

   Views/Home/Article.aspx:
   ```
   <div class="editor-label">
     <%: Html.LabelFor(model => model.Title) %>
   </div>
   <div class="editor-field">
     <%: Html.TextBoxFor(model => model.Title,
         new { disabled = "true" }) %>
     <%: Html.ValidationMessageFor(model => model.Title) %>
   </div>
   ```

2. If we wanted to specify more than one attribute for an HTML element, we do that by adding commas to our object. In this case, we will add some **alt text** to our ID.

   Views/Home/Article.aspx:
   ```
   <div class="editor-label">
     <%: Html.LabelFor(model => model.Title) %>
   </div>
   <div class="editor-field">
     <%: Html.TextBoxFor(model => model.Title,
         new {disabled="true", alt="alt text here"}) %>
     <%: Html.ValidationMessageFor(model => model.Title) %>
   </div>
   ```

How it works...

A feature I particularly like about ASP.NET MVC is the use of anonymous objects to pass in key/value pairs. One potential gotcha that becomes apparent when applying this technique to HTML attributes, though, is C# reserved words, specifically `class`. Whenever you need to pass in a reserved word into an anonymous object property, be sure to prepend an `@` symbol.

```
<%: Html.TextBoxFor(model => model.Postcode,
    new { @class="postcode" }) %>
```

If you don't like this object syntax (some people don't) then you can also pass in a collection that implements `IDictionary` instead, but I find it a bit long-winded.

```
<%: Html.TextBoxFor(model => model.Postcode,
  new Dictionary<string, object> { { "class", "postcode" } }) %>
```

Defining a default button with jQuery

In ASP.NET, you were able to set the default button for a form by simply specifying the name of the button you wanted to use when a user clicked on the *Enter* button. In ASP.NET MVC, we may still want to be able to configure which button we want to use by default. Regardless of need, this exercise will hopefully be a good introduction to using jQuery with your ASP.NET MVC form.

How to do it...

1. Start from any of the previous recipes in this chapter and open up the `HomeController`. We're going to add an additional action called `Article` that takes two parameters—the form data in the form of an `Article` and a string to capture the button that was pressed. The action that captures the `Article` will allow only posts to it, so we'll decorate the action with an `HttpPostAttribute`.

   Controllers/HomeController.cs:

```
[HttpPost]
public ActionResult Article(Article article, string btnSubmit)
{
    return View(article);
}
```

You can have action overloads, just like you can have method overloads, because an action is a method. Compiling isn't the issue, the issue is the application's interpretation of the values passed into the routing dictionary. If you're going to overload your actions, make sure that they're unique enough to not leave any room for interpretation. Avoid multiple action overloads that take the same amount of nullable parameters. Making use of attributes such as `HttpPost` will also help avoid ambiguity.

2. Replace the **Submit** button of your form with the following code. Notice that both the buttons are named `btnSubmit`. This allows us to capture either button when clicked in the controller. The form can be found in `Article.aspx` or `_articleFormFields.ascx`, depending on which recipe you have just finished.

Views/Home/Article.aspx:

```
<input type="submit" name="btnSubmit" id="submitButton"
    value="Submit" />
<input type="submit" name="btnSubmit" id="cancelButton"
    value="Cancel" />
```

3. Next, we need to update the form declaration. We will add attributes that will specify which default button to use and the ID of the form. I've used HTML5 data attributes, as they allow me the freedom to specify custom attributes and still remain compliant. The downside is that you have to pass the attributes as a dictionary, as the hyphen doesn't translate when using anonymous objects.

Views/Home/Article.aspx:

```
<% using (Html.BeginForm("Article", "Home", FormMethod.Post,
    new Dictionary<string, object> { { "data-default",
    "submitButton" }, { "id", "form1" } })) { %>
```

4. With all of this in place, we can now wire up some jQuery to glue it all together. The first step to adding in any jQuery is to open up your `Site.Master` file in the `Views/Shared` directory. Make some whitespace under the `css` link, then expand the `Scripts` directory and drag over the `jquery-1.4.1.js` file.

Views/Shared/Site.Master:

```
<head runat="server">
    . . .
    <script src="/Scripts/jquery-1.4.1.js"
        type="text/javascript"></script>
</head>
```

5. Now we can go back to the `Article.aspx` file. Directly above the content of the `Article` page, (above the default `<h2>` tags) we will add a new `<script>` block. Inside this `script` block, we'll add the script, which will be responsible for capturing the *Enter* key (character 13). Once captured, we'll trigger the `click` event of the button specified in the `data-default` attribute.

Views/Home/Article.aspx:

```
<script type="text/javascript">
  var buttonKeys = { enterKey: 13 };
  $(function () {
    $("#form1").keypress(function (evt) {
      if (evt.which == buttonKeys.enterKey) {
        evt.preventDefault();
        var defaultButtonId = $(this).attr("data-default");
        if (defaultButtonId != null)
          $("#" + defaultButtonId).click();
      }
    });
  });
</script>
```

6. You should now be able to build and run your site. Navigate to `Home/Article` and view the form. Then put your cursor in any of the fields and hit *Enter*. This should submit your form. If you set a break point in your post-handling action, you should be able to see that the `submitButton` is the button that was used.

How it works...

HTML5 data attributes provide an ideal way to add additional information to your markup. When the page is loaded, our jQuery script overrides the `keypress` event of the form with a custom function. If the *Enter* key is pressed, we trigger the `click` event of the specified default button. If you have plain old text areas in your form, you'll need some refinement to avoid creating a new line and inadvertently submitting the form at the same time.

Hijaxing a form with jQuery

In this recipe, we are going to take a look at how we can override the form submission process. Sometimes you may want to enable the user to POST a form without refreshing the whole page. I usually do it because I either want to preserve some other piece of information on the page, or because I want to preserve the page's state within the browser. Examples I can think of might be scroll position, or the form exists within a modal created with JavaScript. You might be tempted to achieve a similar result with an IFRAME, hopefully this recipe will show you that a ASP.NET MVC/jQuery solution is a lot more elegant.

Getting started

In addition to jQuery 1.4.1, we're going to be using one of the official jQuery plug-ins called **jQuery Form**. It's in the source code, but it's also available for the following URL—`http://jquery.malsup.com/form/`.

How to do it...

1. As before, we'll start off with any one of the recipes that we've already created in this chapter. If you've not already done so, create a second action in the home controller called `Article`. The action should look like the following example. The second parameter (`btnSubmit`) is entirely optional; this recipe does not use it.

```
[HttpPost]
public ActionResult Article(Article article, string btnSubmit) {
   return View(article);
}
```

2. We're going to alter that second action in a moment, but first we need to create a new action/view. Upon a successful submission, we'll redirect the user to a page called `ArticleSaved`. So, create a new action in the `HomeController` called `ArticleSaved`.

Controllers/HomeController.cs:

```
public ActionResult ArticleSaved() {
   return View();
}
```

3. Then create a new view (right-click and select **Add View**) and add a message saying something along the lines of **The article was successfully saved!**.

4. With this message view in place, you can now go back to the `Article` action that accepts posts and redirects that action to render the new `ArticleSaved` action.

```
[HttpPost]
public ActionResult Article(Article article, string btnSubmit) {
    return RedirectToAction("ArticleSaved");
}
```

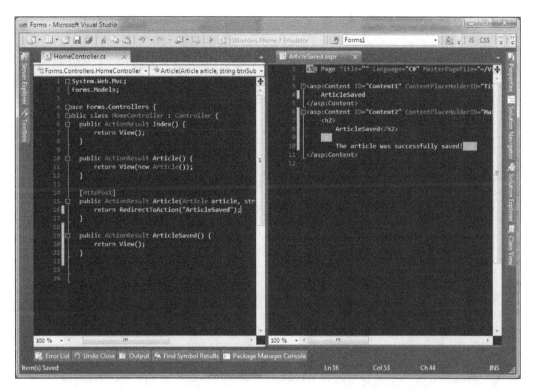

5. With all this in place, you can now run the application. Browsing to **Home/Article** should render your form. When you click on **Submit**, the form should post its data to your `Article` action and then redirect to the `ArticleSaved` view.

We've just implemented a design pattern called **Post/Redirect/Get** or **PRG**. Rather than returning the success message in the initial response to the POST, we redirect to another action first. This technique was introduced to prevent the accidental resubmission of HTML forms. If we didn't redirect first and the user tried to refresh the page, the browser will attempt to resubmit the form. Bad, if you've just bought a car! http://en.wikipedia.org/wiki/Post/Redirect/Get.

6. With this working normally without JavaScript, we can now start to wire in some jQuery to make this form more user-friendly. Start by opening up the `Site.Master` in the `Views/Shared` directory. Make some whitespace after the `css` link. Then drag the `jquery-1.4.1.js` & `jquery.form.js` scripts into the head. You may already have a reference to jQuery.

Views/Shared/Site.Master:

```
<head runat="server">
 <title><asp:ContentPlaceHolder ID="TitleContent" runat="server"/>
</title>
 <link href="/Content/Site.css" rel="stylesheet" type="text/css"/>
 <script src="/Scripts/jquery-1.4.1.js"
    type="text/javascript"></script>
 <script src="/Scripts/jquery.form.js"
    type="text/javascript"></script>
</head>
```

7. Then, towards the top of your article page add a script block to hold your jQuery. This jQuery script will override the form submission, serialize the form data, and then POST the data to the action of the form.

Views/Home/Article.aspx:

```
<script language="javascript" type="text/javascript">
  $(function () {
      $("form").ajaxForm({ target: "#result" });
  });
</script>
```

8. Next we need to add a `div` tag to capture the result of our form submission. This tag can go just above the `form` tag.

Views/Home/Article.aspx:

```
<div id="result"></div>
```

9. Feel free to run the `Article` page as it currently sits. It should technically work as currently configured. However, the result will be a bit unexpected. The response for the post is currently fed into the `div` tag that we just added. The problem is that the current response is an entire page! Let's remedy this by allowing our controller to render a different result depending on the type of request.

10. JavaScript libraries such as jQuery and MS Ajax add a header to server requests; the header identifies the request as an Ajax request. ASP.NET MVC provides a method called `IsAjaxRequest` that checks for this header in incoming requests. We'll use `IsAjaxRequest` to decide which response to send back to the client.

Controllers/HomeControllers.cs:

```
[HttpPost]
public ActionResult Article(Article article) {
    if (Request.IsAjaxRequest())
        return Content("Article Saved!");

    return RedirectToAction("ArticleSaved");
}
```

11. That last step isn't really keeping it DRY, it would be better if we could reuse the Article Saved view that we created earlier. Start by adding a new partial view called _ArticleSaved. Then take the message that we put in the ArticleSaved view, and put it into the partial view. Finally, set the ArticleSaved view to render the _ArticleSaved partial view. At the end, you should have a view called ArticleSaved that references a partial view called _ArticleSaved.

Views/Home/ArticleSaved.aspx:

```
<% Html.RenderPartial("_ArticleSaved"); %>
```

12. Add a new action to the Home controller called `_ArticleSaved`—this action will return our `_ArticleSaved` partial.

```
public ActionResult _ArticleSaved () {
  return PartialView();
}
```

13. Now update the Home controller to redirect to the `_ArticleSaved` action when `IsAjaxRequest()` returns `true`.

Controllers/HomeController.cs:

```
if (Request.IsAjaxRequest())
  return RedirectToAction("_articleSaved");

return RedirectToAction("ArticleSaved");
```

14. Now run the application again. Disabling JavaScript should render the `ArticleSaved` view after submitting the form. But with JavaScript enabled, you should just see the message rendered at the top of the form itself after it is submitted.

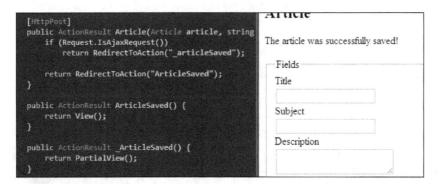

In this recipe, we have created a form that posts to an action as expected. When the form is submitted, it is then redirected to a successful submission page. With the basic form submission working as expected, we then turn our attention to wiring in some JavaScript to handle posting our form behind the scenes in an Ajax fashion. We then make our controller intelligent enough to respond to the form submission differently, based on whether we used JavaScript or not. This is called **progressive enhancement** or **graceful degradation**, depending on whether you are a glass half-full or half-empty sort of developer.

Performing an auto post-back with a select list

In this recipe, we are going to look at how to replicate another standard ASP.NET web forms feature. We frequently need to present a drop-down list as a form of navigation. When the user selects an item from the list, we want the form to post itself so that we can do something with the selected value.

How to do it...

1. Start by opening up one of the previous recipes in the chapter and make sure that jQuery is referenced in the master page.

2. Open the home controller in the `Controllers` directory. We're going to create a little helper method to generate a small list of articles.

   Controllers/HomeController.cs:

   ```
   private List<Article> GetArticles() {
     return new List<Article> {
       new Article {
         ID = Guid.Parse("f4838485-058d-4c82-b4f4-3bd8c81c7d09"),
         Title = "Title 1",
         Description = "Description 1" },
       new Article {
           ID = Guid.Parse("67f19f15-9ba8-4624-91a4-152aec01c5f8"),
           Title = "Title 2",
           Subject = "This one has a subject.",
           Description = "And a description." }
     };
   }
   ```

3. We will create two new actions called `ViewArticle`. Each of the actions grabs the list of articles and adds the list to a `ViewData` dictionary item called `ArticleList`. Also, both the actions send an individual `article1` to the view, using differing LINQ methods. Because no selection has been made when the user first loads the `ViewArticle` view, the GET action will return the first of our dummy articles (`FirstOrDefault()`). When a selection has been made, the POST action will return the desired article (`SingleOrDefault(i => i.ID == article.ID)`).

   ```
   [HttpPost]
   public ActionResult ViewArticle(Guid id) {
     var articles = GetArticles();
     ViewData["ArticleList"] = articles;
     return View(articles.SingleOrDefault(i => i.ID == id));
   ```

```
  }

  public ActionResult ViewArticle() {
    var articles = GetArticles();
    ViewData["ArticleList"] = articles;
    return View(articles.FirstOrDefault());
  }
```

4. Now, right-click on either of the actions that we have just created and select **Add View**. Create a strongly typed view (`Article`) and select **Details** as **View content**.

5. If you run the application at this point and navigate to `/Home/ViewArticle`, you'd see our first dummy article laid out in a `FIELDSET`. But what we want to do is add the ability to select a different article from a drop-down list. Add the following code above the `FIELDSET` tag.

Views/Home/Article.aspx:

```
<% using (Html.BeginForm()) {%>
  <%= Html.DropDownList("id",
    new SelectList(ViewData["ArticleList"] as
    List<Forms.Models.Article>, "ID", "Title"),
    new { onchange = "this.form.submit();"}) %>
  <input type="submit" value="Change" />
<% } %>
```

6. Now you can build and run your application. Navigating to `Home/Article` should show you the drop-down with the first item asking you to **Choose...** an item from the list. Choosing an item from the list should cause the form to post itself.

How it works...

In this recipe, we created a simple details page to view our dummy articles. Setting the onchange event of the drop-down list runs some inline JavaScript that causes the form to submit itself. With this recipe, I want to illustrate how small changes can make a big impact on the user experience.

However, in a real world scenario, I have two concerns with the code in its current state.

▶ The **Submit** button seems unnecessary, but what would you do without JavaScript enabled? In situations like these, I have taken to adding a class (something like nojs) to the unnecessary **Submit** buttons. I'll then hide or remove those buttons with JavaScript to keep the UI clean.

```
$(function() {
  $(".nojs").remove();
});
```

▶ I used a very ugly combination of words a moment ago—*inline* and *JavaScript*. I used inline JavaScript in this recipe to not only keep it to the point, but also to make another point. In reality, I would never inject JavaScript—or CSS for that fact—directly into my HTML markup. A clear separation between layout, presentation, and function will help you as a developer keep your application scalable; and it'll help clients connecting to your site digest only the information they require. A screen reader generally does not care about presentation or function. The following code, added to a document ready function, would enable all (or some) drop-down lists to auto postback.

```
$("select").change(function () {
  $(this).parents("form").submit();
});
```

```
52      </p>
53      <script type="text/javascript">
54          $(function () {
55              $(".nojs").remove();
56              $("select").change(function () {
57                  $(this).parents("form").submit();
58              });
59          });
60      </script>
61  </asp:Content>
62
```

Autocomplete with jQuery UI

We've already seen how well ASP.NET MVC works with jQuery to provide a rich and graceful client user experience. And that collaboration is at its strongest when working with forms. That's not the end of the story though. Where jQuery is a cross-browser enabler with strong DOM and Ajax support, jQuery UI works to improve the interface with powerful widgets—one such widget is called **autocomplete**.

In this recipe, we will see how easy it is to use jQuery UI to add advanced features to an ASP.NET MVC form. We'll do this by allowing the user access predefined subjects, via an autocomplete prompt, directly from the server. The subjects will be requested using Ajax and delivered to the client as JSON.

Getting ready

For this recipe, I'm using jQuery 1.4.1 and jQuery UI 1.8.5, both are provided in the dependencies folder. As we've done previously, we'll be starting off from any one of the previous recipes in this chapter, just make sure that you've got both the scripts added to your site master.

How to do it...

1. In our home controller, we're going to add three actions. The first one is called **Auto**, and like other recipes, this one is going to return a new `Article` as the view model.

    ```
    public ActionResult Auto() {
      return View(new Article());
    }
    ```

2. The second is also called **Auto**, but will additionally take a single parameter (called `article`) and be decorated with an `HttpPostAttribute`. The parameter called `article` will be of type `Article` and will represent our submitted form (more on that later). One final thing in this action, we'll add some text to the `ViewData` dictionary. Again, I'll explain why, later on.

     The `HttpPostAttribute` is saying "I take only POSTs, your GETs can go elsewhere", so this action will be used to deal with our form POST.

    ```
    [HttpPost]
    public ActionResult Auto(Article article) {
      ViewData["message"] = "Subject updated to " + article.Subject;
      return View(article);
    }
    ```

3. The last action is called `Subjects`. The `Subjects` action will be responsible for returning our subject suggestions to the client and will have one parameter called `term`. The name of the parameter is prescribed by the jQuery autocomplete widget and, as it represents the user's text input, `term` will help us filter the results that we send back. The jQuery widget will be using `GET` requests, so remember to allow this in your JSON response.

```
public ActionResult Subjects(string term) {
  var subjects = new[] {
    "Clever Subject",
     "Really Clever Subject", "Running Out Of Ideas",
     "Run Out Of Ideas", "Will Soon Be Reduced To Writing Random
       Words", "Should Every Word Be Capitalised?", "Sausage" };

  if (String.IsNullOrWhiteSpace(term))
   return Json(subjects, JsonRequestBehavior.AllowGet);

  return Json(subjects.Where(s => s.StartsWith(term, true,
    CultureInfo.CurrentCulture)), JsonRequestBehavior.AllowGet);
}
```

4. Okay, let's set up our view really quickly. Right-click on the first action called **Auto** and **Add View**. Make sure that the view is strongly typed to our `Article`, leave **View content** set to **Empty**, and uncheck **Select site master**.

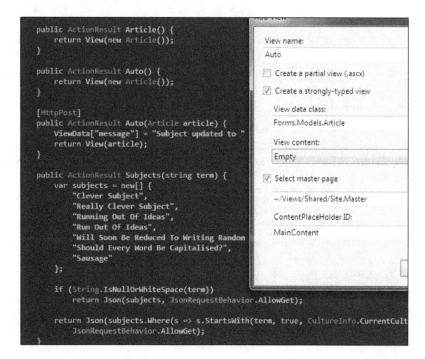

5. So far, we've seen what Visual Studio tooling can offer us by way of templates. We can achieve pretty much the same thing with a helper method called `Html.EditorForModel()`. If you add the following markup to `Auto.aspx` and navigate to it in a browser, you should see the same basic form that we've been using throughout this chapter.

```
<% using (Html.BeginForm()) { %>
  <%: Html.EditorForModel() %>
  <input type="submit" name="submit" value="Submit" />
<% } %>
```

6. We're not done with `Auto.aspx` yet. First, add a reference to the entry you added to the `ViewData` dictionary earlier. Once submitted, we should see a message under our form, reporting the change to the article's subject.

```
<% using (Html.BeginForm()) { %>
<%: Html.EditorForModel() %>
<input type="submit" name="submit" value="Submit" />
<% } %>
<p><%: ViewData["message"] %></p>
```

> At this stage, we have a fully functional form. You type in stuff, hit **Submit**; now watch the form data submit to the server. Remember, there is no validation, so if you type in something that doesn't conform to your strongly typed `Article` model, prepare yourself for an ugly server error. Chuck in some breakpoints to see your form data become an instance of `Article`.

7. Now we want to add the jQuery functionality. Import `jquery-1.4.1.js` and `jquery-ui-1.8.5.custom.min.js` to your `Scripts` folder and drag the references into the `head` tag of `Auto.aspx`.

8. In addition to JavaScript, jQuery UI is dependent on CSS. Import `jquery-ui-1.8.5.custom.css` and the `images` folder into your `Content` folder. Drag the reference to CSS file to the `head` tag of `Auto.aspx`. You should have a block that looks like this.

```
<link href="/Content/jquery-ui-1.8.5.custom.css"
  rel="stylesheet" type="text/css" />
  <script src="/Scripts/jquery-1.4.1.js"
      type="text/javascript"></script>
  <script src="/Scripts/jquery-ui-1.8.5.custom.min.js"
      type="text/javascript"></script>
```

9. In this step, we're going to bring it all together. The following code instructs the jQuery UI autocomplete widget to attach an instance of itself to the textbox called **Subject**. Append the `script` block to the end of the `head` tag.

```
<script type="text/javascript">
  $(function () {
     $("#Subject").autocomplete({
        source: "/home/subjects"
     });
  });
</script>
```

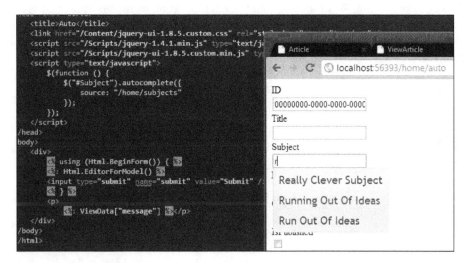

How it works...

The autocomplete widget registers an event handler with a *key press* event on the Subject textbox. When the user starts typing, the handler grabs the value of the textbox and fires it to the server as an Ajax GET request. The Subject's action applies the `term` parameter as a filter to our LINQ statement, returning only the subjects that begin with the contents of `term`. The action then returns any results as a JSON array, which is consumed by the autocomplete widget.

For something once described as rocket science (rather overly dramatically), the whole process was pretty painless.

Not to lose sight of the book's title, ASP.NET MVC was also being exceptionally clever. We generated a complete form using two helper methods and an `input` tag. The `EditorForModel` helper integrates the view model and provides an appropriate HTML block for each public property. Upon submitting the form, ASP.NET MVC utilized its model binders to squeeze the form data into a strongly typed `Article`.

I'd recommend adding breakpoints to the first line of each action, then populate and submit the form using Firefox, with Firebug pointing at the **Console** tab. It's amazing what has been achieved with so little code on our part.

There's more...

Check out the demos over at `http://jqueryui.com/`, the jQuery UI team is doing some great stuff on top of the excellent jQuery library. One of my favorite features of jQuery UI is **ThemeRoller**. The ability to customize the look and feel of all widgets from a simple interface is very impressive.

This idea of incorporating Ajax requests into the population of forms has implications beyond suggestive helpers such as autocomplete. In conjunction with the jQuery forms and Validation plug-ins, ASP.NET MVC can be made to support advanced concepts such as remote validation with a small amount of effort. We will be taking this concept further in *Chapter 8*.

7
Simplifying Complex Applications

In this chapter, we will cover:

- ▶ Centralized formatting of common types with templated helpers
- ▶ Making templated helpers for custom types
- ▶ Using areas to separate application components
- ▶ Creating a "portable" area to use across multiple applications
- ▶ Using the input builders of MVC Contrib
- ▶ Generating forms with `Html.InputForm`
- ▶ Leaving breadcrumbs for your users with `MvcSiteMap`
- ▶ Displaying tabular data in a grid

Introduction

In this chapter, we are going to focus on tools and features that can be used in MVC to make building larger-scale applications easier to manage. In particular, we will take advantage of templated helpers, model binding, and areas. We will also take a look at some of the features offered by the open source project, MVC Contrib—portable areas, input builders, and the grid.

Centralized formatting of common types with templated helpers

In the previous chapter, we saw how you can use HTML helpers for different input types. Additionally, ASP.NET MVC provides intuitive helpers such as **EditiorForModel**, which try to figure out which input types you actually want to use. Helpers such as EditorForModel make these assumptions primarily based on data type, but what if there were a data type that was unaccounted for? In this recipe, we will take a look at how we can override these decisions to centralize the formatting of common types. We will do this by using the built-in templated helpers. Templated helpers allow you to specify how you want to display common types, such as dates and numbers, as well as more complex models.

In this recipe, we will take a look at the `DateTime` type. Instead of asking a person to simply enter a date into a textbox, we will instead provide them with a jQuery date picker. Because we will do this with templated helpers, all dates that are displayed on an input form will use the same date picker.

Getting ready

For this recipe, I'm using jQuery 1.4.1 and jQuery UI 1.8.5, both of which are provided in the dependencies folder. The latest versions of each library can be downloaded from `jquery.com` and `jqueryui.com` respectively.

How to do it...

1. Create a new MVC application.
2. Create a new class called `Person` to hold our test type. We will give the `Person` class a `DateTime` property called `BirthDate`.

   Models/TestClass.cs:
   ```
   public class Person {
     public DateTime BirthDate { get; set; }
   }
   ```

3. We need to create a view to display our `BirthDate` property. To do this, open up the `HomeController` and add a new action called `Edit`. Configure this action to return an instance of our new `Person`.

   Controllers/HomeController.cs:

   ```
   public ActionResult Edit() {
     return View(new Person());
   }
   ```

4. Now build your application (otherwise the `Person` won't show in the list when we try to create a new strongly typed view!). Then right-click anywhere in the new `action` method and add a new strongly typed view based on the `Person`. Specify that the view content will use the `Edit` template.

5. Hit *F5* and navigate to the **Edit** action (**Home/Edit**). You should see a simple textbox that you can type a date into. Close that window and we will start building a new `EditTemplate`.

6. First, change the `TextBoxFor` to an `EditorFor` method call in the **Edit** view.

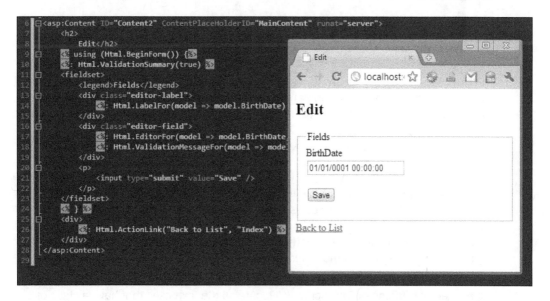

7. Then add an `EditorTemplates` folder to the `Views/Shared` folder (`Views/Shared/EditorTemplates`).

8. Now create a new partial view called `DateTime.ascx` in the `EditorTemplates` directory.

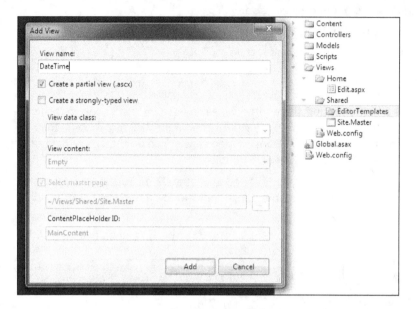

9. In the `DateTime` view we are going to output a textbox. We will also format any date that is passed in to us or provide an empty value in the case that a date is not passed in. Also, we will append a class value to the input box that is created, so that we can access it later.

```
<%: Html.TextBoxFor(model => Model, new { @class = "date" } ) %>
```

10. Now we need to write a bit of jQuery to attach a date picker to our textbox. Start by opening up the `Site.Master` file in the `Views/Shared` directory. Then drag the `jquery-1.4.1.js` file from your `Scripts` directory into the head of your master file. Also drag in the `jquery-ui{version}.js` and the `ui.all.css` file into the head to support a date picker popup (this is included in the source code for this recipe or you can get it on the jQuery site).

11. With jQuery included in the master page, we can now add a bit of script underneath the external references. This script will locate all the textboxes that have a class of *date* and attach a date picker.

Views/Shared/Site.Master:

```
<script type="text/javascript">
    $(function () {
      $("input:text.date").datepicker({
        dateFormat: "MM d, yy"
      });
    });
</script>
```

12. Now build your project and navigate to **Home/Edit**. Clicking into the date field should show the jQuery date picker!

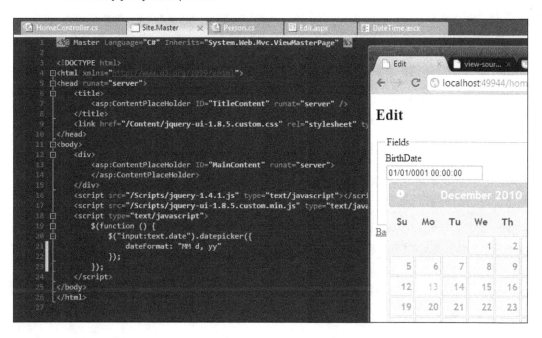

How it works...

The `EditorFor` method will first look in the directory of the view that is executing for an `EditorTemplates` directory for the type it is trying to display. If it doesn't find any templates there, it will move up to the shared directory. If there are no templates in the shared directory, it will move on and display the typed-in question with a default template.

You can test this by renaming the `EditorTemplates` directory that we created! If you rename the directory to `_EditorTemplates`, you will see that the `DateTime` is rendered with a simple textbox as usual.

Making templated helpers for custom types

In this recipe, we will take a look at how we go about creating custom templated helpers for our own types. This is very similar to the previous recipe—in this one we will specify how the template should display our type. But this is different from the previous recipe—we have to tell the view engine how to bind the model of our type to the template; there is just a bit more overhead in this recipe.

How to do it...

1. We'll start by opening a copy of the project that we created in the last recipe.

2. Next, we will build up our `Person` class with a few more basic properties. In addition, we're going to decorate some of the properties with an attribute from the `System.ComponentModel` namespace.

Models/Person.cs:

```
public class Person
using System;
using System.ComponentModel;

namespace ComplexApplications.Models {
  public class Person {
      [DisplayName("First Name")]
      public string FirstName { get; set; }
      [DisplayName("Middle Name")]
      public string MiddleName { get; set; }
      [DisplayName("Last Name")]
      public string LastName { get; set; }
      [DisplayName("Birth Date")]
      public DateTime BirthDate { get; set; }
      public string Email { get; set; }
    public string Phone { get; set; }
      }
}
```

3. Now you need to build your project so that the `Person` type will be available when we go to add a strongly typed view.

4. Once the build is complete, open up the `HomeController` so that we can add a new action. Name this action `AddPerson` and configure it to return a new instance of `Person`. Then create a second action similar to the first. Set this action to accept a `Person` as a parameter and to be accessible only via a form post.

Controllers/HomeController.cs:

```
[HttpPost]
public ActionResult AddPerson(Person person) {
  return View(person);
}

public ActionResult AddPerson() {
  return View(new Person());
}
```

5. Now you can right-click on one of your `AddPerson` actions and select **Add View**. Configure this view so that it is strongly typed based on a `Person`. Also set the content of this view to be an *Edit* view.

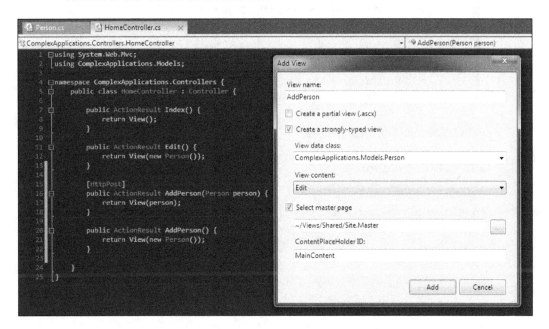

6. In the view that is generated, remove all of the provided `div` tags, HTML helpers, and so on. In their place, put an `Html.EditorForModel` (which is interchangeable with `Html.EditorFor(m=>m)`) to represent the `Person` that will be passed into the view. Also provide a button to submit the form.

Views/Home/AddPerson.ascx:

```
<% using (Html.BeginForm()) {%>
  <%: Html.ValidationSummary(true) %>

  <%= Html.EditorForModel() %>

  <input type="submit" value="Add Person" />
<% } %>
```

7. View that page in a browser and notice that we've still got a jQuery UI date picker attached to our `Birthdate` field (from the first recipe). Also notice that the labels for each property are responding to the `DisplayNameAttribute` that we set earlier.

8. Inside that `EditorTemplates` folder (`Views/Shared` folder), create a partial view called `Person.ascx`.

9. In your `Person` partial view, feel free to go crazy with the way you want to represent the Edit controls for a person. To save time, I simply copied the fieldset from the generated view as a starting point. I also switched the `BirthDate TextBoxFor` for an `EditorFor` helper and removed the **Submit** button.

 Keep in mind: A `TextBoxFor` helper is explicitly saying "I want a textbox". An `EditorFor` helper will at worst give you a textbox, but will look for better alternatives (such as our `DateTime` template) first.

Views/Shared/EditorTemplates:

```
. . .
<div class="editor-label">
    <%: Html.LabelFor(model => model.FirstName) %>
</div>
<div class="editor-field">
    <%: Html.TextBoxFor(model => model.FirstName) %>
    <%: Html.ValidationMessageFor(model => model.FirstName) %>
</div>

<div class="editor-label">
    <%: Html.LabelFor(model => model.LastName) %>
</div>
<div class="editor-field">
    <%: Html.TextBoxFor(model => model.LastName) %>
    <%: Html.ValidationMessageFor(model => model.LastName) %>
</div>
. . .
```

10. You can now run your application, browse to **Home/AddPerson**, and view your new `Person` input form.

How it works...

This is very similar to the previous recipe, in that we are building on top of a feature that is provided for us by the framework. We can build up all sorts of different reusable partial views to represent standard types in the .NET framework, as well as our own custom types.

There's more...

We have been discussing only about creating forms for data input to this point. Of course, the good folks on the MVC team have also provided us with facilities for specifying how we want to display our types. Instead of creating an `EditorTemplates` folder, create a `DisplayTemplates` folder. Everything works the same from that point on!

Using areas to separate application components

If you have ever worked on an application of any size, you would have gotten to a point where having every single line of code in one bucket may become overly cumbersome. Perhaps your routes have started to collide. Or perhaps, one section of your application is considerably different in form and function from the other (think about an administration console for example). These sorts of issues are easy to solve by introducing *areas* into your project. An **area** is basically an ASP.NET MVC project within another.

How to do it...

1. For consistency, I'm going to start off with a copy of the previous recipe. But there is dependency on what has come before, so you should be able to work with an empty project just as easily.

2. Right-click on your project and select **Add New Area**.

3. Name your area **Administration**. This will add a new **Administration** area to a folder called `Areas`.

4. Now open up your `Global.asax` file. Notice that there is an `AreaRegistration.RegisterAllAreas()` call, which scans your application looking for any registration classes.

    ```
    protected void Application_Start() {
        AreaRegistration.RegisterAllAreas();

        RegisterRoutes(RouteTable.Routes);
    }
    ```

5. When you created the **Administration** area, a new folder structure called `Areas` was created. Take a look in the root of your `Administration` folder and you will see a file called `AdministrationAreaRegistration.cs`. Open up that file and you will see that the call from the `Global.asax` is actually registering the routes for your area. This allows you to specify a different set of routes for your areas from that of your root application.

6. Notice that the route definition for your area is a bit different from that of the routes configured for the rest of your application. In the `AdministrationAreaRegistration` class, you will notice that its default route specifies an *area key* along with its controller, action, and ID.

    ```
    public override void RegisterArea(AreaRegistrationContext context)
    {
        context.MapRoute(
            "Administration_default",
    ```

```
            "Administration/{controller}/{action}/{id}",
            new { action = "Index", id = UrlParameter.Optional }
              );

    }
```

How it works...

Areas are a nice and convenient way to isolate aspects of your application. This allows you to have subapplications in your application that can be controlled in a totally separate manner from your primary application. The MVC framework quickly scans the application for any classes that inherit from `AreaRegistration` and then calls the `RegisterArea` method on each of your area registration classes. This is a great way to keep multiple facets of a complex application within a single file structure. Prior to areas, I would have kept my Admin area (for instance) in a separate project that was then added to IIS as a virtual folder.

There's more...

Be sure to also take a look at the fact that areas don't have to be created inside your application. You can also create areas in separate projects and still register them inside your primary application.

Creating a "portable area" to use across multiple applications

In this recipe, we will see how we can create self-contained easily distributable widgets called portable areas. A **portable area** is very similar to a regular MVC area in an external project with a few added bits to make it portable. Thanks to the makers of `MvcContrib`, a portable area is very easy to create and considerably more portable, or distributable, than a regular area. A **regular area project** is just a collection of files contained in an external project. A portable area's project outputs a single assembly that can be consumed by any other application—ASP.NET or ASP.NET MVC. A portable area therefore allows you to create widgets, which can easily be shared across many websites reducing code duplication and allowing you to publish updates on a per widget basis.

How to do it...

1. We'll need two applications for this recipe: one application will act as the portable area, which we will name the `CommentsWidget`, and the other application will act as the host for our comments widget. Both will work from the empty ASP.NET MVC 2 project template; for the host I've used a copy of the last recipe.

2. Now delete the `Global.asax` file from the `CommentsWidget` project.

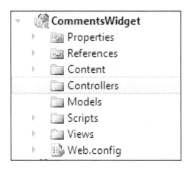

3. Next, we need to add a reference to `MvcContrib` and NBuilder to our `Widget` project. `MvcContrib` has all the bits to make our portable area work. NBuilder will help us to mock up some data, so that we can have a list of comments. Both of these can be found in the dependencies folder.

4. Add a `CommentsRegistration.cs` file to the root of our `CommentsWidget` project to take care of registering our portable areas routes. This class will need to inherit from `PortableAreaRegistration` in the `MvcContrib.PorableAreas` namespace. Inheriting from `PortableAreaRegistration` requires that we create a method, `RegisterArea`, and a property, `AreaName`. `RegisterArea` will hold the routes we want to configure for this widget. `AreaName` tells the framework what our area is called. Also, and probably the most important, it is the area of code that is highlighted. The call to `RegisterAreaEmbeddedResources` tells MVC how to find our views and resources (which we will eventually embed into our portable area).

CommentsRegistration.cs:

```
public class CommentsRegistration : PortableAreaRegistration {
  public override void RegisterArea(
    AreaRegistrationContext context, IApplicationBus bus) {
      context.MapRoute("commentsRoute",
        "CommentsWidget/{controller}/{action}/{id}",
          new { controller = "links", action = "index",
            id = UrlParameter.Optional });

      this.RegisterAreaEmbeddedResources();
  }

  public override string AreaName {
    get {
        return "CommentsWidget";
    }
  }
}
```

5. In order for us to provide any functionality, we will need to create some objects to work with. A comments widget would naturally need a `Comment` class to render. Let's create that in the `CommentsWidget` project.

```
public class Comment {
  public string Name { get; set; }
  public string Email { get; set; }
  public string Subject { get; set; }
  public string Body { get; set; }
}
```

6. Next, we will create a new `CommentsController` in our `CommentsWidget` project. This controller will have one action called `ShowComments`. The `ShowComments` action will work off of an `HTTP GET` request and shall take in an ID attribute (to simulate getting comments for a blog post or something similar).

Controllers/CommentsController.cs:

```
public class CommentsController : Controller {
  public ActionResult GetComments(int id) {
    List<Comment> comments =
      Builder<Comment>.CreateListOfSize(5).Build().ToList();
    return View(comments);
  }
}
```

7. With our new action created, we are ready to create a new view that corresponds to it. Do this by right-clicking on the action and selecting **Add a new view**. Make this a partial view that is strongly typed to our `Comment` class. Also, set this view to be a details view. When the new view comes up, edit the type of class we inherit from and change it to `ViewUserControl<List<CommentsWidget.Models.Comment>>`.

8. Then we need to wrap the HTML that was generated for us with a `foreach` iteration block, so that we can show all of the items that were passed to the view.

Views/Comments/GetComments.ascx:

```
<%@ Control Language="C#"
 Inherits="System.Web.Mvc.ViewUserControl<
    List<CommentsWidget.Models.Comment>>" %>
<%@ Import Namespace="CommentsWidget.Models" %>

<fieldset>
  <legend>Comments</legend>

  <% foreach (Comment comment in Model)
  { %>
    <div class="display-label">Name</div>
    <div class="display-field"><%: comment.Name%></div>
```

```
    <div class="display-label">Email</div>
    <div class="display-field"><%: comment.Email%></div>

    <div class="display-label">Subject</div>
    <div class="display-field"><%: comment.Subject%></div>

    <div class="display-label">Body</div>
    <div class="display-field"><%: comment.Body%></div>
    <hr />
  <% } %>

</fieldset>
```

9. Now we can add an `Extensions` class to our `CommentsWidget` project. This class will be responsible for extending the HTML class that we often use in an MVC application. In there, we will create a `GetComments` method that takes in a `postId`. This will allow our consuming application to work very easily with the functionality exposed by the `CommentsWidget`.

Extensions.cs:

```
public static class Extensions
{
  public static void GetComments(this HtmlHelper htmlHelper,
    int postId)
  {
    htmlHelper.RenderAction("GetComments", "Comments",
      new { area = "CommentsWidget", id = postId });
  }
}
```

The previous method relies on an extension method called `RenderAction`, which can be found in the `System.Web.Mvc.Html` namespace. I, for one, have let Visual Studio make me very lazy. I let the IDE work which namespaces are needed (and which aren't), VS even orders them for me. To my knowledge though, VS still can't resolve the namespaces of extension methods. I'm starting to sound like a man whose batteries in his TV remote, have just run out. I'm sure there is a solution in the works, if not already completed.

10. The last, and probably most important piece to our `CommentsWidget` project, is that we need to alter the project's configuration in the `CommentsWidget.csproj` file. Do this by opening the file in a text editor such as Programmer's Notepad or just plain old Notepad. Then scroll down to the **Build** section and add the following snippet to insure that all of our views and other resources are compiled into the widget assembly. This step allows us to not have to distribute a bunch of files to the consuming application but instead allows us to just distribute one DLL.

```
<Target Name="BeforeBuild">
  <ItemGroup>
    <EmbeddedResource Include="**\*.aspx;
      **\*.ascx;
      **\*.gif;
      **\*.jpg;
      **\*.png;
      **\*.css;
      **\*.js" />
  </ItemGroup>
</Target>
```

11. With all of this work completed in the `CommentsWidget` project, we are now ready to turn our attention to the host project. In the host project, we need to add a reference to `MvcContrib` (in the dependencies folder) and we need to add a reference to our `CommentsWidget` project (though if you don't, that is ok too, just make sure that the `CommentsWidget dll` gets into the `bin` folder of your host application).

12. Now we need to tell our host application how to get to our `CommentsWidget`. We do this in the `Global.asax` file by calling the into the `MvcContrib` library. You'll need to add a reference to the `MvcContrib.UI.InputBuilder` namespace, in order to access a method called `BootStrap()`. `BootStrap` works a bit like `RegisterAllAreas`, gathering up our portable areas.

```
protected void Application_Start()
{
    AreaRegistration.RegisterAllAreas();

    RegisterRoutes(RouteTable.Routes);

    InputBuilder.BootStrap();
}
```

13. Then we can open up any view (I've created a **home/index controller/view** combo) in the application and type **Html.GetComments(3)**; we should see a list of ten randomly generated comments displayed on the page.

Views/Home/Index.aspx:

```
<asp:Content ID="Content2" ContentPlaceHolderID="MainContent"
  runat="server">
```

```
    . . .
    <p>
        <% Html.GetComments(3);%>
    </p>
</asp:Content>
```

14. We need to do two final things in the host application for all of this to work.

   ❑ In order for the GetComments extension method to work as described, we
   will need to add a namespace reference to the Web.config file.

   ```
   <add namespace="System.Web.Routing" />
   <add namespace="CommentsWidget.Helpers" />
       </namespaces>
   </pages>
   ```

   ❑ Copy the Web.config from your Views folder to a new folder called Areas.

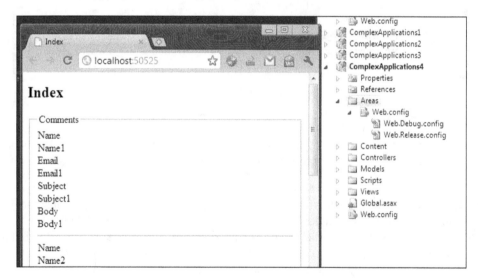

15. Now build and run your application and you should see a list of comments displayed
   on the home page.

How it works...

The portable area builds on the concept of the ASP.NET MVC external project areas. A couple
of things are different between a portable area and a regular area. One is that a portable area
embeds its resources into an assembly rather than leaving them scattered about on the disk,
meaning that a portable area only needs to be referenced as a DLL. And lastly, regular areas
interact with our MVC applications in the normal way, whereas portable areas can use the
MvcContrib service bus concepts (which we didn't directly cover in this recipe).

The next important bit is that we have to be able to register our areas routes. Because our portable area project may or may not be directly referenced by a host application, it is important that we expose a way for the routes in our portable area to be consumed and added to the routing table. Regular areas are referenced and brought into the `bin` directory of a host application. The assemblies of other areas are automatically scanned and configured into the host application with very little fuss. In order for us to achieve the same magic, we have to use some `MvcContrib` classes and calls to get this done for us.

Lastly, though not specific to the concept of the portable area, is the service bus that comes with `MvcContrib`. A suggested practice to use with portable areas is to communicate with the host application using messages. This is sort of a publish-subscribe type pattern where the portable area puts a message on the bus when it does something, such as registering the portable area, creating a comment, sending an email, and so on. Then the host application can use a message handler to subscribe to specific messages that it cares about. In this way, the host application is loosely coupled to the portable area and vice versa.

> The service bus of `MvcContrib` is a bit different from something like **NService Bus** or **BizTalk**, in that it is a synchronous process model whereas most service bus implementations are asynchronous. (Just an FYI.)

There's more...

The topic of portable areas hasn't gotten too much coverage, as cool as they are. The best way to see some different examples of these is to go download the `MvcContrib` examples here: `http://mvccontrib.codeplex.com/`.

Also, the ability to work in a regular MVC web application to build portable areas instead of working in a class library (you don't want to know what a pain it is to work without IntelliSense!) is thanks to Steve Michelotti. You can read about his portable areas' tinkering at `geekswithblogs.net/michelotti`. Things of interest are how to interact with compiled resources, such as CSS and images, and also how to go about using a master page inside your portable area!

Using input builders of MvcContrib

We have seen how templating works with MVC's templated helpers, and will see how these concepts enable validation in the next chapter. But while we're on the subject of `MvcContrib`, let's take a look at a slightly different approach using input builders. **Input builders** are similar to templated helpers, in that we can dictate how we want a certain piece of code to look when it is displayed on a form. We can use data annotations and other attributes in the `MvcContrib` project to specify how we want our data to appear and perform.

How to do it...

1. Create an empty ASP.NET MVC application, or start from where we left the last recipe.

2. Add a reference to `MvcContrib` and NBuilder, if not already there.

3. Then we need to import the input builder templates from the `MvcContrib` project into our project. This is in the dependencies folder (or you can download it from the `MvcContrib` site). Simply select all of the `InputBuilderTemplates` and drag them into your solution into the `Shared` folder inside the `Views` folder.

4. Then we need to create a class to demonstrate how input builders work. We will create a class called `ExampleModel` and place it in the `Models` folder. The attributes that decorate really drive all the extra fun features. But similar to the templated helpers, the type of data (for the most part) drives how the property is laid out on the screen.

   Models/ExampleModel.cs:

```
public class ExampleModel {
    public Guid Key { get; set; }

    [Required]
    public string FirstName { get; set; }

    [Required]
    public string LastName { get; set; }

    [Required]
    [Label("What type of example is this?")]
    public ExampleTypes ExampleType { get; set; }

    [Label("Please enter your birthday")]
    [Example("mm/dd/yyyy")]
    public DateTime BirthDate { get; set; }

    [DataType(DataType.MultilineText)]
    public string Biography { get; set; }
}

public enum ExampleTypes {
    Man = 1,
    Woman = 2,
    Boy = 3,
    Girl = 4,
    Baby = 5
}
```

5. Now we need to create a new action in our `HomeController` called `ShowExample`; this will return a new instance of our new `ExampleModel` class.

Controllers/HomeController.cs:

```
public ActionResult ShowExample() {
    ExampleModel model = Builder<ExampleModel>
        .CreateNew()
        .Build();
    return View(model);
}
```

6. Create a new view from your new action. Right-click on the action and select **Add View**. Make a strongly type view for our `ExampleModel` class and make a Details view. Notice all the fluff that was created for us. You can remove everything between the `legend` and the closing `fieldset` tag.

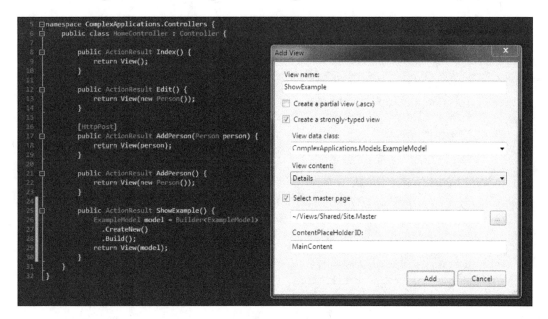

7. Enter an `Html.Input(m=>m.{property})` for each of the properties exposed on your model.

Views/Home/ShowExample.aspx:

```
<fieldset>
    <legend>A form created with Input Builders</legend>
    <% Html.BeginForm(); %>
    <%= Html.Input(m=>m.Key) %>
    <%= Html.Input(m=>m.FirstName) %>
```

```
<%= Html.Input(m=>m.LastName) %>
<%= Html.Input(m=>m.ExampleType) %>
<%= Html.Input(m=>m.BirthDate) %>
<%= Html.Input(m=>m.Biography) %>
<div style="clear:both;">
    <input type="submit" value="Submit" /></div>
<% Html.EndForm(); %>
</fieldset>
```

8. Be sure to add the following two lines to your `Web.config`.

```
<add namespace="CommentsWidget.Helpers" />
<add namespace="MvcContrib.UI" />
 <add namespace="MvcContrib.UI.InputBuilder.Views" />
</namespaces>
</pages>
```

9. Now you can build your application and see the form displayed appropriately.

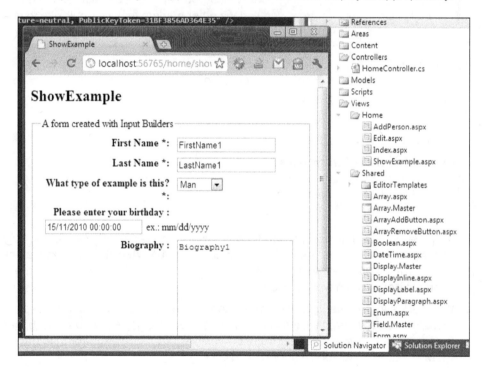

How it works...

Similar to the templated helpers, there is a view that specifies how a certain type should be displayed. If you have views that don't relate directly to a given type, you can specify a view for a property using a `[PartialView("{viewName}")]` attribute. Also, there are non-template related bits, such as when a `[Required]` attribute is placed on a property, which also triggers logic to be executed. For the required attribute specifically, if you look in the `Field.Master` view, you will see a check for whether a required attribute is present or not. If the required attribute is present, an asterisk will be displayed.

Generating forms with Html.InputForm()

In the previous recipes, we have taken a look at templated helpers and the `MvcContrib` input builders. But those forms of streamlining your UI pale in comparison to the `MvcContrib InputForm` functionality, which is similar to that of ASP.NET MVC's own `Html.EditorForModel`. With one single line of code, you are able to generate an entire form with all of its fields, input controls, and various other markup that we would like to have, as defined by the input builders.

How to do it...

1. Start by creating a copy of the project from the last recipe.

2. We will add a `New()` method to the `HomeController`, which will return an instance of our new `ExampleModel`.

    Controllers/HomeController.cs:
    ```
    public ActionResult New() {
        return View(new ExampleModel());
    }
    ```

3. Then we need to generate the view for our new action. Be sure to build your project first, so that your `ExampleModel` is available in the **Add View** dialog. Then right-click on the action and select **Add View**. Make this a strongly typed view based on the **ExampleModel** and have Visual Studio create an empty view.

4. With our view generated, we are almost ready for the magic. There is one last step though, we need to drag in all the input builder views from the `MvcContrib` project (located in `Dependencies/MvcContrib/InputBuilderTemplates`) to the `Views/Shared` directory in our MVC project.

5. Inside the view, we can now add the magic that is the `Html.InputForm()` call. Add this under the `h2` tag that was generated for you.

   Views/Home/New.aspx:

   ```
   <%= Html.InputForm() %>
   ```

6. Now you can hit *F5* to run your application. Then navigate to `/home/new` and see your magic new input form.

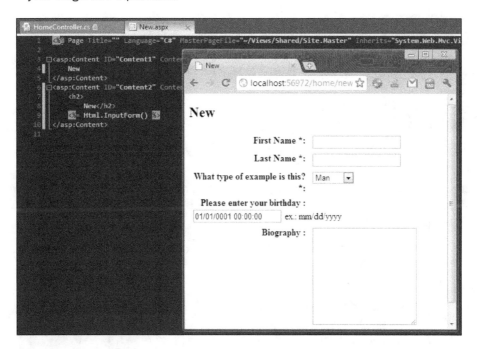

How it works...

This functionality is built on top of the `MvcContrib` input builders that we covered earlier. Each type has its own view. The `InputForm` extension method loads the `Form.aspx` view, which in turn makes a call to `Html.InputFields`, which then lays out all of the items of the model that is passed into the `InputForm`.

There's more...

Eric Hexter has a great blog series on `InputBuilder` (including the `InputForm`) located here: `http://www.lostechies.com/blogs/hex/archive/2009/06/09/opinionated-input-builders-for-asp-net-mvc-using-partials-part-i.aspx`.

Leaving breadcrumbs for your users with MvcSiteMap

In this recipe, we are going to take a look at how to implement a breadcrumb trail using the open source project `MvcSiteMap`.

Getting ready

The key to making this recipe work is getting the latest from the `MvcSiteMap` project here: `http://mvcsitemap.codeplex.com/`.

How to do it...

1. Kick off from a copy of the last recipe, or a new project.

2. Add a reference to the `MvcSiteMap`.

3. Then open up your `web.config` file and add a new provider for the `SiteMap`. You can add this directly after the `<system.web>` block.

   Web.config:

```
<siteMap defaultProvider="MvcSiteMapProvider" enabled="true">
  <providers>
    <clear />
    <add name="MvcSiteMapProvider"
        type="MvcSiteMapProvider.DefaultSiteMapProvider,
          MvcSiteMapProvider"
        siteMapFile="~/Mvc.Sitemap"
        securityTrimmingEnabled="true"
        cacheDuration="5"
        enableLocalization="true"
        scanAssembliesForSiteMapNodes="true"
        skipAssemblyScanOn=""
        attributesToIgnore="bling"
        nodeKeyGenerator="
          MvcSiteMapProvider.DefaultNodeKeyGenerator,
          MvcSiteMapProvider"
        controllerTypeResolver="
          MvcSiteMapProvider.DefaultControllerTypeResolver,
          MvcSiteMapProvider"
        actionMethodParameterResolver="
          MvcSiteMapProvider.DefaultActionMethodParameterResolver,
          MvcSiteMapProvider"
        aclModule="MvcSiteMapProvider.DefaultAclModule,
          MvcSiteMapProvider"
```

```
        siteMapNodeUrlResolver="
          MvcSiteMapProvider.DefaultSiteMapNodeUrlResolver,
          MvcSiteMapProvider"
        siteMapNodeVisibilityProvider="
          MvcSiteMapProvider.DefaultSiteMapNodeVisibilityProvider,
          MvcSiteMapProvider"
      />
    </providers>
  </siteMap>
```

4. Now you can add a `SiteMap` file to your application in the root called `Mvc.sitemap`.

 The name is important, because that is what is configured in the site map provider configuration!

5. In the new site map file, you can select all the existing code and delete it. Then enter the following site map, which corresponds to the default application's controllers and views (**Home**, **Account**, **LogOn**, **Register**, and so on).

   Web.sitemap:
```
<?xml version="1.0" encoding="utf-8" ?>
<mvcSiteMap
  xmlns="http://mvcsitemap.codeplex.com/schemas/
    MvcSiteMap-File-2.0" enableLocalization="true">
  <mvcSiteMapNode title="Home" controller="Home"
    action="Index" changeFrequency="Always"
    updatePriority="Normal">
  <mvcSiteMapNode title="Edit Person" controller="Home"
      action="Edit" />
</mvcSiteMapNode>
</mvcSiteMap>
```

6. Now all you need to do is to start using the functionality that is offered with the `MvcSiteMap`. We will add a breadcrumb trail by adding a call to `MvcSiteMap()`. `SiteMapPath()` in the `Site.Master`.

   Views/Shared/Site.Master:
```
<div id="main">
  <%= Html.MvcSiteMap().SiteMapPath(" &gt; ") %>
  <asp:ContentPlaceHolder ID="MainContent" runat="server" />
```

7. Add the following line to your `Web.config`.
```
        <add namespace="MvcSiteMapProvider.Web.Html" />
          <add namespace="MvcSiteMapProvider.Web.Html.Models" />
        </namespaces>
    </pages>
```

8. Now you can build the application and click around. You should see the breadcrumb trail build itself as you move from one view to the next.

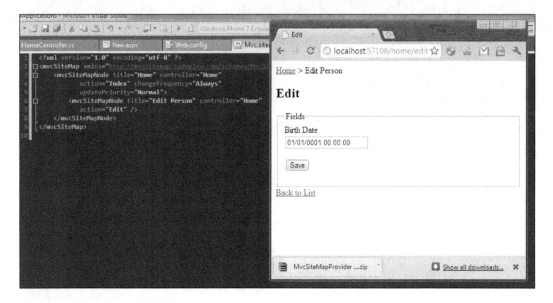

How it works...

Maarten Balliauw (`http://blog.maartenballiauw.be/`) had one of the first custom providers to take care of the lack of good support for the concept of the ASP.NET SiteMap back in 2008 (`http://blog.maartenballiauw.be/post/2008/08/29/Building-an-ASPNET-MVC-sitemap-provider-with-security-trimming.aspx`). He has since expanded on that little blog post to create a full blown open source project with loads of additional functionality. This code is available at `http://mvcsitemap.codeplex.com/`, if you are curious about the internals of it.

There's more...

For an idea of all the nodes that you have access to with this SiteMap provider, take a look here: `http://mvcsitemap.codeplex.com/wikipage?title=Creating%20a%20first%20sitemap&referringTitle=Home`.

Displaying tabular data in a grid

In this recipe, we are going to tackle the usually quite complex task of displaying grid data for a collection of data objects. Rather than using a looping structure and manually configuring how the data should be displayed, we will instead use the MvcContrib grid. This gets us close to the traditional style of the ASP.NET grid.

How to do it...

1. Start by creating a new empty ASP.NET MVC application.

2. Then add references to MvcContrib and NBuilder.

3. Next, we need to create a model to work with. In this case, we will work with the concept of a product. Add a new class to the Models directory called Product. Then add the following properties to represent our product.

   Models/Product.cs:

```
public class Product {
  public Guid ProductID { get; set; }
  public string ProductName { get; set; }
  public double Price { get; set; }
}
```

4. Then we need to add a new action to our HomeController called ListProducts. This action will be responsible for creating a collection of products with NBuilder and returning that collection to the view.

   Controllers/HomeController.cs:

```
public ActionResult ListProducts() {
  List<Product> products =
    Builder<Product>.CreateListOfSize(10).Build().ToList();

  return View(products);
}
```

5. Build the project so that when we add our new view, we can create a strongly typed view of type `Product`. Then right-click on the new `ListProducts` action and add a view. Make this a strongly typed empty view based on `Product`. Change the `Inherits` declaration to be a list of products rather than just a `Product`.

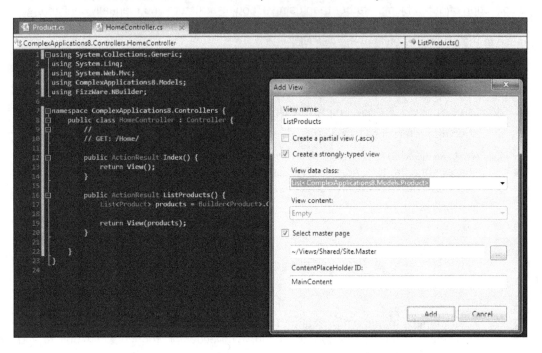

6. Now we can drop in the grid from `MvcContrib`. Do this by importing `MvcContrib.UI.Grid`. Then drop a call to the grid.

Views/Home/ListProducts.aspx:

```
...
<%@ Import Namespace="MvcContrib.UI.Grid" %>

<asp:Content ID="Content1" ContentPlaceHolderID="TitleContent"
    runat="server">
    ListProducts
</asp:Content>

<asp:Content ID="Content2" ContentPlaceHolderID="MainContent"
    runat="server">

  <h2>ListProducts</h2>

  <%= Html.Grid(Model) %>

</asp:Content>
```

7. Next, we need to configure the columns and their data for the given model. In this case, we want to display the product's price, name, and ID.

```
...
<%= Html.Grid(Model).Columns
    (c=>
        {
            c.For(m => m.Price);
            c.For(m => m.ProductName);
            c.For(m => m.ProductID);
        }
    ) %>
...
```

8. Now click, build, and run your application. Then navigate to `Home/ListProducts` to see the new grid.

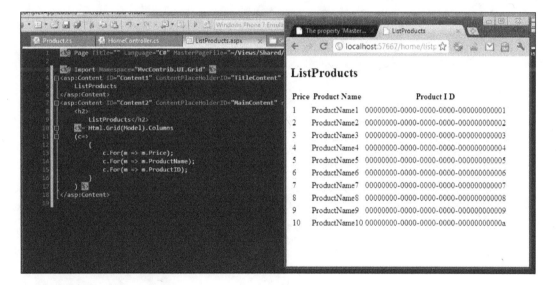

`MvcContrib` extends an already robust framework with some great functionality. The Grid is no exception, simple but effective. The Grid extension helper iterates through a collection and outputs a table. What I really like a lot about this helper and the direction of .NET projects in general, is its fluent approach—the grid is created in the first method, and columns (using lambda expression) are applied in the second.

8
Validating MVC

In this chapter, we will cover:

- ▶ Basic input validation
- ▶ Data annotations
- ▶ Client-side validation with jQuery
- ▶ Custom validators
- ▶ Remote validation with jQuery

Introduction

ASP.NET MVC provides a simple, but powerful, framework for validating forms. In this chapter, we will be building upon what has been learned in the previous two chapters. We'll start by creating a simple form, and then incrementally extend the functionality of our project to include client-side validation, custom validators, and remote validation.

Basic input validation

The moment you create an action to consume a form post, you're validating. Or at least the framework is. Whether it is a textbox validating to a `DateTime`, or checkbox to a Boolean, we can start making assumptions on what should be received and making provisions for what shouldn't. Let's create a form.

How to do it...

1. Create an empty ASP.NET MVC 2 project and add a master page called
   `Site.Master` to `Views/Shared`.

2. In the `models` folder, create a new model called `Person`. This model is just an
   extended version of the `Person` class that we used in the last chapter.

   Models/Person.cs:
   ```
   public class Person {
        [DisplayName("First Name")]
      public string FirstName { get; set; }
      [DisplayName("Middle Name")]
      public string MiddleName { get; set; }
      [DisplayName("Last Name")]
      public string LastName { get; set; }
      [DisplayName("Birth Date")]
      public DateTime BirthDate { get; set; }
      public string Email { get; set; }
      public string Phone { get; set; }
      public string Postcode { get; set; }
      public string Notes { get; set; }
   }
   ```

3. Create a controller called `HomeController` and amend the `Index` action to return
   a new instance of `Person` as the view model.

   Controllers/HomeController.cs:
   ```
   public ActionResult Index() {
       return View(new Person());
   }
   ```

4. Build and then right-click on the action to create an `Index` view. Make it an empty
   view that strongly types to our `Person` class.

5. Create a basic form in the `Index` view.

   Views/Home/Index.aspx:
   ```
   <% using (Html.BeginForm()) {%>
   <%: Html.EditorForModel() %>
   <input type="submit" name="submit" value="Submit" />
   <% } %>
   ```

6. We'll go back to the home controller now to capture the form submission. Create a
   second action called `Index`, which accepts only POSTs.

   Controllers/HomeController.cs:
   ```
   [HttpPost]
   public ActionResult Index(...
   ```

7. At this point, we have options. We can consume our form in a few different ways, let's have a look at a couple of them now:

Controllers/HomeController.cs (Example):

```
// Individual Parameters
public ActionResult Index(string firstName, DateTime birthdate...

// Model
Public ActionResult Index(Person person) {
```

8. Whatever technique you choose, the resolution of the parameters is roughly the same. The technique that I'm going to demonstrate relies on a method called `UpdateModel`. But first we need to differentiate our POST action from our first catch-all action. Remember, actions are just methods, and overrides need to take sufficiently different parameters to prevent ambiguity. We will do this by taking a single parameter of type `FormCollection`, though we won't necessarily make use of it.

Controllers/HomeController.cs:

```
[HttpPost]
public ActionResult Index(FormCollection form) {
  var person = new Person();

  UpdateModel(person);

  return View(person);
}
```

The `UpdateModel` technique is a touch more long-winded, but comes with advantages. The first is that if you add a breakpoint on the `UpdateModel` line, you can see the exact point when an empty model becomes populated with the form collection, which is great for demonstration purposes.

The main reason I go back to `UpdateModel` time and time again, is the optional second parameter, `includeProperties`. This parameter allows you to selectively update the model, thereby bypassing validation on certain properties that you might want to handle independently.

9. Build, run, and submit your form. If your page validates, your info should be returned back to you. However, add your birth date in an unrecognized format and watch it bomb. `UpdateModel` is a temperamental beast.

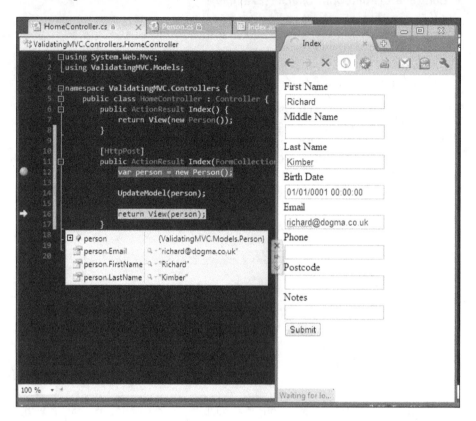

10. Switch your `UpdateModel` for `TryUpdateModel` and see what happens. `TryUpdateModel` will return a Boolean indicating the success or failure of the submission. However, the most interesting thing is happening in the browser.

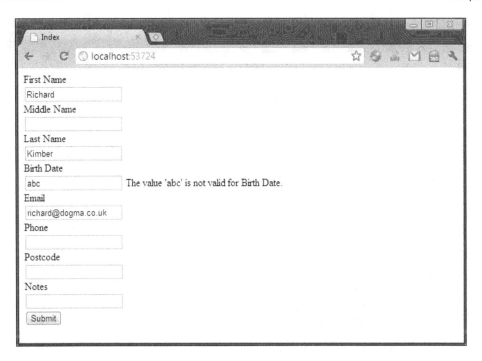

How it works...

With ASP.NET MVC, it sometimes feels like you're stripping the development process back to basics. I think this is a good thing; more control to render the page you want is good. But there is a lot of clever stuff going on in the background, starting off with **Model Binders**.

When you send a request (GET, POST, and so on) to an ASP.NET MVC application, the query string, route values and the form collection are passed through model binding classes, which result in usable structures (for example, your action's input parameters). These model binders can be overridden and extended to deal with more complex scenarios, but since ASP.NET MVC2, I've rarely made use of this. A good starting point for further investigation would be with DefaultModelBinder and IModelBinder.

What about that validation message in the last screenshot, where did it come from? In previous chapters, we've talked only about LableFor and EditorFor, but we also have ValidationMessageFor. If the model binders fail at any point to build our input parameters, the model binder will add an error message to the model state. The model state is picked up and displayed by the ValidationMessageFor method, but more on that later.

Data annotations

Okay, given the minimal effort we put into creating our form, getting that validation message on the birth date was impressive. You would also get an error message if you didn't send a date at all because `DateTime` cannot be null.

The question that we will answer in this recipe however, is how do we add validation that is not implied by type? One way is to use data annotations. **Data annotations** are a collection of attributes that allow you to describe your model in terms of what is required, or what a property might be used for, among other things.

How to do it...

1. Starting from our previous recipe, let's go to our `Person` model and make the following amendments:

   Models/Person.cs:
   ```
   public class Person {
       [DisplayName("First Name"), StringLength(50)]
       public string FirstName { get; set; }
       [DisplayName("Middle Name"), StringLength(50)]
       public string MiddleName { get; set; }
       [DisplayName("Last Name"), StringLength(50), Required]
       public string LastName { get; set; }
       [DisplayName("Birth Date"), DataType(DataType.Date)]
       public DateTime BirthDate { get; set; }
       [DataType(DataType.EmailAddress), Required]
       public string Email { get; set; }
       public string Phone { get; set; }
       public string Postcode { get; set; }
       [DataType(DataType.MultilineText)]
       public string Notes { get; set; }
   }
   ```

2. Build the project and then reload the form to see the changes. We can already see a neater date (**Birth Date**) and a text area instead of a textbox (**Notes**). Submit though, and we start getting feedback as well.

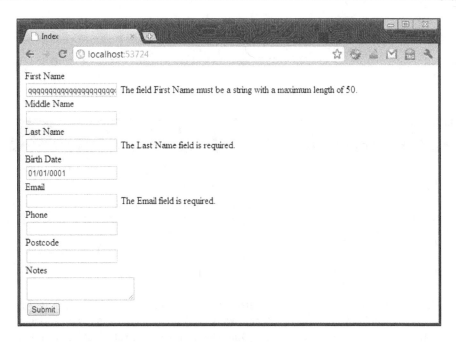

3. Validation attributes such as `Required` and `StringLength` inherit from `ValidationAttribute`, which contains additional properties that allow you to customize the error message or attach the attribute to a resource. In the following screenshot, I've amended the error message of the `MiddleName` property.

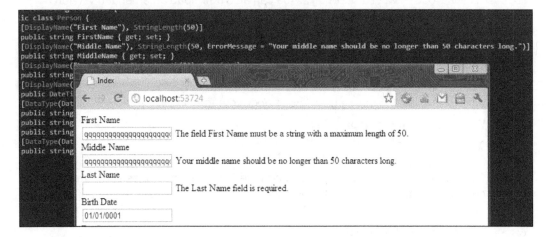

How it works...

The default model binder in ASP.NET MVC uses reflection to interrogate target types for attributes that fall under the namespace `DataAnnotations`. Using the additional metadata provided by the attributes, the model binder can generate a more comprehensive set of tests.

Client-side validation with jQuery

We're already running quite a tight ship with our form, but it's a little frustrating to receive the error messages only after we submit the form. Think about thousands of people constantly submitting incorrect data to your site. It's an unnecessary use of your valuable resources. Client-side validation goes some way to prevent this, but used to be a real bind to implement; with ASP.NET MVC though, it's remarkably easy.

Getting ready

Up until about ASP.NET MVC 2 RC, there were two options for implementing client-side validation—Microsoft Ajax and jQuery. Of the two, the jQuery option was mysteriously absent from the final release. It will be the jQuery option that we will focus on in this recipe. Beyond the jQuery files already contained within any new ASP.NET MVC 2 project, this recipe has a requirement for the somewhat elusive jQuery connector. I've given up trying to track down the file's permanent residence, so will simply say that it is included within the book's source code, and can be tracked down (with some effort) on Google by searching for `MicrosoftMvcJQueryValidation.js`. You can also download an amended version from `http://blog.dogma.co.uk`.

How to do it...

1. Starting from the previous recipe, let's add a call to `Html.EnableClientValidation()` above our form in `Views/Home/Index.aspx`.

   Views/Home/Index.aspx:
   ```
   <% Html.EnableClientValidation(); %>
   <% using (Html.BeginForm()) {%>
   ```

2. Open up your `Site.Master` file and add the following three lines above the closing `body` tag, assuming that you added the connector file to the root of your `Scripts` folder.

   Views/Shared/Site.Master:
   ```
   <script src="/Scripts/jquery-1.4.1.min.js"
      type="text/javascript"></script>
   <script src="/Scripts/jquery.validate.min.js"
     type="text/javascript"></script>
   <script src="/Scripts/MicrosoftMvcJQueryValidation.js"
      type="text/javascript"></script>
   ```

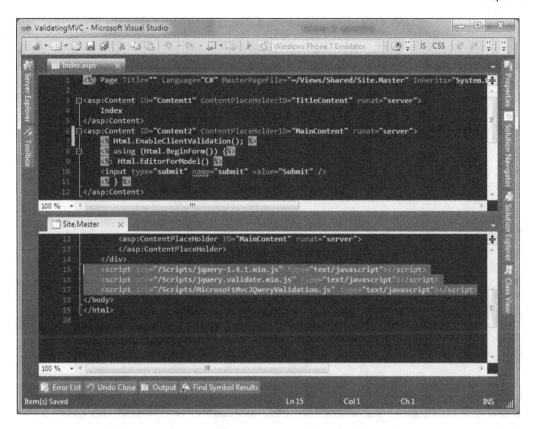

3. Build and run your project, then submit your form. Unless you've filled in all the required fields, you wouldn't be able to make a submission. jQuery, with the help of our connector (`MicrosoftMvcJQueryValidation.js`), has prevented the POST. What's more, if you start correcting the mistakes, the error messages will disappear without having to attempt resubmission.

How it works...

In the first step, we added a call to an HTML helper called `EnableClientValidation`. The `EnableClientValidation` method should be added just above the targeted form and it basically tells the form to render some extra information. The extra information is a **JSON** (**JavaScript Object Notation**) map containing all the validation conditions for the form within a `script` block. The `script` block is placed directly beneath the form and attaches the map to a window object called `mvcClientValidationMetadata`. Have a look at the HTML source of your form for a complete example.

Home/Index (View Source):

```
if (!window.mvcClientValidationMetadata) {
    window.mvcClientValidationMetadata = []; }
```

```
window.mvcClientValidationMetadata.push({ "Fields": [{
    "FieldName": "FirstName",
    "ReplaceValidationMessageContents": true,
    "ValidationMessageId": "FirstName_validationMessage",
    "ValidationRules": [{
        "ErrorMessage": "The field First Name must be a string
          with a maximum length of 50.",
        "ValidationParameters": {
            "minimumLength": 0, "maximumLength": 50 },
        "ValidationType": "stringLength"
    }]
    },
    . . .
```

The validation itself is handled by a very robust jQuery plug-in called **jQuery Validation**. At this point though, the validation plug-in needs to be initiated and, as the `mvcClientValidationMetdata` object is a Microsoft invention that means nothing to jQuery, we need a bridge. Enter `MicrosoftMvcJQueryValidation.js` (the connector). This file consumes the JSON map and reformats it as an `options` object that the validation plug-in can understand. The connector then calls the validation plug-in into action.

So far, we have mirrored validation on the client and server with a small amount of effort. What else can we do?

Custom validators

We can create our own validation rules. I've got a couple of issues with our code so far.

▸ We've told ASP.NET MVC that our `email` field is an e-mail field, but I can type in any old junk.

▸ I'm British (that is not the issue), so I've got a postcode and I want to validate it!

I've already mentioned the `ValidationAttribute` class and some of the attributes that inherit from it, another is `RegularExpressionAttribute`. We'll derive a couple of attributes from the `RegularExpressionAttribute` to resolve my two immediate issues.

How to do it...

1. From our last recipe, we'll create a new folder called `Helpers` and a class within, called `Attributes`.

2. In `Attributes.cs`, create a new class called `EmailAttribute`, which inherits from `RegularExpressionAttribute`.

3. Override the base constructor with the following code. Of particular note here is the regular expression used, `^[a-zA-Z0-9._%+-]+@(?:[a-zA-Z0-9-]+\.)+[a-zA-Z]{2,6}$`, which is passed in as the sole parameter. We then provide a default error message within the constructor.

Helpers/Attributes.cs:

```
public class EmailAttribute : RegularExpressionAttribute {
  public EmailAttribute() : base(
  @"^[a-zA-Z0-9._%+-]+@(?:[a-zA-Z0-9-]+\.)+[a-zA-Z]{2,6}$") {
  ErrorMessage = "Email is invalid";
  }
}
```

4. We'll now switch our attention to the `Person` model in the `models` folder. Make the following adjustment, remembering to resolve your namespaces. We're saying that this property should conform to the regular expression specified.

Models/Person.cs:

```
public DateTime BirthDate { get; set; }
[DataType(DataType.EmailAddress), Required, Email]
public string Email { get; set; }
```

5. Build and run your project. Fill out the form and submit with and without a correctly formatted e-mail address. Your first observation should be that it is not working on the client-side, but is on the server.

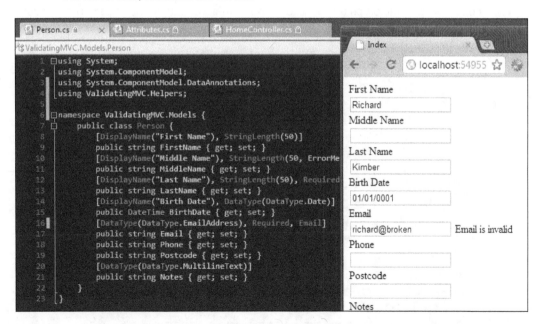

6. Our e-mail validation is not working on the client because ASP.NET MVC doesn't know what an `EmailAttribute` is. The framework does know what a `RegularExpressionAttribute` is, though. So, within the `Global.asax.cs` file, our final step for e-mail validation will be to tell ASP.NET MVC to make this connection.

Global.asax.cs :

```
protected void Application_Start() {
  AreaRegistration.RegisterAllAreas();

  RegisterRoutes(RouteTable.Routes);

  DataAnnotationsModelValidatorProvider.RegisterAdapter(
    typeof(EmailAttribute),
    typeof(RegularExpressionAttributeAdapter));
}
```

7. Build your project and reload your form. You should now have client-side e-mail validation.

8. The process required for a postcode validation is almost identical, except this time you use a different regular expression.

Helpers/Attributes.cs :

```
([Gg][Ii][Rr] 0[Aa]{2})|((([A-Za-z][0-9]{1,2})|(([A-Za-z][A-Ha-hJ-
Yj-y][0-9]{1,2})|(([A-Za-z][0-9][A-Za-z])|([A-Za-z][A-Ha-hJ-Yj-
y][0-9]?[A-Za-z])))) {0,1}[0-9][A-Za-z]{2})
```

9. Follow each of the steps that we did for our e-mail validation and you should end with something like this:

How it works...

We could have just used a vanilla `RegularExpressionAttribute` to satisfy both cases. But what we have now is two very useful attributes that can be reapplied across multiple models and projects. For the client-side validation to work, there needs to be a translation between the server and client environments. The translation happens in an `AttributeAdapter` that is registered in the `DataAnnotationsModelValidatorProvider`. It is these two components that ultimately decide the shape of the JSON map identified in the last recipe. We cover this concept in more detail in the next recipe.

Remote validation with jQuery

In a lot of cases, validation is a static formula, something definable like a formula or regular expression. Sometimes however, validation requires an external source (like a database). In cases like this, putting the logic in an attribute is possible but not always ideal. And what happens to the client-side? It's not so easy to tell the browser to connect to a database before allowing a form submission. Well, it's actually a lot easier than I thought.

Getting ready

In this recipe, we'll think of our form as a registration form. We've been getting a lot of duplicate registrations, so we'd like to prevent users from registering an e-mail address more than once.

How to do it...

1. Start from our last recipe and open up the home controller.

2. Add the following method called `IsEmailAlreadyRegistered` to the top of the home controller class. This method will act as a list of e-mails that have already been registered. You will need to add a reference to the `System.Linq` namespace.

   Controllers/HomeController.cs:

```
private bool IsEmailAlreadyRegistered(string email) {
  return new string[] { "test@test.com", "example@example.com",
    "richard@dogma.co.uk" }.Contains(email);
}
```

3. Now we need to add some code to the `Index` action (the one that accepts only POSTs) to validate against our list of e-mail addresses. Before we attempt to validate against our e-mail list, we'll make sure that the rest of the model has validated successfully. If the e-mail does already exist, we'll add an error message to the `ModelState` object. Add the following code after the `TryUpdateModel` call.

Controllers/HomeController.cs :

```
if (ModelState.IsValid && IsEmailAlreadyRegistered(person.Email))
{
  var propertyName = "email";
  ModelState.AddModelError(propertyName, "Email address is already
    registered");
  ModelState.SetModelValue(propertyName,
    ValueProvider.GetValue(propertyName));
}
```

 The `ModelState` object represents the state of the models before they're sent to the view. The model state contains the validation message and the current values. If you provide a model error without a model value, you can run into unexpected errors further down the line.

4. Let's see how this works. Build and run the project.

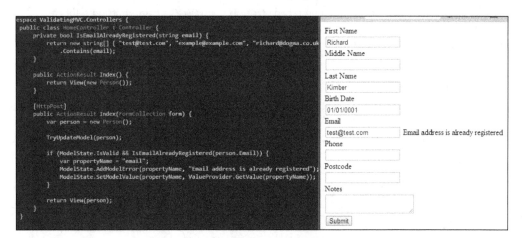

5. We should now be preventing duplicate registrations on the server, but ideally, we'd like this on the client as well. We'll do this by using remote validation, which generally involves an Ajax call to the server. First, we need to tell ASP.NET what remote validation is. Let's create a new attribute in our `Attributes.cs` file called `RemoteAttribute`.

Helpers/Attributes.cs :

```
public class RemoteAttribute : ValidationAttribute { }
```

6. jQuery's validation plug-in will need a URL to connect to, in order to establish whether the e-mail has already been registered or not; so we'll add a URL property. Also, because this attribute is not going to be validating on the server, we'll override the `IsValid` method to always return true.

Helpers/Attributes.cs:

```
public class RemoteAttribute : ValidationAttribute {
    public string Url { get; set; }

    public RemoteAttribute() {
        ErrorMessage = "Email address is already registered";
    }

    public override bool IsValid(object value) {
        return true;
    }
}
```

7. Now before we go and decorate our `Person` model with our shiny new attribute, we need a URL for our client validation to validate against. Go back to the home controller and create a new action called `EmailCheck`.

Controllers/HomeController.cs:

```
public ActionResult EmailCheck(string email) {
    return Json(!IsEmailAlreadyRegistered(email),
        JsonRequestBehavior.AllowGet);
}
```

8. We can now decorate our model. Open up the `Person` class and make the following amendment.

Models/Person.cs:

```
[DataType(DataType.EmailAddress), Required, Email,
    Remote(Url = "/home/emailcheck")]
public string Email { get; set; }
```

9. At this stage we have an attribute, a URL, and we've decorated our model. Now we need an attribute adapter. Create a new class in your `Helpers` folder called `RemoteAttributeAdapter`, which will inherit from `DataAnnotationsModelValidator<RemoteAttribute>`.

Helpers/RemoteAttributeAdapter.cs:

```
public class RemoteAttributeAdapter :
    DataAnnotationsModelValidator<RemoteAttribute> { }
```

10. `DataAnnotationsModelValidator<>` doesn't have a parameter-less constructor, so we'll need to create a new constructor for our class.

Helpers/RemoteAttributeAdapter.cs:

```
public class RemoteAttributeAdapter :
    DataAnnotationsModelValidator<RemoteAttribute> {
    public RemoteAttributeAdapter(ModelMetadata metadata,
```

```
        ControllerContext context, RemoteAttribute attribute) :
        base(metadata, context, attribute) { }
}
```

11. I mentioned in the last recipe that the adapter had its part to play in what was rendered on the client; this happens in a method called `GetClientValidationRules`. You'll see from the following code that we can add custom parameters to relate to our new attribute.

Helpers/RemoteAttributeAdapter.cs:

```
public class RemoteAttributeAdapter :
    DataAnnotationsModelValidator<RemoteAttribute> {
  public RemoteAttributeAdapter(ModelMetadata metadata,
    ControllerContext context, RemoteAttribute attribute) :
    base(metadata, context, attribute) { }

    public override IEnumerable<ModelClientValidationRule>
      GetClientValidationRules() {
        var rule = new ModelClientValidationRule {
          ErrorMessage = ErrorMessage,
          ValidationType = "remote"
      };

      rule.ValidationParameters["url"] = Attribute.Url;
      rule.ValidationParameters["type"] = "get";

      return new[] { rule };
  }
}
```

 `GetClientValidationRules` returns a collection of `ModelClientValidationRules`. These rules are special because when serialized, they make up the structure of the JSON map that we identified two recipes ago, called `mvcClientValidationMetdata`.

12. In the last step, we created a rule with a validation type of `remote`. Remote validation is baked straight into the jQuery validation plug-in—the Microsoft connector (`MicrosoftMvcJQueryValidation.js`) however, has no idea what remote validation is. So, we will need to make some changes. Open up the `MicrosoftMvcJQueryValidation.js` in your `Scripts` folder.

13. The connector file is a series of functions that respond to different validation types. Our first job will be to create a function to respond to the remote validation type (or rule). When you look at the following code, you will see that it acts like a mirror for the `GetClientValidationRules` method that we created a second ago. It consumes the custom parameter's set on the server and produces a jQuery-friendly `options` object.

Scripts/MicrosoftMvcJQueryValidation.js:

```
function __MVC_ApplyValidator_Remote(object, validationParameters,
    fieldName) {
    var obj = object["remote"] = {};
    var props = validationParameters.additionalProperties;

    obj["url"] = validationParameters.url;
    obj["type"] = validationParameters.type;

    if (props) {
        var data = {};

        for (var i = 0, l = props.length; i < l; ++i) {
            var param = props[i];
            data[props[i]] = function () {
                return $("#" + param).val();
            }
        }

        obj["data"] = data;
    }
}
```

14. We're almost there. We just need to connect the remote validation type to our function, as well as pass the correct parameters. Our new function makes use of the name of the field being validated. The factory method (__MVC_CreateRulesForField) that associates the validation type to the function currently has no knowledge of this, so we'll need to pass it in as an additional parameter.

Scripts/MicrosoftMvcJQueryValidation.js:

```
function __MVC_CreateValidationOptions(validationFields) {
    var rulesObj = {};
    for (var i = 0; i < validationFields.length; i++) {
        var validationField = validationFields[i];
        var fieldName = validationField.FieldName;
        rulesObj[fieldName] =
            __MVC_CreateRulesForField(validationField, fieldName);
    }

    return rulesObj;
}
```

15. Now we want to tell the factory method to make use of the additional parameter, and apply it to our new function.

Scripts/MicrosoftMvcJQueryValidation.js:

```
function __MVC_CreateRulesForField(validationField, fieldName) {
    var validationRules = validationField.ValidationRules;
```

```
       // hook each rule into jquery
       var rulesObj = {};
       for (var i = 0; i < validationRules.length; i++) {
         var thisRule = validationRules[i];
         switch (thisRule.ValidationType) {
           case "range":
               __MVC_ApplyValidator_Range(rulesObj,
                   thisRule.ValidationParameters["minimum"],
                    thisRule.ValidationParameters["maximum"]);
             break;

           case "regularExpression":
               __MVC_ApplyValidator_RegularExpression(rulesObj,
                   thisRule.ValidationParameters["pattern"]);
             break;

           case "required":
               __MVC_ApplyValidator_Required(rulesObj);
             break;

           case "stringLength":
               __MVC_ApplyValidator_StringLength(rulesObj,
                   thisRule.ValidationParameters["maximumLength"]);
             break;

           case "remote":
               __MVC_ApplyValidator_Remote(rulesObj,
                 thisRule.ValidationParameters, fieldName);
             break;

           default:
               __MVC_ApplyValidator_Unknown(rulesObj,
                   thisRule.ValidationType,
                   thisRule.ValidationParameters);
             break;
       }
        }

     return rulesObj;
   }
```

16. If we build and run this form in Firefox (with FireBug switched on), we should be able to see our remote validation in action.

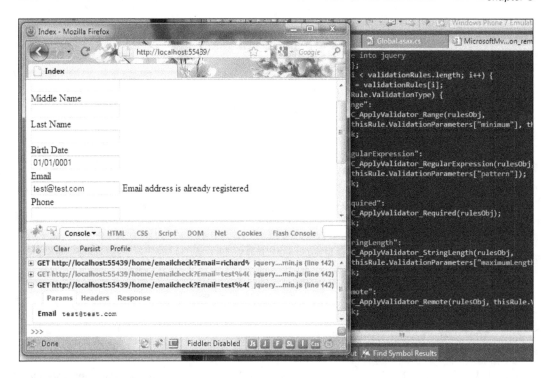

How it works...

The validation plug-in of jQuery is a comprehensive collection of rules, which can be triggered in any number of ways. The most common approach is through the use of class names applied to the input field; where a textbox decorated with the class `required` would result in the surrounding form not being able to submit without the said textbox being filled in. Another way to initiate the validation plug-in is through the use of an `options` object. The `options` object is a schema for how the form should be validated.

ASP.NET MVC's client-side validation was not built with jQuery's specific schema in mind, so the `MicrosoftMvcJQueryValidation.js` file was written to bridge the JavaScript injected by ASP.NET MVC (`mvcClientValidationMetdata`) with the jQuery `options` object, then initializing the validation plug-in.

Scripts/MicrosoftMvcJQueryValidation.js :

```
function __MVC_EnableClientValidation(validationContext) {
    // this represents the form containing elements to be validated
    var theForm = $("#" + validationContext.FormId);

    ...

    var options = {
        errorClass: "input-validation-error",
```

```
        . . .
          $(messageSpan).removeClass("field-validation-error");
        }
    };

    // register callbacks with our AJAX system
    var formElement =
      document.getElementById(validationContext.FormId);
    var registeredValidatorCallbacks =
      formElement.validationCallbacks;
    if (!registeredValidatorCallbacks) {
      registeredValidatorCallbacks = [];
      formElement.validationCallbacks = registeredValidatorCallbacks;
    }
    registeredValidatorCallbacks.push(function () {
      theForm.validate();
      return theForm.valid();
    });

    theForm.validate(options);
}
```

Baked into jQuery's validation plug-in is this concept of remote validation. **Remote validation** is validation where not all the variables are known at implementation, so there is a requirement to source that information from a remote location. When dealing with remote validation it is preferable to try and retrieve any information without disrupting the user's workflow; for this reason we use an Ajax request to the server. As the user types in his/her e-mail address, the client-side script silently fires off requests to our URL (or endpoint) to unobtrusively validate the input.

We enabled jQuery's remote validation functionality by passing through the URL of an action, which will return a Boolean based on the existence of the entered e-mail within our dummy method. jQuery took care of the rest with a simple GET request to our endpoint.

Validation was something I didn't particularly enjoy in ASP.NET web forms, but now relish in ASP.NET MVC. It is another great example of the extensibility of the new framework.

9
Data Access and Storage

In this chapter, we will cover:

- ▶ Mocking your data layer with NBuilder
- ▶ Adding support for LINQ to SQL
- ▶ Going old school with ADO.NET
- ▶ XML documents as a data store

Introduction

In this chapter, we are going to focus more on the various flavours of data access and data storage, which are accessible to you when building an MVC application. To do this without taking too much time away from our focus on the data story, we will use a single MVC application across all recipes. To make our application flexible enough to easily swap our data access around, we will use **StructureMap**, the inversion of control pattern, and the repository pattern. At the end of this chapter, we should have one application with several different forms of data storage and methods of data access.

Mocking your data layer with NBuilder

In order for us to get started with other recipes in this chapter, we need to first build the application that we will be using in each of the following recipes. Oddly enough, the ability to build out your entire application without having any data storage or data access already in place is a common occurrence. You might not be on the team that builds the data-access layer or you might work in a dev shop where the database is under tight control of the database administrators. There are many scenarios where mocking or faking out the database and data access layer may come in handy or be a requirement.

In this recipe, we will be building a simple blog post and commenting system. We will create an application that allows the user to add, edit, and delete posts. With each post the user will also have the ability to add and delete comments to and from a blog post. This is going to be a simple system for the sole purpose of demonstrating data storage functionality. Primarily, we will be looking at how to perform select, insert, update, joins, and delete statements in various environments using all sorts of tools.

Getting ready

In this recipe, we will be using StructureMap and NBuilder. Both of these are in the dependencies folder. You may be interested in getting the latest copies of both of these tools, as they are constantly being updated!

How to do it...

1. Let's get started by creating a new ASP.NET MVC application using the default application (rather than the empty template); we named ours AccessAndStorage.

2. Add references to StructureMap and NBuilder.

3. We need to add some folders to the existing `Models` directory. This will help us stay organized as we build out our solution. Add a `Domain`, `Repository`, and a `StructureMap` directory to the `Models` directory. The `Domain` folder will hold the domain (business) objects for our application. The `Repository` folder will hold each of the new recipes form of data access.

4. Inside the `Repository` directory, create a `MockRepository` folder. The `MockRepository` folder will hold the data access for this recipe—the NBuilder implementation.

5. Next we are going to move to creating our domain objects. Specifically, we need to create `Post` and `Comment` classes. The `Post` object will represent our blog post. The `Comment` class will represent a comment being added to a `Post`. Create these two new classes in the `Models/Domain` folder.

   Models/Domain/Post.cs:

```
public class Post {
  public Guid PostID { get; set; }
  public DateTime CreateDate { get; set; }
  public string Title { get; set; }
  public string Body { get; set; }
  public string Slug { get; set; }
  private List<Comment> comments { get; set; }
  public List<Comment> Comments {
     get {
        //implementation discussed later...
           throw new NotImplementedException();
        }
     }
}
```

   Models/Domain/Comment.cs:

```
public class Comment {
  public Guid CommentID { get; set; }
  public Guid PostID { get; set; }
  public string Body { get; set; }
  public DateTime CreateDate {get; set; }
}
```

6. With our two business objects created, we can now create some interfaces that will represent the functionality that all of our data access classes should implement. The first interface for us to create is the `IRepositoryConfiguration` in the `Repository` folder. This will provide us with a hook for any data access tool that we might use that will need configuration performed when our application starts up. We will expose one method called `Configure`.

   Models/Repository/IRepositoryConfiguration.cs:

```
public interface IRepositoryConfiguration {
  void Configure();
}
```

7. Next, we will create the `IPostRepository` interface, again in the `Repository` folder. This interface will require the following methods to be created: `AddPost`, `UpdatePost`, `DeletePost`, `GetPost`, and `GetPosts`.

Models/Repository/IPostRepository.cs:

```
public interface IPostRepository {
   void AddPost(Post post);
   void UpdatePost(Post post);
   void DeletePost(Post post);
   Post GetPost(Guid postId);
   List<Post> GetPosts();
}
```

8. Lastly, we will create the `ICommentRepository` interface, which will require the following methods: `AddComment`, `DeleteComment`, `GetComment`, and `GetCommentsByPostID`.

Models/Repository/ICommentRepository.cs:

```
public interface ICommentRepository {
   void AddComment(Comment comment);
   void DeleteComment(Comment comment);
   Comment GetComment(Guid commentId);
   List<Comment> GetCommentsByPostID(Guid postId);
   void DeleteComments(Guid postId);
}
```

9. Now that we know what we are working to build, we can start to build out our first implementation. The first class that we can create is `MockRepositoryConfiguration`, which will implement `IRepositoryConfiguration`. All we need is a placeholder here, as the mock implementation doesn't actually require any pre-configuration. Place this file in the `MockRepository` folder.

Models/Repository/MockRepository/MockRepositoryConfiguration.cs:

```
public class MockRepositoryConfiguration :
   IRepositoryConfiguration
{
   public void Configure() {
   }
}
```

10. Next we will create the `MockPostRepository`. This is the most important repository of our repositories, as it will help us to manage and display our posts. As we are creating only a mock implementation so that we can create our application, we only really need to fake out the display side of our implementation. We will do this by creating new posts and new lists of posts using NBuilder. As you will see shortly, the NBuilder syntax is very simple.

Models/Repository/MockRepository/MockPostRepository.cs:

```
public class MockPostRepository : IPostRepository {
  public void AddPost(Post post) {

  }

  public void UpdatePost(Post post) {

  }

  public void DeletePost(Post post) {

  }

  public Post GetPost(Guid postId) {
    return Builder<Post>.CreateNew().With(
        p => p.PostID = postId).Build();
  }

  public List<Post> GetPosts() {
      return Builder<Post>.CreateListOfSize(10).Build().ToList();
  }
}
```

11. This leaves us with one more repository class to create, the `MockCommentRepository` class, which will handle the display of comments for each post. There is a bit of logic baked into this though, as I wanted to create a variable number of comments for each post. To do this, I used a random number to generate a random length list of comments.

Models/Repository/MockRepository/MockCommentRepository.cs:

```
public class MockCommentRepository : ICommentRepository {
  public void AddComment(Comment comment) {

  }

  public void DeleteComment(Comment comment) {

  }
```

```
public Comment GetComment(Guid commentId) {
  return Builder<Comment>.CreateNew().With(
    c => c.CommentID == commentId).Build();
}


public List<Comment> GetCommentsByPostID(Guid postId) {
  int init = Convert.ToInt32(String.Format("{0:ffffff}",
    DateTime.Now));
  Random r = new Random(init);
  int listSize = r.Next(1,10);
  List<Comment> result = Builder<Comment>.CreateListOfSize(
    listSize).WhereAll().Have(c => c.PostID =  postId).
    Build().ToList();
  return result;
}


public void DeleteComments(Guid postId) {


}
}
```

Now that we have our business objects, interfaces, and implementation created, we can start to wire StructureMap into place. By using interfaces, we have detached the implementation of our data layer for the rest of our application. StructureMap will allow us to plug in any data layer, which implements our interfaces.

A more comprehensive description of the **Inversion of Control** (**IoC**) pattern, as implemented by StructureMap, is beyond the scope of this recipe. As you'll see from this recipe though, once the basics are grasped, the pattern is easy to implement (when using a library like StructureMap). For further information, you could do a lot worse than to look at the article by Martin Fowlers at http://martinfowler.com/articles/injection.html.

Let's take a look at what is required to get StructureMap working. We will start by creating a `MockRepositoryRegistry` class in the `Models/StructureMap` folder. This class will inherit from the `StructureMap.Configuration.DSL.Registry` class, which provides us with the ability to map our `MockRepository` classes to the repository interfaces that we created. We will also create a `Registry` method that will actually tell StructureMap to use our configuration.

Models/StructureMap/MockRepositoryRegistry.cs:

```
public class MockRepositoryRegistry : Registry {
  public MockRepositoryRegistry() {
    For<ICommentRepository>()
      .Use<MockCommentRepository>();
    For<IPostRepository>()
      .Use<MockPostRepository>();
    For<IRepositoryConfiguration>()
      .Use<MockRepositoryConfiguration>();
  }

  public static void Register() {
    ObjectFactory.Initialize(x => x.AddRegistry(
      new MockRepositoryRegistry()));
  }
}
```

12. With this configuration helper class created, we now need to add a line of code to our `Global.asax.cs` file to configure StructureMap when the application first starts. The call to our registry is what tells StructureMap which implementation to use for the given interface. Open the `Global.asax.cs` file. In the `Application_Start()` method add the following lines:

Global.asax.cs:

```
protected void Application_Start() {
  AreaRegistration.RegisterAllAreas();

  RegisterRoutes(RouteTable.Routes);

  MockRepositoryRegistry.Register();
}
```

13. While we are in the `Global.asax.cs` file, we can also add a call to our `MockRepositoryConfiguration.Configure()` method. We will do this with StructureMap syntax using the `ObjectFactory` entry point. This is the class that provides us with access to all of our classes. Directly under the call to our `MockRepositoryRegistry`, add the following line, which will call the appropriate `Configure` method on whatever data access we are using at the time (which is controlled by the registry that we called earlier).

`ObjectFactory.GetInstance<IRepositoryConfiguration>().Configure();`

```
8   namespace AccessAndStorage {
9       public class MvcApplication : HttpApplication {
10          public static void RegisterRoutes(RouteCollection routes) {
11              routes.IgnoreRoute("{resource}.axd/{*pathInfo}");
12
13              routes.MapRoute(
14                  "Default", // Route name
15                  "{controller}/{action}/{id}", // URL with parameters
16                  new { controller = "Home", action = "Index", id = UrlParameter.Optional }
17              );
18          }
19
20          protected void Application_Start() {
21              AreaRegistration.RegisterAllAreas();
22
23              RegisterRoutes(RouteTable.Routes);
24
25              MockRepositoryRegistry.Register();
26
27              ObjectFactory.GetInstance<IRepositoryConfiguration>().Configure();
28          }
29      }
30  }
```

14. With StructureMap wired into place and all of our interfaces and repositories mocked out, we now need to revisit our `Post` class. It has a property on it called `Comments`, which should return the list of related comments. It is not currently implemented. Let's implement it by making a call to our new `MockCommentRepository`.

Models/Domain/Post.cs:

```
public List<Comment> Comments {
  get {
    if (comments == null) {
      if (PostID != Guid.Empty)
        comments = ObjectFactory
        .GetInstance<ICommentRepository>()
        .GetCommentsByPostID(PostID);
      else comments = new List<Comment>();
    }
```

```
    return comments;
  }
  set {
    comments = value;
  }
}
```

15. At this point, you should be able to build and run your application. The normal MVC starter template application should appear. When the application begins, StructureMap should be configured. Then the `Configure` method will be called (which does nothing in this implementation). If this works, we can now start to mock out our UI.

16. This application will largely be a scaffolding of our objects. By that I mean we will create actions in our `HomeController` to add, edit, and delete our posts. We will also have actions to add and delete our comments. We will entirely rely upon StructureMap to provide us with the correct implementation of a given interface, which will allow us to swap out data-access methods in later recipes. Here is our `HomeController`. The only place that you might need to pay some special attention is in the `add` actions, as they generate a custom ID for the new record, as well as set the create date (something that might be better handled in a service layer rather than in the controller). Let's first see the post-oriented actions and the home page action (index).

Controllers/HomeController.cs:

```
public class HomeController : Controller {
  public ActionResult Index() {
    ViewData["Message"] = "Welcome to ASP.NET MVC!";
    List<Post> result =
      ObjectFactory.GetInstance<IPostRepository>().GetPosts();
    return View(result);
  }


  public ActionResult AddPost() {
    return View(new Post());
  }


  [HttpPost]
  public ActionResult AddPost(Post post) {
    post.CreateDate = DateTime.Now;
    post.PostID = Guid.NewGuid();
    ObjectFactory.GetInstance<IPostRepository>().AddPost(post);
    return RedirectToAction("Index");
  }


  public ActionResult EditPost(Guid id) {
```

```
      Post post =
        ObjectFactory.GetInstance<IPostRepository>().GetPost(id);
     return View(post);
    }


    [HttpPost]
    public ActionResult EditPost(Post post) {
      ObjectFactory.GetInstance<IPostRepository>().UpdatePost(post);
      return RedirectToAction("Index");
    }


    public ActionResult DeletePost(Guid id) {
      Post post =
        ObjectFactory.GetInstance<IPostRepository>().GetPost(id);
    return View(post);

  }


    [HttpPost]
    public ActionResult DeletePost(Guid id, FormCollection form) {
      ObjectFactory.GetInstance<IPostRepository>().DeletePost(
        new Post { PostID = id });
      return RedirectToAction("Index");
    }}
```

17. The comment-oriented actions are pretty much identical.

Controllers/HomeController.cs:

. . .

```
    public ActionResult AddComment(Guid id) {
      return View(new Comment { PostID = id });
    }


    [HttpPost]
    public ActionResult AddComment(Guid id, Comment comment) {
      comment.CreateDate = DateTime.Now;
      comment.CommentID = Guid.NewGuid();
      comment.PostID = id;
      ObjectFactory.GetInstance<ICommentRepository>().AddComment(
        comment);
      return RedirectToAction("Index");
    }


    public ActionResult DeleteComment(Guid id) {
```

```
    Comment comment =
        ObjectFactory.GetInstance<ICommentRepository>().
        GetComment(id);
      return View(comment);
    }

    [HttpPost]
    public ActionResult DeleteComment(Guid id, FormCollection form)
    {
        ObjectFactory.GetInstance<ICommentRepository>().
            DeleteComment(new Comment { CommentID = id });
        return RedirectToAction("Index");
    }
}
```

18. With all of our actions defined, you can now right-click each of the unique action names and add a new strongly typed view. Even the home page has been updated to a list of posts as its model! For the most part, the views that are in my application are from the wizard's template generation (take a look at the provided source code). The home page is probably the only view worth looking at, in that it displays a collection of Posts, as well as each Post's comments. I started this page by generating a details page for a `Post`. I then wrapped the generated details view with a `foreach` loop and then put another loop at the bottom of the details view to show the comments.

Views/Home/Index.aspx:

```
<%@ Page Title="" Language="C#"
    MasterPageFile="~/Views/Shared/Site.Master"
    Inherits="System.Web.Mvc.ViewPage<List<AccessAndStorage.Models.
        Domain.Post>>" %>


<asp:Content ID="Content1" ContentPlaceHolderID="TitleContent"
    runat="server">
    Index
</asp:Content>
<asp:Content ID="Content2" ContentPlaceHolderID="MainContent"
    runat="server">
  <h2>
    Index
  </h2>
  <fieldset>
    <legend>Posts</legend>
    <% foreach (AccessAndStorage.Models.Domain.Post post in Model)
    {%>
        <div class="display-label">
          PostID
        </div>
        <div class="display-field">
          <%: post.PostID %></div>
        ...
        <div class="display-label">
          Comments</div>
        <div class="display-field">
          <blockquote>
            <% foreach (AccessAndStorage.Models.Domain.Comment
                comment in post.Comments)
            { %>
              <p>
                <%= comment.Body %>
                <br />
                <%= String.Format("{0:MM/dd/yyyy}",
                  comment.CreateDate) %>
                -
                <%= Html.ActionLink("Delete", "DeleteComment",
                  new {id = comment.CommentID}) %>
              </p>
            <% } %>
            <p>
                <%= Html.ActionLink("Add new comment", "AddComment",
                  new {id=post.PostID}) %></p>
```

```
      </blockquote>
    </div>
    <hr />
    <% } %>
  </fieldset>
  ...
</asp:Content>
```

Be aware that this implementation of showing data is not performance-oriented. We are loading the comments for a post in a lazy loading fashion, one `Post` object at a time. If you display 50 posts on one page then you are possibly making 51 requests to the database at a time. You are making one query for the list of posts and one query for each set of comments for each post. Some data access tools may handle this eloquently...others may not.

19. You should now be able to run your application and click through adding posts, editing posts, deleting posts, adding comments, and so on. None of this is real, obviously, as our data access is totally mocked out using NBuilder!

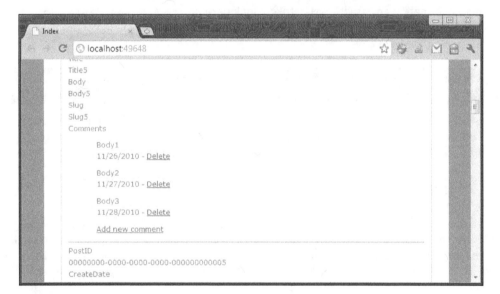

How it works...

There are two all stars in this recipe—StructureMap and NBuilder. StructureMap has allowed us to build our application in a manner that will let us swap out our data access implementation easily. NBuilder has let us create mocks of our future repository implementation. It has also allowed us to generate the presentation side of our application by providing us with placeholder data.

StructureMap is usually the more complex and confusing topic, so let's start there. StructureMap, if you are not already familiar with it, is an Inversion of Control (sometimes referred to as **Dependency Injection**) container that takes care of handing us the appropriate implementation of a given type, based on the requested interface.

By creating interfaces that define generic functionality and then wiring in the actual implementation later, the implementation is isolated from the rest of the application. At the end of this chapter, we will have several implementations and registries that can easily be swapped in and out with each other. Using StructureMap in this manner will make your application considerably easier to test, too.

NBuilder has all sorts of purposes. Any place that you might need to be able to generate some data of a given type, consider using NBuilder. I find myself using it most frequently for creating mock data sources. I also use it for proof of concepts and demos where I don't want to have to worry about creating a data store and data-access code. The NBuilder tool is quite flexible and allows for all sorts of custom scenarios.

There's more...

For more information on StructureMap take a look here: `http://structuremap.github.com/structuremap/`. For more information regarding NBuilder take a look here: `http://nbuilder.org/`.

Adding support for LINQ to SQL

In this recipe, we are going to take the initial base application that we built in the first recipe and add a LINQ to SQL data access layer to the project. As the first project didn't require a database, we will have to also create a database to support this application.

Getting ready

This recipe requires that you copy the existing code base from the previous recipe. We will work from that recipe and spot weld in the new LINQ to SQL data access. You will also need to add a reference to a library called `AutoMapper`. More information, as well as the DLL, can be found at `http://automapper.codeplex.com/`. Basically, `AutoMapper` will allow us to map our domain models to the ones generated by LINQ to SQL.

How to do it...

1. The first thing that we need to do to get LINQ to SQL working is to create our SQL database. Right-click the `App_Data` folder and select **Add | New Item**. Create a database called `Database1.mdf`.

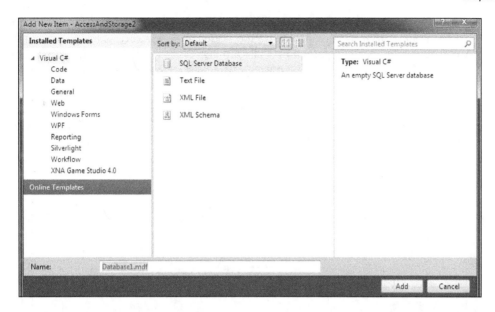

2. Double-click on the `Database1.mdf` file. This will open the database in the **Server Explorer** | **Data Connections** section. You can then expand the database, where you will see a list of database objects.

3. We need to create some tables to hold our data. Create a table called `comments` and one called `posts`. Match the schema as I've indicated in the following screenshot. I've also added a foreign key constraint between the two tables.

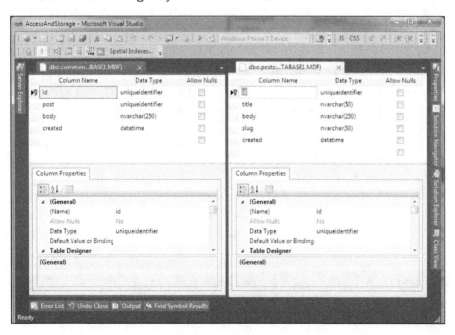

4. With the database created, we can now get LINQ to SQL up and running. Do this by adding an `L2SRepository` folder to the `Models/Repository`. Inside of our new `L2SRepository` folder, add a new LINQ to SQL Classes file. Name this `Blog.dbml`, which will expose an object called `BlogDataContext`; we'll be using this further down the line.

5. Once you have your `Blog.dbml` file added to Visual Studio, you should see a new designer window opened up. Drag the two table items from the **Data Connections** pane onto the design surface. This will generate two LINQ to SQL objects for you to work within your data access.

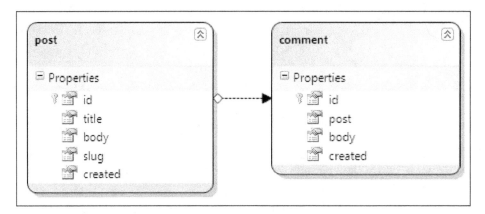

6. Build the application to generate your LINQ to SQL classes.

7. Next we will create some new LINQ to SQL repository classes that will implement the interfaces that we created earlier. We will start by creating the `L2SPostRepository`. Add a new class called `L2SPostRepository` to the `L2SRepository` folder. Then make that repository implement the `IPostRepository` interface. Once that is done, you can right-click on the interface and choose `Implement` Interface. This should generate a bunch of empty methods that are defined by the `IPostRepository`.

Models/Repository/L2SRepository/L2SPostRepository.cs:

```
public class L2SPostRepository : IPostRepository {
  public void AddPost(Domain.Post post) {
    throw new NotImplementedException();
  }

  public void UpdatePost(Domain.Post post) {
    throw new NotImplementedException();
  }

  public void DeletePost(Domain.Post post) {
    throw new NotImplementedException();
```

```
  }

  public Domain.Post GetPost(Guid postId) {
    throw new NotImplementedException();
  }

  public List<Domain.Post> GetPosts() {
    throw new NotImplementedException();
  }
}
```

8. Next we can create the other repository, `L2SCommentRepository`, in the same fashion. Add a new `L2SCommentRepository` to the `Models/Repository/ L2SRepository` folder. Have the class implement the `ICommentRepository` interface. Then right-click on the interface and choose to implement the interface.

9. With our two repositories created, all that is left to conform to our interfaces scheme is to create an `L2SRepositoryConfiguration` class. This goes in the same directory as our repository classes. Set this class to implement from the `IRepositoryConfiguration` interface. Then make that class implement that interface.

10. Now that our repositories are implementing their interfaces, we are ready to start putting LINQ to SQL to work for us. As we are actually going to be interacting with a database, this time we will need to create some type of connection object so that we can control how we communicate with our database. But before we create the connection object, we need to first devise a way to manage our connection string. We will do this by first adding a new connection string to our `Web.config` in the **connections** section.

   Web.config:

```
<connectionStrings>
  ...
  <add name=" Database1ConnectionString"
    connectionString="Data Source=.\SQLEXPRESS;
    AttachDbFilename=|DataDirectory|\Database1.mdf;
    Integrated Security=True; User Instance=True"
    providerName="System.Data.SqlClient" />
</connectionStrings>
```

11. Then you need to add a reference to `System.Configuration` by right-clicking on your project and choosing to add a reference. Then locate the `System. Configuration` namespace and add it to your project.

12. Now we need to create a class that will wrap the `ConfigurationManager` class provided to us by .NET. This class will be called `ConfigurationService` and will live in the root of our `Models` folder. This class will currently have two methods—one to get keys from our config, and another to give us methods to hide the magic string key away from our application.

Models/ConfigurationService.cs:

```
public class ConfigurationService {
  public string GetBlogDBConnectionString() {
    return GetConfigValue("Database1ConnectionString");
  }

  private string GetConfigValue(string key) {
    return ConfigurationManager.ConnectionStrings[key].ToString();
  }
}
```

13. With our new `ConfigurationService` created, we need to create a new registry file for our new repository implementations. Add a new class file called `L2SRepositoryRegistry.cs`.

Models/StructureMap/L2SRepositoryRegistry.cs:

```
public class L2SRepositoryRegistry : Registry {
  public L2SRepositoryRegistry() {
    For<ICommentRepository>().Use<L2SCommentRepository>();
    For<IPostRepository>().Use<L2SPostRepository>();
    For<IRepositoryConfiguration>()
        .Use<L2SRepositoryConfiguration>();
  }

  public static void Register() {
    ObjectFactory.Initialize(x => x.AddRegistry(
      new L2SRepositoryRegistry()));
  }
}
```

14. Before we move on the `DataContext` mappings, we should point our application to our new LINQ to SQL data layer. We do this by making the following change to the `Global.asax.cs` file:

Global.asax:

```
protected void Application_Start() {
    AreaRegistration.RegisterAllAreas();

    RegisterRoutes(RouteTable.Routes);

    L2SRepositoryRegistry.Register();

    ObjectFactory.GetInstance<IRepositoryConfiguration>().
        Configure();
}
```

15. With everything wired into place, we are now ready to create a new class in the `Models/Repository/L2SRepository` folder called `Connection.cs`. Our connection object is essentially a wrapper to our `BlogDataContext`, which was generated by our LINQ to SQL classes object. We don't want our data-access choice to leak out into our application, yet we need to be able to control when a connection is opened, closed, or when to submit the changes made in our data context.

 I have used this class on a few projects and so it has a few methods in it that we won't be using in this recipe. I figured that you might like to see some of the other capabilities that can be handled by this class though, such as rolling back changes.

Models/Repository/L2SRepository/Connection.cs:

```
public class Connection : IDisposable {
  private BlogDataContext _dc;
  private string _connectionString;

  public Connection(ConfigurationService configurationService) {
    _connectionString =
      configurationService.GetBlogDBConnectionString();
  }

  public BlogDataContext Context {
    get { return _dc; }
    set { _dc = value; }
  }

  public void Open() {
```

```
      _dc = new BlogDataContext(_connectionString);
   }


   public void Close() {
     if (_dc != null) {
       _dc.SubmitChanges();
       _dc.Dispose();
       _dc = null;
     }
   }

   public void SubmitChanges() {
     _dc.SubmitChanges();
   }

   public void RollbackChanges() {
     _dc.Transaction.Rollback();
   }

   public void Dispose() {
     Close();
   }
 }
```

16. Now that our `Connection` object is ready for consumption in our application, we can turn our attention to the mappings between our data layer and the `L2S` classes. We will use our `L2SRepositoryConfiguration` class to describe the mapping between our **POCO** (**Plain Old CLR Object**) domain models and the L2S-generated models. This configuration simply tells `AutoMapper` to expect mappings from object A to object B and vice versa.

Models/Repository/L2SRepository/L2SRepositoryConfiguration.cs:

```
public class L2SRepositoryConfiguration : IRepositoryConfiguration
{
   public void Configure() {
     ConfigureAutoMapper();
   }

   public void ConfigureAutoMapper() {
     Mapper.CreateMap<Models.Domain.Post,
       Models.Repository.L2SRepository.post>()
     .ForMember(dest => dest.id, opt => opt.MapFrom(
       src => src.PostID))
     .ForMember(dest => dest.created, opt => opt.MapFrom(
         src => src.CreateDate));
```

```
Mapper.CreateMap<Models.Repository.L2SRepository.post,
  Models.Domain.Post>().ForMember(dest => dest.PostID,
    opt => opt.MapFrom(src => src.id))
  .ForMember(dest => dest.CreateDate,
    opt => opt.MapFrom(src => src.created));

Mapper.CreateMap<Models.Domain.Comment,
  Models.Repository.L2SRepository.comment>()
  .ForMember(dest => dest.id, opt => opt.MapFrom(
    src => src.CommentID))
  .ForMember(dest => dest.post, opt => opt.MapFrom(
    src => src.PostID))
  .ForMember(dest => dest.created, opt => opt.MapFrom(
    src => src.CreateDate));

Mapper.CreateMap<Models.Repository.L2SRepository.comment,
  Models.Domain.Comment>().ForMember(dest => dest.CommentID,
    opt => opt.MapFrom(src => src.id))
  .ForMember(dest => dest.PostID, opt => opt.MapFrom(
    src => src.post))
  .ForMember(dest => dest.CreateDate, opt => opt.MapFrom(
    src => src.created));
  }
}
```

17. With `AutoMapper` referenced and configured, we can create the `RepositoryBase` class in the `Models/Repository/L2SRepository` folder. I found a variation of this base class some while back and have been tweaking it over time. It is a generic class that works by being told what POCO object you are working with and which entity class (LINQ to SQL class) that POCO maps to. This then allows the base class to focus its attention on those two types when it is performing its various duties. When it is done running a query on an entity type, it can map the result to a POCO type and can return business objects, rather than LINQ to SQL objects. This base class allows you to remove a great deal of CRUD and mapping code from your application.

Models/Repository/L2SRepository/RepositoryBase.cs:

```
public abstract class RepositoryBase<T, P>
  where T : class, new() //entity
  where P : class, new() //poco
{
  private Connection _connection;
  public RepositoryBase(Connection connection) {
    _connection = connection;
  }

  public void DeleteByQuery(Expression<Func<T, bool>> query) {
    T entity = GetEntity(query);
```

```
        if (entity != null)
          _connection.Context.GetTable<T>().DeleteOnSubmit(entity);
    }


    public void Add(P poco) {
      T entity = Mapper.Map(poco, new T());

      _connection.Context.GetTable<T>().InsertOnSubmit(entity);
    }


    public void Update(P poco, bool commitNow = false) {
      T entity = Mapper.Map(poco, new T());

      _connection.Context.GetTable<T>().Attach(entity, true);
    }


    public void Update(P poco, Expression<Func<T, bool>> query) {
      T entity = Mapper.Map(poco, new T());

      object propertyValue = null;
      T entityFromDB = _connection.Context.GetTable<T>().
        Where(query).SingleOrDefault();
      if (null == entityFromDB)
        throw new NullReferenceException("Query Supplied to " +
          "Get entity from DB is invalid, NULL value returned");
      PropertyInfo[] properties =
        entityFromDB.GetType().GetProperties();
      foreach (PropertyInfo property in properties) {
        propertyValue = null;
        if (null != property.GetSetMethod()) {
          PropertyInfo entityProperty =
            entity.GetType().GetProperty(property.Name);
        if (entityProperty.PropertyType.BaseType ==
            Type.GetType("System.ValueType") ||
            entityProperty.PropertyType ==
              Type.GetType("System.String"))

        propertyValue =
          entity.GetType().GetProperty(property.Name).
          GetValue(entity, null);
        if (null != propertyValue)
          property.SetValue(entityFromDB, propertyValue, null);
        }
      }
    }
```

```
public P Get(Expression<Func<T, bool>> query) {
  T t = GetEntity(query);
  if (t == null)
    return null;
    return Mapper.Map(t, new P());
}

private T GetEntity(Expression<Func<T, bool>> query) {
 T t = _connection.Context.GetTable<T>().
    Where(query).FirstOrDefault();
 if (t == null)
    return null;
    return t;
}

public virtual IEnumerable<P> GetAll(Expression<Func<T,
   bool>> query) {
  IEnumerable<T> list = null;

 if (null == query)
    list = _connection.Context.GetTable<T>();
 else
    list = _connection.Context.GetTable<T>().Where(query);

 if (list.Count() == 0)
    return new List<P>();

 return Mapper.Map(list, new List<P>());
 }
}
```

18. Let's open up our `L2SPostRepository` and provide the actual implementation. First, we need to inherit from our `RepositoryBase` class.

Models/Repository/L2SRepository/L2SPostRepository.cs:

```
public class L2SPostRepository :
  RepositoryBase<Models.Repository.L2SRepository.post,
  Models.Domain.Post>, IPostRepository {
```

19. Now that we have our `RepositoryBase` in place, we can work with its functionality. Let's take a look at the implementation in our repository. I think most of the methods are self-explanatory; we are opening a connection, passing information about the domain model, and then closing down the connection again. The `DeletePost` method is a touch more involved, as we first remove the corresponding comments before deleting the post.

Models/Repository/L2SRepository/L2SPostRepository.cs:

```csharp
private Connection _connection;
public L2SPostRepository(Connection connection) : base(connection)
{
    _connection = connection;
}

public void AddPost(Domain.Post post) {
    _connection.Open();
    base.Add(post);
    _connection.Close();
}

public void UpdatePost(Domain.Post post) {
    _connection.Open();
    base.Update(post, p => p.id == post.PostID);
    _connection.Close();
}

public void DeletePost(Domain.Post post) {
    _connection.Open();

    ObjectFactory.GetInstance<ICommentRepository>()
      .DeleteComments(post.PostID);

    _connection.SubmitChanges();

    base.DeleteByQuery(p => p.id == post.PostID);
    _connection.Close();

}

public Domain.Post GetPost(Guid postId) {
    Domain.Post result;

    _connection.Open();
    result = base.Get(p => p.id == postId);
    _connection.Close();

    return result;
}

public List<Domain.Post> GetPosts() {
    List<Domain.Post> results;

    _connection.Open();
    results = base.GetAll(p => p.id != Guid.Empty).ToList();
    _connection.Close();

    return results;
}
```

20. With the new implementation of `IPostRepository` out of the way, we can turn our attention to the implementation of `ICommentRepository`. This will pretty much be exactly like our `L2SPostRepository`.

Models/Repository/L2SRepository/L2SCommentRepository.cs:

```
public class L2SCommentRepository :
  RepositoryBase<Models.Repository.L2SRepository.comment,
    Models.Domain.Comment>, ICommentRepository {
      private Connection _connection;
      public L2SCommentRepository(Connection connection)
        : base(connection) {
          _connection = connection;
      }

  public void AddComment(Domain.Comment comment) {
    _connection.Open();
    base.Add(comment);
    _connection.Close();
  }

  public void DeleteComment(Domain.Comment comment) {
    _connection.Open();
    base.DeleteByQuery(c => c.id == comment.CommentID);
    _connection.Close();
  }

  public void DeleteComments(Guid postId) {
    _connection.Open();
    base.DeleteByQuery(c => c.post == postId);
    _connection.Close();
  }

  public Domain.Comment GetComment(Guid commentId) {
    Domain.Comment result;

    _connection.Open();
    result = base.Get(c => c.id == commentId);
    _connection.Close();

    return result;
  }

  public List<Domain.Comment> GetCommentsByPostID(Guid postId) {
    List<Domain.Comment> results;

    _connection.Open();
    results = base.GetAll(c => c.id == postId).ToList();
    _connection.Close();

    return results;
  }
}
```

21. You should now be able to build your application and add posts and comments, as well as edit posts and delete both posts and comments.

> **Fields**
>
> PostID
> 660ce823-6c11-4610-9c41-ba9a05ade1b2
> CreateDate
> 26/11/2010 13:00
> Title
> Test
> Body
> Test Body
> Slug
> test-slug
>
> [Delete] | Back to List

How it works...

Notice that we were able to pretty easily snap in a new form of data access using only StructureMap, pre-determined interfaces, and AutoMapper. By providing ourselves with a configuration hook, we were able to wire up AutoMapper to handle mapping LINQ to SQL types to our POCO classes. This allowed us to continue working with our domain objects, rather than inflicting its LINQ to SQL entities on our application. And because our application was built on the assumption that our repository classes provided a specific set of methods, we were able to add LINQ to SQL-specific implementation in our repository classes, as well as some other classes with very little change to our actual application. Most importantly, we can easily swap back to the mocked-out version of our application by changing one line in our `Global.asax.cs` file.

Global.asax.cs:

```
protected void Application_Start() {
    AreaRegistration.RegisterAllAreas();

    RegisterRoutes(RouteTable.Routes);

    L2SRepositoryRegistry.Register();

    ObjectFactory.GetInstance<IRepositoryConfiguration>().
        Configure();
}
```

Going old school with ADO.NET

In this recipe, we are going to take a look at what it takes to use some basic ADO.NET skills to make an old school data-access layer. We will continue with our repository and IoC concepts and shoehorn some inline SQL into our application.

Getting ready

As with all the other recipes in this chapter, start by copying the previous recipes code base. This will give you the core application that we created in the first recipe. From there we will build a new repository that uses ADO.NET to access the underlying data.

How to do it...

1. The first thing that we need to do is to create a new folder for our new repository. Expand `Models/Repository` and add a new folder called `ADORepository`.

2. Then create four new classes in that folder: `ADOCommentRepository.cs`, `ADOPostRepository.cs`, `ADORepositoryConfiguration.cs`, and `Connection.cs`. These four files will be our ADO data access layer.

3. With these new empty classes in place, we can now start to work with our existing interfaces. Set `ADOCommentRepository` to inherit `ICommentRepository`, `ADOPostRepository` to inherit from `IPostRepository`, and `ADORepositoryConfiguration` to inherit from `IRepositoryConfiguration`.

4. With all three classes inheriting the appropriate interfaces, we can now start to build out our data access. To get started, right-click on each interface and choose to implement the interface. Do this for each interface of our ADO Repository classes. This will generate empty methods for us to fill in later.

5. We now have enough information to wire our new classes into StructureMap. We will do this by creating a new class named `ADORepositoryRegistry.cs`. This class will handle adding the appropriate configuration to StructureMap that we can then attach to our application initialization.

   Models/StructureMap/ADORepositoryRegistry.cs:

   ```
   public class ADORepositoryRegistry : Registry {
     public ADORepositoryRegistry() {
       For<ICommentRepository>().Use<ADOCommentRepository>();
       For<IPostRepository>().Use<ADOPostRepository>();
       For<IRepositoryConfiguration>()
         .Use<ADORepositoryConfiguration>();
     }
   ```

```
    public static void Register() {
      ObjectFactory.Initialize(x => x.AddRegistry(
        new ADORepositoryRegistry()));
    }
  }
```

6. Now we are ready to add our new registry class into the `Global.asax` file. We will add this configuration underneath the last recipe's configuration, so that we can simply uncomment the repository that we are interested in using.

Global.asax.cs:

```
protected void Application_Start() {
  AreaRegistration.RegisterAllAreas();

  RegisterRoutes(RouteTable.Routes);

  //MockRepositoryRegistry.Register();

  //L2SRepositoryRegistry.Register();

  ADORepositoryRegistry.Register();

  ObjectFactory.GetInstance<IRepositoryConfiguration>().
    Configure();
}
```

7. With everything wired into place, we can turn our attention to building up the connection object. Open the `Connection.cs` file and add the following implementation. We'll be using the database that we created in the previous recipe for the sake of convenience.

Models/Repository/ADORepository/Connection.cs:

```
public class Connection : IDisposable {
  private SqlConnection _context;
  private ConfigurationService _configurationService;

  public Connection(ConfigurationService configurationService) {
    _configurationService = configurationService;
  }

  public SqlConnection Context {
    get { return _context; }
  }

  public void Open() {
    _context = new SqlConnection();
```

```
    _context.ConnectionString =
       _configurationService.GetBlogDBConnectionString();
    _context.Open();
  }

  public void Close() {
    if (_context != null) {
      _context.Close();
      _context = null;
    }
  }

  public void Dispose() {
    if (_context != null) {
      _context.Close();
      _context = null;
    }
  }
}
```

8. Once our connection is operational, we can turn our attention to implementing the `ADOPostRepository` class. This class is responsible for all the CRUD (create, read, update, delete) operations on our database using standard ADO.NET code. First, we'll create an instance of our `Connection` class.

Models/Repository/ADORepository/ADOPostRepository.cs:

```
private Connection _connection;
public ADOPostRepository(Connection connection) {
   _connection = connection;
}
```

9. Now we'll look at a couple of the individual methods, starting with the `AddPost` method, which constructs an `insert` statement and executes it against the database.

Models/Repository/ADORepository/ADOPostRepository.cs:

```
public void AddPost(Post post) {
  try {
    _connection.Open();

    string sql = "insert into posts (id, created, title, body,
      slug) " + "values (@PostID, @CreateDate, @Title, @Body,
      @Slug)";

    SqlCommand cmd = _connection.Context.CreateCommand();
    cmd.CommandText = sql;
```

```
      cmd.Parameters.Add("@PostId",
         SqlDbType.UniqueIdentifier).Value = post.PostID;
         cmd.Parameters.Add("@CreateDate", SqlDbType.DateTime).Value
            = DateTime.Now;
         cmd.Parameters.Add("@Title", SqlDbType.VarChar, 150).Value
            = post.Title;
      cmd.Parameters.Add("@Body", SqlDbType.VarChar, 2000).Value =
         post.Body;
      cmd.Parameters.Add("@Slug", SqlDbType.VarChar, 200).Value =
         post.Slug;

      cmd.ExecuteNonQuery();
   }
   finally {
      _connection.Close();
   }
}
```

10. Next, we will look at the `UpdatePost` method, which is responsible for creating an `update` statement and executing it against the database.

Models/Repository/ADORepository/ADOPostRepository.cs:

```
public void UpdatePost(Post post) {
   try {
      _connection.Open();

      string sql = "update posts set created = @CreateDate, " +
         "title =  @Title, body = @Body,
         slug = @Slug where id = @PostID";

      SqlCommand cmd = _connection.Context.CreateCommand();
      cmd.CommandText = sql;

      cmd.Parameters.Add("@PostID",
         SqlDbType.UniqueIdentifier).Value = post.PostID;
      cmd.Parameters.Add("@CreateDate", SqlDbType.DateTime).Value =
         post.CreateDate;
      cmd.Parameters.Add("@Title", SqlDbType.VarChar, 150).Value =
         post.Title;
      cmd.Parameters.Add("@Body", SqlDbType.VarChar, 2000).Value =
         post.Body;
      cmd.Parameters.Add("@Slug", SqlDbType.VarChar, 200).Value =
         post.Slug;

     cmd.ExecuteNonQuery();
   }
```

```
finally {
    _connection.Close();
  }
}
```

11. Then we can create our `DeletePost` method. As you may have guessed, this method constructs a `delete` statement and runs it against the database.

    Models/Repository/ADORepository/ADOPostRepository.cs:

```
public void DeletePost(Post post) {
  try {
    //delete all comments first
    ObjectFactory.GetInstance<ICommentRepository>().
        DeleteComments(post.PostID);

    _connection.Open();

    string sql = "delete from posts where id = @PostID";

    SqlCommand cmd = _connection.Context.CreateCommand();
    cmd.CommandText = sql;

    cmd.Parameters.Add("@PostID",
      SqlDbType.UniqueIdentifier).Value = post.PostID;

    cmd.ExecuteNonQuery();
    }
  finally {
    _connection.Close();
  }
}
```

12. You probably get the idea from this point. There are two other methods to fill out—`GetPost` and `GetPosts`. In addition to that, there is also an `AssemblePostFromReader` method that takes in a reader and constructs the appropriate `Post` object. This allows us to use this in both the `GetPost` and `GetPosts` methods.

    Models/Repository/ADORepository/ADOPostRepository.cs:

```
public Post GetPost(Guid postId) {
  try {
    _connection.Open();

    var sql = "select * from posts where id = @PostID";

    var cmd = _connection.Context.CreateCommand();
```

```
        cmd.CommandText = sql;

        cmd.Parameters.AddWithValue("@PostID", postId);

        var reader = cmd.ExecuteReader();
        if (reader.Read())
          return AssemblePostFromReader(reader);

        return null;
      }
      finally {
        _connection.Close();
      }
    }

    public List<Post> GetPosts() {
      try {
        _connection.Open();

        var sql = "select * from posts";

        var cmd = _connection.Context.CreateCommand();
        cmd.CommandText = sql;

        var reader = cmd.ExecuteReader();
        var results = new List<Post>();
        while (reader.Read())
          results.Add(AssemblePostFromReader(reader));

        return results;
      }
      finally {
        _connection.Close();
      }
    }

    private Post AssemblePostFromReader(SqlDataReader reader) {
      int PostIDPosition = reader.GetOrdinal("id");
      int CreateDatePosition = reader.GetOrdinal("created");
      int TitlePosition = reader.GetOrdinal("title");
      int BodyPosition = reader.GetOrdinal("body");
      int SlugPosition = reader.GetOrdinal("slug");

      Post post = new Post() {
        PostID = (Guid)reader.GetSqlGuid(PostIDPosition),
        Body = reader.GetString(BodyPosition),
        CreateDate = reader.GetDateTime(CreateDatePosition),
```

```
        Slug = reader.GetString(SlugPosition),
        Title = reader.GetString(TitlePosition)
    };

    return post;
}
```

13. All that is left from this point is to implement the `ADOCommentRepository` class. This class looks almost identical to the `ADOPostRepository`, with the exception that it works with the `Comment` object and `Comments` table. Look at the source for details.

14. You should now be able to run the application and see the blog application using the new ADO data access layer.

How it works...

This particular recipe has absolutely nothing fancy going on in it. This is raw unadulterated ADO code. This new ADO repository plugs into the rest of the system using StructureMap in the same fashion as the previous two recipes.

XML documents as a data store

In this recipe, we are going to look at a non-SQL-oriented solution. There are times when you might not need a full blown SQL server backend or you might just not have access to one. In those times, storing the data on the filesystem might be more appropriate. For that reason we will take a look at how to remove SQL server from the picture and plug in an XML data store in its place. We will see that even with this drastically different infrastructure on the backend, we can still work within the boundaries of our existing solution and easily plug in this new data store.

Getting ready

The only thing we need to do to get started with this recipe is prepare our new data storage. We want to swap out our existing SQL server database and make an XML data store. To do this, all we need to do is create an XML folder inside of the App_Data folder. This will be the location we will write our XML documents to.

With that out of the way, we next need to discuss how these XML documents will look. In this recipe, we will write one XML file per `Post`. This `Post` document will contain a collection of `Comments` inside of it. The reason for this is that a `Post` is important on its own. A `Comment` by itself means nothing without its parent `Post`. When talking about document stores, especially where the item being stored is as simple as our `Comment`, we can store our value types (`Comment`) with our entities (`Post`) directly.

Working with .NET like we are, creating XML directly from our objects is as easy as serializing them directly to the filesystem. When we need to read the XML back into our program, we simply reverse the process and de-serialize our file back into an object. In order to locate the appropriate post, we will use the Post's Id, which is a `Guid` as the filename.

Keep in mind that the system that we are creating in this recipe is not an absolute best practice. It is prone to several issues, such as file locking and write-access restrictions. Also, finding a `Post` is easy enough, as we named the file with the Post's identifier. But locating other data, such as a specific `Comment`, becomes problematic (we will look at this shortly). Having said that, this solution may be just the one you need! Just make sure you weigh the pros and cons prior to choosing the filesystem for your data storage mechanism.

How to do it...

1. Create a copy of the previous recipe's solution.

2. Open the solution. Then expand the `App_Data` folder. Create a new folder inside there called `XML`.

3. Next, we need to add a new method to the `ConfigurationService` class called `GetXmlConnectionString`. This method will determine the file path to the root of our application. It will then append `App_Data\Xml` to that path, so that we can get to our XML store.

   Models/ConfigurationService.cs:

   ```
   . . .
   public string GetXmlConnectionString() {
      string path = HttpContext.Current
         .Request.PhysicalApplicationPath + "App_Data\\Xml\\";
      return path;
   }
   . . .
   ```

4. In an XML-based data store, we don't really need a `Connection` object. Instead we need something to manage access to the filesystem. When dealing with files, we don't want more than one thread accessing a file at a time (as that will throw an exception). In that case, we need to create a class that controls the number of allowed instances that are created across our entire application. We will use the *singleton* pattern to do this. Create a new class called `XmlStore` in a new `Models/Repository/XmlRepository` directory. Create a private constructor to ensure that no instances can be created directly. Also, create a static property to control the instance that is initially created and create a lock to allow us to check and create our instance.

   Models/Repository/XmlRepository/XmlStore.cs:

   ```
   public sealed class XmlStore {
      static XmlStore instance = new XmlStore();
   ```

```
    static readonly object padlock = new object();

    XmlStore() { }

    public static XmlStore Instance {
      get {
       lock (padlock) {
       return instance;
       }
      }
    }
}
```

5. With our class controlling the number of instances that are created, we can now move to creating some helper methods to control accessing the filesystem. The first method that we will create is a `Delete` method, which will take the ID of the `Post` to be deleted.

Models/Repository/XmlRepository/XmlStore.cs:

```
...
public void Delete(Guid postId) {
    string file = new
      ConfigurationService().GetXmlConnectionString()
    + postId + ".xml";

    if (File.Exists(file)) {
        File.Delete(file);
    }
}
...
```

6. The next thing that we need is the ability to write a file to the filesystem. This will be handled with a `Write` method. This method will create a serializer to handle our `Post` object. Then we will attempt to serialize the object to the filesystem using a TextWriter.

Models/Repository/XmlRepository/XmlStore.cs:

```
public void Write(Post post) {
    string file = new
      ConfigurationService().GetXmlConnectionString()
      + post.PostID + ".xml";

    // Force Domain Model to check for comments first.
    var comments = post.Comments;

    var s = new XmlSerializer(typeof(Post));
```

```
        var fs = new FileStream(file, FileMode.Create);
        TextWriter w = new StreamWriter(fs, new UTF8Encoding());

        try {
            s.Serialize(w, post);
        }
        catch (Exception e) {
            Console.WriteLine(e.Message);
        }
        finally {
            w.Close();
        }}
```

7. The `Read` method is basically `Write` in reverse. We create a `FileStream` to consume the XML file and an `XmlSerializer` to deserialize the resulting stream into our `Post` object.

Models/Repository/XmlRepository/XmlStore.cs:

```
public Post Read(Guid id) {
    var file = new ConfigurationService().GetXmlConnectionString()
        + id.ToString() + ".xml";

    // Assume Comments precache
    if (!File.Exists(file))
        return new Post { PostID = id, Comments = new List<Comment>()
};

    var stream = new FileStream(file, FileMode.Open);
    Post result;
    try {
        result = (Post)new
            XmlSerializer(typeof(Post)).Deserialize(stream);
    }
    catch (Exception e) {
        result = new Post();
        Console.WriteLine(e.Message);
    }
    finally {
        stream.Close();
        stream.Dispose();
        stream = null;
    }

    return result;
}
```

8. Now that we are able to create a file, delete a file, and read a file, you might think we have all that we need. However, we need to also be able to read all of the files in the store. This `ReadAll` method will simply iterate through all the files in the directory and reconstitute each of them as `Post` objects.

Models/Repository/XmlRepository/XmlStore.cs:

```
public List<Post> ReadAll() {
  List<Post> result = new List<Post>();
  string path = new
      ConfigurationService().GetXmlConnectionString();
  DirectoryInfo di = new DirectoryInfo(path);
  FileInfo[] rgFiles = di.GetFiles("*.xml");
  foreach (FileInfo fi in rgFiles) {
    result.Add(Read(Guid.Parse(fi.Name.Split('.')[0])));
  }

  return result;
}
```

9. The final method that we need to create is one to allow us to look beyond posts. We also need the ability to locate a comment within a post. This is where our current data store scheme starts to let us down a bit. If this were a real-world application, we might create a `Lucene` index, which would allow us to search for a `CommentID` and map it to our `PostID`, thereby allowing us to load the specific file that contains the comment we are interested in. But as this is a simple demo, we will instead need to iterate through each `Post` and search the collection of comments within the `Post`. If we find the comment, we then return it.

Models/Repository/XmlRepository/XmlStore.cs:

```
public Comment SearchForComment(Guid commentId) {
   Comment result = null;
   string path = new
     ConfigurationService().GetXmlConnectionString();
   DirectoryInfo di = new DirectoryInfo(path);
   FileInfo[] rgFiles = di.GetFiles("*.xml");
   foreach (FileInfo fi in rgFiles) {
      Post post = Read(Guid.Parse(fi.Name.Split('.')[0]));
      result = post.Comments
         .Where(c => c.CommentID == commentId).FirstOrDefault();

      if (result != null)
         return result;
   }

   return result;
}
```

10. Now we are finally ready to stand up our `Post` and `Comment` repositories. Start by creating the `XmlPostRepository` and `XmlCommentRepository` classes. Next, configure those classes to implement the `IPostRepository` and `ICommentRepository` interfaces.

11. Now create an `XmlRepositoryConfiguration` file and set it to implement the `IRepositoryConfiguration` interface. Then generate the appropriate methods by making the `XmlRepositoryConfiguration` class implement the interface.

12. With the base framework in place for our new `XmlRepository`, we now need to configure StructureMap, so that it is aware of our new repository. Do this by creating a new class called `XmlRepositoryRegistry` class in the `Models/StructureMap` directory. In this class, we will configure all the mappings that are needed for our host application.

Models/StructureMap/XmlRepositoryRegistry.cs:

```
public class XmlRepositoryRegistry : Registry {
  public XmlRepositoryRegistry() {
     For<ICommentRepository>().Use<XmlCommentRepository>();
     For<IPostRepository>().Use<XmlPostRepository>();
     For<IRepositoryConfiguration>()
       .Use<XmlRepositoryConfiguration>();
  }


  public static void Register() {
     ObjectFactory.Initialize(x => x.AddRegistry(
       new XmlRepositoryRegistry()));
    }
}
```

13. With our registry created, we can then map the StructureMap registry into the start of our application.

Global.asax.cs:

```
protected void Application_Start() {
  AreaRegistration.RegisterAllAreas();

  RegisterRoutes(RouteTable.Routes);

  XmlRepositoryRegistry.Register();

  //run any data access configuration that might be needed
  ObjectFactory.GetInstance<IRepositoryConfiguration>()
    .Configure();
}
```

14. With all of our framework and plumbing set up, we are now ready to add the appropriate implementation to our repository classes. With the majority of the work performed by our `XmlStore`, the actual code in our repository classes is on the light side.

Models/Repository/XmlRepository/XmlPostRepository.cs:

```
public class XmlPostRepository : IPostRepository {
  private XmlStore _xmlStore;
  public XmlPostRepository() {
     _xmlStore = XmlStore.Instance;
  }

  public void AddPost(Post post) {
    post.PostID = Guid.NewGuid();
    post.CreateDate = DateTime.Now;
    _xmlStore.Write(post);
  }

  public void UpdatePost(Post post) {
    _xmlStore.Write(post);
  }

  public void DeletePost(Post post) {
     _xmlStore.Delete(post.PostID);
  }

  public Post GetPost(Guid postId) {
     return _xmlStore.Read(postId); ;
  }

  public List<Post> GetPosts() {
     return _xmlStore.ReadAll();
  }
}
```

15. Now we can build the `XmlCommentRepository`. Oddly enough, there is more actual work to do in the comment repository, as we need to find the right post file to perform the appropriate actions on a comment.

Models/Repository/XmlRepository/XmlCommentRepository.cs:

```
public class XmlCommentRepository : ICommentRepository {
  private IPostRepository _postRepository;
  private XmlStore _xmlStore;
  public XmlCommentRepository(IPostRepository postRepository) {
     _postRepository = postRepository;
```

```
      _xmlStore = XmlStore.Instance;
    }

    public void AddComment(Comment comment) {
      Post post = _postRepository.GetPost(comment.PostID);
      List<Comment> comments = post.Comments;
      comments.Add(comment);
      post.Comments = comments;
      _postRepository.UpdatePost(post);
    }

    public void DeleteComment(Comment comment) {
      Post post = _postRepository.GetPost(comment.PostID);
      List<Comment> comments = post.Comments;
      comments = comments.Where(c => c.CommentID !=
        comment.CommentID).ToList();
      post.Comments = comments;
      _postRepository.UpdatePost(post);
    }

    public Comment GetComment(Guid commentId) {
        return _xmlStore.SearchForComment(commentId);
    }

    public List<Comment> GetCommentsByPostID(Guid postId) {
      Post post = _postRepository.GetPost(postId);
      if (post != null)
        return post.Comments;
      return new List<Comment>();
    }

     public void DeleteComments(Guid postId) {
        Post post = _postRepository.GetPost(postId);
        post.Comments = new List<Comment>();
        _postRepository.UpdatePost(post);
     }
  }
```

16. Because we are not working with a database here, I also found that the `DeleteComment` view doesn't quite provide us with enough information to allow us to quickly locate the appropriate post in our XML data store. For that reason, I had to add one more hidden field in the `DeleteComment` view exposing the `PostId` in the form post.

Views/Home/DeleteComment.aspx:

```
...
<% using (Html.BeginForm()) { %>
<p>
    <%= Html.HiddenFor(m=>m.PostID) %>
    <input type="submit" value="Delete" />
    |
    <%: Html.ActionLink("Back to List", "Index") %>
</p>
<% } %>
...
```

17. A small change is also required to the home controller.

Controllers/HomeController.cs:

```
[HttpPost]
public ActionResult DeleteComment(Guid id, Guid postId) {
    ObjectFactory.GetInstance<ICommentRepository>().
    DeleteComment(new Comment { CommentID = id, PostID = postId });
    return RedirectToAction("Index");
}
```

18. You should now be able to run the application and manage posts and comments as you were able to in any of the other recipes prior to this one.

How it works...

In this recipe, we swapped out our previous use of a SQL server database for data storage on the filesystem using XML files. The key to this process is the ability to serialize our existing POCO classes directly to the filesystem.

10
Application, Session, Cookies, and Caching

In this chapter, we will cover:

- ▸ Keeping track of anonymous visitors versus logged-in users
- ▸ Maintaining a user's information while at your site
- ▸ Remembering a previous visitor
- ▸ Caching your product catalog for faster response times
- ▸ Using output caching to cache an entire page
- ▸ Using partial views to cache pieces of a page individually
- ▸ Exposing an application API to your presentation layer

Introduction

In this chapter, we are going to take a look at managing data at a framework level. Specifically, we are going to look at how to control data at the application, session, caching, and cookie level. We very rarely build a web application that doesn't use at least one or two of these every time.

Keeping track of anonymous visitors versus logged-in users

In this recipe, we are going to take a look at a common task for most sites. We want to be able to keep track of how many users are present on our site at any given time. We will also attempt to distinguish between known (logged-in users) and unknown (anonymous) users. To keep track of users as they come to our site, we will need to attach some of the events, such as `Session_Start` and `Session_End`, which our application exposes. To distinguish between the known and unknown users, we will have to tap into our membership functionalities, such as registration, logging on, and logging off.

How to do it...

1. Start by creating a new default ASP.NET MVC 2 application.

2. Next, we will need to create a class to help us keep track of our users. We will call this class `SiteVisitors` and place it in the `Models` directory. The `SiteVisitors` class will provide us with the ability to keep track of how many visitors of each type are on our site at a given time. As we only ever want one instance of this class to exist at any one time during the lifetime of our application, we will use the *singleton pattern* to control the number of instances that are created. In its most simple form, the *singleton pattern* requires us to have a private constructor (so that no one can instantiate an instance of the class directly) and a static method, which will return an instance of the class to us. In this static method, we will check if we have created an instance or not and behave accordingly.

Models/SiteVisitors.cs:

```
public class SiteVisitors {
  private static SiteVisitors instance = new SiteVisitors();

  private SiteVisitors() { }

  public int UnknownVisitorCount { get; private set; }
  public int KnownVisitorCount { get; private set; }

  public static SiteVisitors Instance {
    get {
        return instance;
        }
    }
}
```

3. Now we need to create an `Enum` that will provide a method for us to identify the two different types of users—**known** and **unknown**. We will do this by creating a new `Enum` in the `Models` folder called `VisitorTypes.cs`.

Models/VisitorTypes.cs:

```
public enum VisitorTypes {
  UnknownVisitor = 0,
  KnownVisitor = 1
}
```

4. Once we have a manner in which to identify between the two types of users, we need to have the ability to assign the type to each visitor. We will do this by setting a value into each user's session called `VisitorType`. Rather than working directly with the session all over our application, we will create a wrapper class to handle this functionality for us. Therefore, we need to create a new class called `SessionWrapper.cs` in the `Models` folder. This class will have two methods—one method each to set the two different types into a user's session depending on who we think they are at the time, and another method to get the user's current type.

```
public static class SessionWrapper {
  private const string c_visitorType = "VisitorType";

  public static void SetUnknownType() {
    HttpContext.Current.Session.Add(c_visitorType,
      VisitorTypes.UnknownVisitor);
  }

  public static void SetKnownType() {
    HttpContext.Current.Session.Add(c_visitorType,
      VisitorTypes.KnownVisitor);
  }

  public static new VisitorTypes GetType() {
    VisitorTypes result = VisitorTypes.UnknownVisitor;
    if (HttpContext.Current.Session[c_visitorType] != null)
      result = (VisitorTypes)HttpContext.Current.Session
        [c_visitorType];

    return result;
  }
}
```

5. With this groundwork set in place, we can now return to our `SiteVisitors` class to provide a bit more functionality. Currently, we are able to get an instance of the `SiteVisitors` class on which we have two properties from which we can read values. We now need to expose some helper methods that allow our application to toggle certain actions as an unknown user becomes known, a user leaves the site, and so on.

```
public class SiteVisitors {
   ...

   //user arrives
   public void UnknownVisitorArrived() {
      SessionWrapper.SetUnknownType();
      UnknownVisitorCount++;
   }

   //known user arrives
   public void KnownVisitorArrives() {
      SessionWrapper.SetKnownType();
      KnownVisitorCount++;
   }

   //user logs in
   public void UnknownVisitorLoggedOn() {
      SessionWrapper.SetKnownType();
      UnknownVisitorCount--;
      KnownVisitorCount++;
   }

   //user logs out
   public void KnownVisitorLoggedOut() {
      SessionWrapper.SetUnknownType();
      UnknownVisitorCount++;
      KnownVisitorCount--;
   }

   //user session expires
   public void VisitorLeft() {
      if (SessionWrapper.GetType() ==
         VisitorTypes.KnownVisitor)
         KnownVisitorLeft();
      else
         UnknownVisitorLeft();
   }
```

```
//anon user session expires
private void UnknownVisitorLeft() {
  UnknownVisitorCount--;
}

//logged in user session expires
private void KnownVisitorLeft() {
  KnownVisitorCount--;
  }
}
```

6. With all of these helper functions in place, we are now able to wire our user tracker into our site. We will start by tapping into our application events in the `Global.asax`. We need to increment our user count when a user comes to the site. We also need to decrement our counts when a user's session expires.

 Keep in mind that when a user leaves the site, we won't be informed immediately. The session timeout is a value generally set by the web server. Usually, this value is set for 20 minutes. This means that you won't know a user left until 20 minutes after they actually left.

```
protected void Session_Start() {
  if(Request.IsAuthenticated)
    SiteVisitors.Instance.KnownVisitorArrives();
  else
    SiteVisitors.Instance.UnknownVisitorArrived();
}

protected void Session_End() {
    SiteVisitors.Instance.VisitorLeft();
}
```

7. The next place for us to tap into is in the registration, logging in, and logging out code. This code is provided by default in the MVC application, so I used that framework for this recipe. Start by opening up the `AccountModels.cs` file (`Models` folder). In there, you will find a few classes and interfaces. Look for the `FormsAuthenticationService`. This is where the `SignIn` and `SignOut` functions can be attached to. For each of those methods, we need to move some of our numbers around, either from known to unknown or unknown to known.

```
public class FormsAuthenticationService :
  IFormsAuthenticationService {
  public void SignIn(string userName, bool createPersistentCookie)
  {
    if (String.IsNullOrEmpty(userName)) throw new
    ArgumentException("Value cannot be null or empty.",
    "userName");
```

```
    FormsAuthentication.SetAuthCookie(userName,
      createPersistentCookie);

    SiteVisitors.Instance.UnknownVisitorLoggedOn();
  }

  public void SignOut() {
    FormsAuthentication.SignOut();
    SiteVisitors.Instance.KnownVisitorLoggedOut();
  }
}
```

8. With our counter framework in place, we are now ready to display some of the information to our users. We can most easily do this by opening up the `Site.Master` page and adding to our display for all pages in one shot.

```
<div id="logindisplay">
  <% Html.RenderPartial("LogOnUserControl"); %><br />
  Known visitor count: <%:
    StateExamples.Models.SiteVisitors.Instance
      .KnownVisitorCount %> - Unknown visitor count:
    <%:
    StateExamples.Models.SiteVisitors.Instance.UnknownVisitorCount
      %>
</div>
```

9. Now you can run the application. The first window that opens up should show that an unknown user is on the site. If you copy the URL and open up a different browser program and paste your URL, you should see that you have two unknown users on the site. Then, in one of the browsers, you can register for a new account. Once you complete the registration process, you should see one unknown user and one known user.

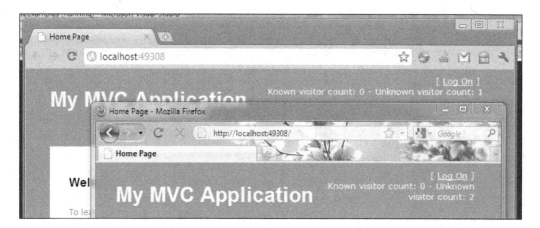

How it works...

This recipe takes advantage of our application events, session, and the fact that the static instance we get from our singleton class stays accessible during the entire lifetime of the application. With these components, we are able to increment and decrement users from our counts, keep track of the state of users as they move around on our site, and display some stats to our users.

Maintaining a user's information while at your site

This recipe is all about keeping track of a user's information while on your site. Generally, once you have identified a user on your site, there will be bits of information that you will need with almost every request that the user makes. This type of information is usually best stored in a session (either on the server they are on, or in some external state server). In this recipe, we will take a look at how we can create a wrapper for the session and get strongly typed objects out of it easily. This will allow us to interact with the objects stored in our session in a very easy fashion.

How to do it...

1. Start by creating a new default ASP.NET MVC 2 application.

2. We will create an `Account` class (in the `Models` folder) that will keep track of things such as the account's ID, e-mail address, username, and so on.

   Models/Account.cs:

   ```
   public class Account {
     public Guid AccountId { get; set; }
     public string Username { get; set; }
     public string Email { get; set; }
     public List<string> Roles { get; set; }
   }
   ```

3. Next, we will create an `AccountService` to get some mock data out of. This class will have a `GetAccountByUsername` and return an `Account` for us to work with. For the sake of simplicity, I've put this class in the `Models` folder, as well.

   Models/AccountService.cs:

   ```
   public class AccountService {
     public Account GetAccountByUsername(string username) {
       Account result = new Account();
       result.AccountId = Guid.NewGuid();
       result.Email = username + "@hotmail.com";
   ```

```
      result.Username = username;
      result.Roles = new List<string>() { "Administrator",
        "Publisher", "Dude"};

      return result;
   }
}
```

4. Now we are ready to create our `SessionWrapper` class, which we will use to put data into and get out of our `Session` for a given user. This class will have several private methods, such as `GetStringFromSession`, `GetIntFromSession`, `GetObjectFromSession`, and `SetItemInSession`, for accessing the session. But most importantly, it will have strongly typed properties and methods for use by our application, so that we never have to worry about casting data out of our session outside of this one class. And we will also manage session cleanliness in our session by removing keys when a property is set to null.

Models/SessionWrapper.cs:

```
public static class SessionWrapper {
   private const string c_account = "Account";

   public static Account Account {
      get { return GetObjectFromSession(c_account) as Account; }

      set {
         if (value == null)
            ClearItemFromSession(c_account);
         else
            SetItemInSession(value, c_account);
      }
   }

   private static string GetStringFromSession(string key) {
      return GetObjectFromSession(key).ToString();
   }

   private static int GetIntFromSession(string key) {
      return (int)GetObjectFromSession(key);
   }

   private static object GetObjectFromSession(string key) {
      return HttpContext.Current.Session[key];
   }

   private static void SetItemInSession(object item, string key) {
```

```
        HttpContext.Current.Session.Add(key, item);
    }

    private static void ClearItemFromSession(string key) {
        HttpContext.Current.Session.Remove(key);
    }
}
```

5. Having come this far, we are now ready to wire things up. We will do this by going into the `Models\AccountModels.cs` file, where we will find the `SignIn` and `SignOut` methods on the `FormsAuthenicationService` class. When a user signs in, we want to get their account from the database (mocked up in this case) and set the user's `Account` into the session for future use. Also, we want to clean up after ourselves when a user logs out.

Models/AccountModels.cs:

```
public void SignIn(string userName, bool createPersistentCookie) {
    if (String.IsNullOrEmpty(userName)) throw new
      ArgumentException("Value cannot be null or empty.",
      "userName");

    FormsAuthentication.SetAuthCookie(userName,
     createPersistentCookie);

    SessionWrapper.Account = new AccountService()
      .GetAccountByUsername(userName);
}

public void SignOut() {
    FormsAuthentication.SignOut();

    SessionWrapper.Account = null;
}
```

6. With our `Account` instance being spun up for us and stuffed into the user's session when he/she logs in, we are now ready to interact with the session in other areas of our application. Let's open up the `Site.Master` file and add some recognition of the user to our display. Right under the `LogOnUserControl` rendering, we will place our own little welcome message.

Views/Shared/Site.Master:

```
<div id="logindisplay">
  <% Html.RenderPartial("LogOnUserControl"); %><br />
  <%= StateExamples.Models.SessionWrapper.Account != null
    ? "Welcome " +
    StateExamples.Models.SessionWrapper.Account.Username + "
   from session wrapper!"  : "" %>
</div>
```

7. Now you can run the application. Prior to creating a new account and logging in, notice that there is no welcome message. Now create an account and you should see a welcome message.

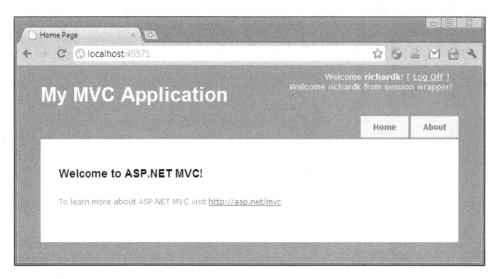

How it works...

This recipe is more of an example on how to create a simple wrapper for your session than anything else. Wrapping any framework dependency is important, as you may want to swap out the framework's way of handling sessions at some point in time for another technology, storage mechanism, or for testing purposes. With just the basic wrapper in place, it is pretty easy to plug in inversion of control (IoC) to allow for quick swapping of implementation on the fly. To best enable IoC though, you will probably want to inject your `SessionWrapper` class into your controllers, rather than accessing the wrapper directly! The method discussed here is perfect for a non-IoC project.

Remembering a previous visitor

If you are the sort of developer that doesn't tend to use the profiles and membership facilities (for whatever reason...) provided by the .NET framework, then odds are that you will be making your registration process and logging-in facilities. Part of this is the ability to drop a cookie and remember the users when they come and go from your site. There are many approaches to this, some better than others. You could drop an encrypted cookie on the user's computer with the user's ID in it and, upon re-entering the site, you simply log them in and allow them to exist in the system, as if they hadn't left (as is done with Gmail). Another approach is to store their username and the like in a cookie and let the user think that you have remembered them. Then, when the user attempts to take an action that really requires them to identify themselves, you can prompt them to log in again (as LinkedIn appears to do).

How to do it...

1. Start by creating a new default ASP.NET MVC 2 application.

2. As this recipe is all about the cookie, we will create a helper class for working with cookies first. Create a `CookieWrapper` class in the `Models` folder. This class will handle getting, setting, and destroying cookies for us. More than that, we will expose properties, of this class that will give us the data in a strongly typed format, so that we don't have to worry about converting strings all over our application.

Models/CookieWrapper.cs:

```
public class CookieWrapper {
  private void SetCookie(string key, string value,
    bool thisSessionOnly) {
    HttpCookie cookie = new HttpCookie(key, value);

    if(!thisSessionOnly)
       cookie.Expires = DateTime.Now.AddMonths(1);

       HttpContext.Current.Response.Cookies.Add(cookie);
  }

  private string GetCookie(string key) {
    if (HttpContext.Current.Request.Cookies[key] != null)
       return HttpContext.Current.Request.Cookies[key].Value;

   return String.Empty;
  }

  private void RemoveCookie(string key) {
     HttpContext.Current.Response.Cookies.Remove(key);
  }
}
```

3. With the helper functions in place, we can now add two properties for the things that we are interested in remembering. We will have an `AccountID` that will return a `Guid` and we will have a `Username` property that will return the user's username.

Models/CookieWrapper.cs:

```
public class CookieWrapper {
  private const string c_accountId = "AccountId";
  private const string c_username = "Username";

  public Guid AccountID {
    get {
      string value = GetCookie(c_accountId);
```

```
            if (!String.IsNullOrEmpty(value))
                return new Guid(value);

           return Guid.Empty;
       }

       set {
         if (value == Guid.Empty)
            RemoveCookie(c_accountId);
         else
            SetCookie(c_accountId, value.ToString(), false);
       }
     }

   public string Username {
      get { return GetCookie(c_username); }
      set {
         if (String.IsNullOrEmpty(value))
            RemoveCookie(c_username);
          else
            SetCookie(c_username, value, false);
      }
    }
    ...
}
```

4. That is technically all we need for our cookie wrapper to work. Now we can add some logic to our application to demonstrate how this works. We will work in the `Home/Index` view for our display purposes. But we will also create a new action called `CookieAction` in `HomeController.cs`, which will handle a handful of operations for setting and getting our data out of cookies. These operations will be triggered by some links that we will add to the home page of our application.

Controllers/HomeController.cs:

```
public ActionResult CookieAction(string id) {
   var cookieJar = new CookieWrapper();

   switch(id) {
      case "SetAccountId":
          cookieJar.AccountID = Guid.NewGuid();
          break;

      case "SetUsername":
          cookieJar.Username = "asiemer";
          break;
```

```
        case "RemoveAccountId":
            cookieJar.AccountID = Guid.Empty;
            break;

        case "RemoveUsername":
            cookieJar.Username = String.Empty;
            break;
    }
    return RedirectToAction("Index");
}
```

5. In order for us to get our data to the home page, we need to set the `Username` and `AccountID` into the `ViewData` for our home page in the `Index` action of the home controller.

Controllers/HomeController.cs:

```
public ActionResult Index() {
    ViewData["Message"] = "Welcome to ASP.NET MVC!";

    var cookieJar = new CookieWrapper();
    ViewData["AccountId"] = cookieJar.AccountID;
    ViewData["Username"] = cookieJar.Username;

    return View();
}
```

6. The only thing left at this point is to create the links that trigger the values to be retrieved or destroyed, as well as to display the current values of the cookies. Make the following changes to `Views\Home\Index.aspx`:

Views/Home/Index.aspx:

```
<asp:Content ID="Content2" ContentPlaceHolderID="MainContent"
    runat="server">
    <h2><%: ViewData["Message"] %></h2>
    <p>
        To learn more about ASP.NET MVC visit
        <a href="http://asp.net/mvc" title="ASP.NET MVC Website">
            http://asp.net/mvc</a>.
    </p>
    <p>
        <%: Html.ActionLink("Set AccountId cookie", "CookieAction",
            new { @id="SetAccountId"}) %>
        <br />
        <%: Html.ActionLink("Remove AccountId cookie", "CookieAction",
            new { @id="RemoveAccountId"}) %>
    </p>
```

```
<p>
  <%: Html.ActionLink("Set Username cookie", "CookieAction",
      new { @id = "SetUsername" })%>
  <br />
  <%: Html.ActionLink("Remove Username cookie", "CookieAction",
      new { @id = "RemoveUsername" })%>
</p>
<fieldset>
  <legend>Cookie Jar</legend>
    Username: <%: ViewData["Username"] %>
    <br />
    AccountId: <%: ViewData["AccountId"] %>
</fieldset>
</asp:Content>
```

7. Now you can run the application. Clicking on the links to set and destroy the data should write the contents to the cookies or remove the values all together. Because we opted to persist the cookies in the `CookieWrapper`, these cookies will by default be set for a month. Each time you write the cookie, this date will be updated. When closing the browser window and then opening it again, you should see that the state of your cookies have been "remembered".

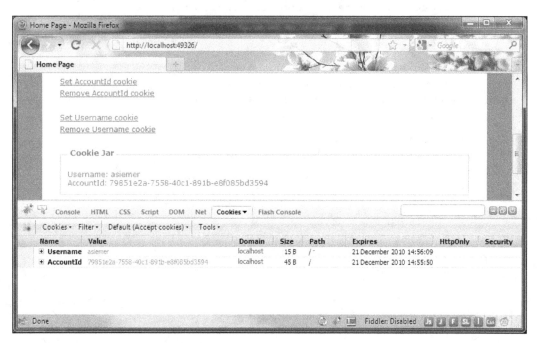

How it works...

As with our session wrapper in the previous recipe, we have opted to wrap the framework's concept of a cookie, which is exposed by `HttpContext`. This gives us a couple of benefits. First and foremost, all of our dealings with the concept of a cookie happen in one place—helping to keep our code DRY. Also, it limits the exposure of magic strings that working with cookies often presents in the cookie's dependency on strings for keys. This makes the code that uses our cookie wrapper less fragile and more easily refactorable. All of these things then lead up to one more key strength in wrapping dependencies like this, in that we can easily swap out this implementation for something else for testing purposes or otherwise using an Inversion of Control container, such as `StructureMap`.

Caching your product catalog for faster response times

There are a lot of applications that are built these days with data that doesn't change all that much. A **product catalog** is usually a good example of that. There may be updates here or there, but not every five minutes. With fairly static data like this, why do we feel the need to make a request from the controller, through a service class of some type, to a repository, which then reaches out to some form of infrastructure such as a database or the filesystem? In cases like these, we can save ourselves a lot of pain by doing that big reach once and then stuffing the results into the cache for a while. With the next request, we can then just fetch the data directly from the cache.

In this recipe, we will see how to create a simple wrapper for the standard .NET cache. We will create the ability to stash and get a single item from the cache. We will also create some methods that allow us to fetch a group of items, as well as store a group of items. Similar to other wrapper classes, the one key thing that we have created for these wrappers to do is expose strongly typed results rather than cache-oriented items. This will mean that our application won't know anything about the idea of cache. Ultimately, this gives us the ability to pick and choose how we want to cache our items down the road.

How to do it...

1. Start by first creating a new default ASP.NET MVC 2 application.
2. Then add a reference to NBuilder, which we will use to generate some product data for us.

3. Next, because we are building a product catalog, we need to build the idea of a product. We will do this by adding a new `Product` class to the `Models` directory.

Models/Product.cs:

```
public class Product {
  public string Name { get; set; }
  public decimal Price { get; set; }
}
```

4. Then we can create a `ProductService` class to help us generate some products to work with. This class will use NBuilder to generate 100 fictitious products to work with.

Models/ProductService.cs:

```
public class ProductService {
  public List<Product> GetProducts() {
    List<Product> result = Builder<Product>
      .CreateListOfSize(100)
      .Build()
      .ToList();

    return result;
  }
}
```

5. With the added ability, we easily get a list of products. We can then create the wrapper we will use for accessing the cache. This class will provide us with methods to add items to the cache both one at a time and in groups. It will also allow us to get items from the cache one at a time and in groups.

Models/CacheWrapper.cs:

```
public class CacheWrapper
public class CacheWrapper {
  private List<object> GetCacheItems(string[] keys) {
    IDictionaryEnumerator theCache =
      HttpContext.Current.Cache.GetEnumerator();
    List<object> results = new List<object>();
    while (theCache.MoveNext()) {
      if (keys.Contains(theCache.Key))
        results.Add(theCache.Value);
    }

    return results;
  }

  private object GetCachItem(string key) {
```

```
    if (HttpContext.Current.Cache[key] != null)
      return HttpContext.Current.Cache[key];

    return null;
  }

  private void AddCacheItems(Dictionary<string, object> items) {
    foreach (KeyValuePair<string, object> item in items) {
      AddCacheItem(item.Key, item.Value);
    }
  }

  private void AddCacheItem(string key, object item) {
   HttpContext.Current.Cache.Add(key, item, null, //dependencies
      DateTime.MaxValue, //absolute expiration
      new TimeSpan(0, 1, 0, 0), //sliding expiration
      CacheItemPriority.Default, //priority
      null); //callback
  }
}
```

6. Once we have the ability to put items into and get them out of the cache, we can start to add additional abilities. Specifically, we want to be able store a list of products in the cache and get a list of products out of the cache. To do this, we will need two new methods.

Models/CacheWrapper.cs:

```
public class CacheWrapper {
  public void PutProducts(List<Product> products) {
    Dictionary<string, object> itemsToCache = new
        Dictionary<string, object>();
    foreach (Product product in products) {
      itemsToCache.Add(product.Name, product);
    }

    AddCacheItems(itemsToCache);
  }

  public List<Product> GetProducts(string[] productNames) {
    List<Product> results = new List<Product>();

    List<object> cacheItems = GetCacheItems(productNames);
    foreach (object cacheItem in cacheItems) {
      results.Add(cacheItem as Product);
    }
```

```
        return results.OrderBy(p => p.Name).ToList();
    }


    . . .


}
```

7. From this point, there are various ways to actually put our products in the cache. My preferred way is to use an IoC container such as StructureMap, so that when my presentation code calls for products, it first goes through a cache layer and, if the cache doesn't have the needed items, it then goes through the products service. In this case, we are keeping things a bit more simplified though. We will load up our entire product catalog (100 products in all) when the application first starts. Being a demo of how the cache wrapper works, this should suit our purposes just fine!

Global.asax:

```
protected void Application_Start() {
    AreaRegistration.RegisterAllAreas();

    RegisterRoutes(RouteTable.Routes);

    PreLoadProductCatalog();
}

private void PreLoadProductCatalog() {
    List<Product> products = new ProductService().GetProducts();
    new CacheWrapper().PutProducts(products);
}
```

8. Once our `Product` catalog is placed firmly into the cache, we are ready to create a new action and view to display our catalog. We will start by first adding a new action called `CachedProducts` to the home controller. This action will put in a query to our `CacheWrapper` for a select set of products based on their names, and then pass that result down to the view.

Controllers/HomeController.cs:

```
public ActionResult CachedProducts() {
    List<Product> products = new CacheWrapper().GetProducts(new[] {
        "Name1", "Name5", "Name98", "Name39", "Name88", "Name34"
    });

    return View(products);
}
```

9. Now we are ready to generate a view from this action. Be sure to compile your code so that your `Product` is in the list of strongly typed items. Set this view to be a list of products.

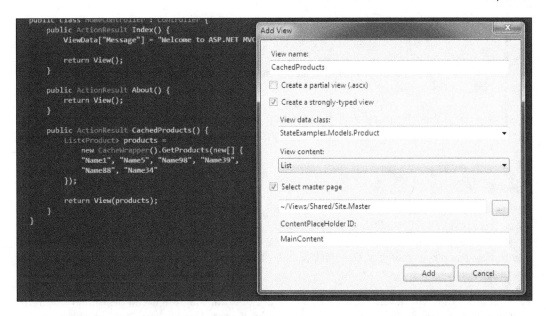

10. Now you can build and run your application. If you debug your application, you will see that the products are generated only once when the application starts up. When you browse to the cached products page, you will see that the products are actually retrieved from cache only.

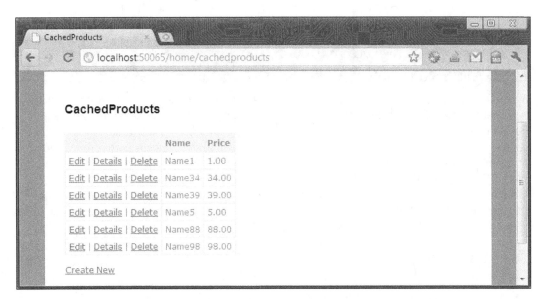

Be aware that, in this recipe, the cached items are set to expire after an hour if they are not used. You would want to expose this property to the methods in your cache wrapper, so that it could be set depending on the required usage. Also, for items that are loaded when the app starts, you would want to make sure that, if the item is not in the cache, you can get them from some other source.

How it works...

In this recipe, we created a cache wrapper, which we then used to preload our product catalog when the application first started. Then down the road when we accessed our `CacheWrapper` to get a list of products, we were working directly with products loaded in memory. This allows you to bypass calls to a database server where you then run possibly complex queries to get a set of products.

Keep in mind that when working with a cached set of data, the data could disappear out from under you. This means that you usually need your full cache implementation (not the cache wrapper per se) to first check the cache for items and then take action upon those results. If cached items are found, they are returned. If they are not found, then you need to get the items in another manner and then cache those results, so that they are ready for the next request.

Using output caching to cache an entire page

In this very short recipe, we are going to see how to use output caching. **Output caching** is a very easy way to implement caching for an entire page in your application. The difference between setting output caching on a view and caching items from the database is that you are caching at a higher level of processing. The reason to cache data access is to remove the cost of communicating with the server and then running a complex, possibly long-running query. Working with cached data will certainly save you some time on getting your requests turned around. However, output caching caches not only the data access, but also the processing of that data into a view. With output caching, you are caching the final result of the request. This is the ultimate way to turn a request around quickly.

How to do it...

1. Start by creating a new default ASP.NET MVC 2 application.
2. Then we need to add a reference to NBuilder (in the dependencies folder), so that we can generate some products for testing purposes.

3. Next, we need to create a `Product` class in the `Models` directory.

   Models/Product.cs:

```
public class Product {
  public Guid ProductID { get; set; }
  public string Name { get; set; }
  public decimal Discount { get; set; }
  public decimal Retail { get; set; }
  public decimal Tax { get; set; }
  public decimal Price {
    get {
      decimal finalCost = Retail;
      if(Discount > 0)
          finalCost = finalCost - (finalCost * Discount);

      finalCost = finalCost + (finalCost * Tax);
      return finalCost;
    }

    private set { }
  }
}
```

4. Once we have the `Product` class in place, we can then create a `ProductService` class to generate 1000 products. We will set each product to have a different discount rate (to add time to our page creation), as well as a tax value of 10 cents. Also, I added two lines to make the current thread sleep for a second to replicate the idea of communicating with an external server, as well as running a complex product query.

   Models/ProductService.cs:

```
public class ProductService {
  public List<Product> GetProducts() {
      Thread.Sleep(1000); //connect to the database
      Thread.Sleep(1000); //run a query and return data
      Random rnd = new Random(99);
      return Builder<Product>
         .CreateListOfSize(1000)
         .WhereAll()
         .Have(p => p.Discount = Convert.ToDecimal("." +
             rnd.Next(1,99)))
         .WhereAll()
         .Have(p => p.Tax = new decimal(.10))
         .Build()
         .ToList();
  }
}
```

5. Now, we can create a new action called `Products` in the home controller, which will be responsible for returning a list of products.

   Controllers/HomeController.cs:

   ```
   [OutputCache(Duration = (60 * 60), VaryByParam = "none")]
   public ActionResult Products() {
       List<Product> products = new ProductService().GetProducts();
       return View(products);
   }
   ```

6. The next obvious step is to create a new view called `Products`. This will be a strongly typed view, which we will configure to show a list of products.

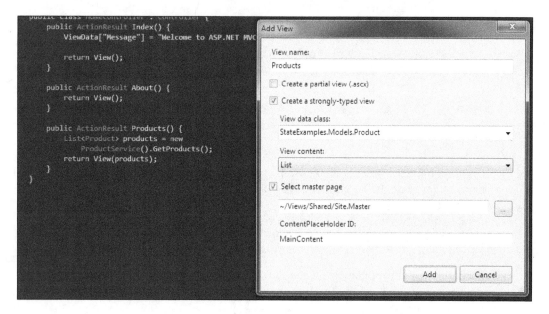

7. If you run the application as it is now, you will notice that loading the **Products** page will take a little over two seconds. The quickest and easiest way to combat page slowness like this is to cache it. An easy way to cache a whole view like this is to add an `OutputCache` attribute above the action in the home controller. We will set the duration of our cached view to one hour. The easiest way to figure out the amount of time a resource will be cached it to say 60 (seconds) times 60 (minutes), which is an hour.

   Controllers/HomeController.cs:

   ```
   [OutputCache(Duration = (60 * 60), VaryByParam = "none")]
   public ActionResult Products() {
       Stopwatch sw = new Stopwatch();
       sw.Start();
   ```

```
List<Product> products = new ProductService().GetProducts();
sw.Stop();
Response.Write(sw.ElapsedMilliseconds);
return View(products);
}
```

8. Now you can run the application again. The first time you view the **Products** view, you will see that the page still takes a couple of seconds to load. But after refreshing the page, you will see that it comes back almost immediately!

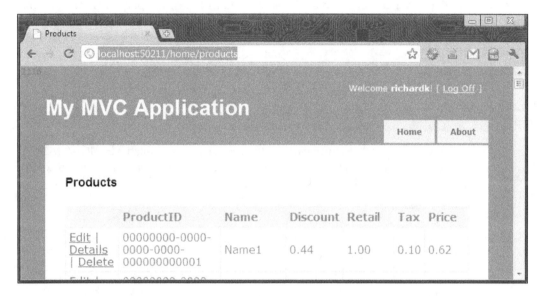

How it works...

The output cache is a carry-over from the ASP.NET framework. It allows us to easily cache an entire resource without too much thought on our part. As the request goes through the pipeline, the output cache attribute is recognized and the cache is checked for the requested resource.

There's more...

There is a problem with this approach though. With our previous example, run the application, browse to the products page to see the two second load time, and then refresh the page to see the instant response time. Now click the **Log On** link. Then click the register page and create a new account. Notice that you are now logged in and that your username is in the upper-right part of the page. Now navigate back to the **Products** page. What happened? Full-page caching is exactly that...full-page caching. If you have any bits on your website that need to be cached separately, or not cached at all, full-page caching is not the solution you need!

Using partial views to cache pieces of a page individually

In this recipe, we will take a look at how we can use the `RenderAction` method to get a partial view. We will do this by creating a shared partial view that is capable of rendering any action in which we might be interested. We will then create an `extension` method, which is capable of calling our helper view and converting that into a string. This string can then be cached. Best of all, this particular approach allows us to use the appropriate controller to take care of the requirements for each of the views being rendered.

How to do it...

1. Start by creating a new default ASP.NET MVC 2 application.

2. Then add a reference to NBuilder, so that we can generate a huge list of data. This huge list of data should give us a slow page to be cached later.

3. Next, we will create a `Product` class in the `Models` folder, which we will use to hold the data in our list. We will also have some properties, which we will use to do some calculations for each displayed product.

    Models/Product.cs:

```
public class Product {
  public Guid ProductId { get; set; }
  public string Name { get; set; }
  public decimal Discount { get; set; }
  public decimal Retail { get; set; }
  public decimal Tax { get; set; }
  public decimal Price {
    get {
       decimal finalCost = Retail;
       if(Discount > 0)
          finalCost = finalCost - (finalCost * Discount);

       finalCost = finalCost + (finalCost * Tax);
       return finalCost;
    }

    private set { }
  }
}
```

4. Now we need to create a `ProductService` class in the `models` folder to generate our list of data. We will use NBuilder to generate a list of 1000 products. Each product will have a value of 10 cents for the tax property and we will randomly generate a discount for each product.

Models/ProductService.cs:

```
public class ProductService {
  public List<Product> GetProducts() {
      Thread.Sleep(1000); //connect to the database
      Thread.Sleep(1000); //run a query and return data
      Random rnd = new Random(99);
      return
        Builder<Product>.CreateListOfSize(1000)
          .WhereAll()
          .Have(p => p.Discount = Convert.ToDecimal("." +
            rnd.Next(1,99)))
          ..WhereAll()
          ..Have(p => p.Tax = new decimal(.10))
          ..Build()
          ..ToList();
  }
}
```

5. With the ability to generate a list of products, we need to be able to show them in a view. To do this, we will create a new action in our home controller called `Products`. In this action, we will get a list of products and return that list to the view as its model. Knowing that this list of data is going to take a while to generate, we need to add an output cache attribute to cache the data for an hour.

Controllers/HomeController.cs:

```
[OutputCache(Duration = (60*60), VaryByParam = "none")]
public ActionResult Products() {
  List<Product> products = new ProductService().GetProducts();
  return PartialView(products);
}
```

6. Then we need to generate a partial view to display our list of products. Do this by right-clicking on the action and adding a new view. This view will be a strongly typed partial view of type `Product`, which will show a list of the products.

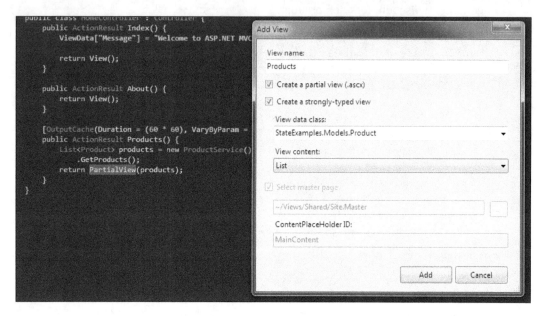

7. Now we need to create a view to render our cached products to. We will create a new action in our home controller called `CachedByAttribute`. This action will simply return the view.

Controllers/HomeController.cs:

```
public ActionResult CachedByAttribute() {
    return View();
}
```

8. Then right-click on the action and add a new view. This view will be a simple no-frills view with nothing in it. Inside of it, we will make a call to `Html.RenderAction`. I also wrapped it with a stopwatch to see how long the page takes to render with the products list inside of it.

Views/Home/CachedByAttribute.aspx:

```
<asp:Content ID="Content2" ContentPlaceHolderID="MainContent"
    runat="server">

    <h2>Cached By Attribute</h2>
    <p>A non cached bit of data on this page: <%= DateTime.Now %>
    </p>
    <%System.Diagnostics.Stopwatch sw = new
            System.Diagnostics.Stopwatch();
```

```
      sw.Start();
   %>
   <% Html.RenderAction("Products"); %>

    <% sw.Stop(); %>

     <%= "Getting 1000 products took " + sw.ElapsedMilliseconds +
         " milliseconds."%>
   </asp:Content>
```

9. Now you are ready to see the cached listing of products. Browse to `/Home/` `CachedByAttribute`; you should see the list of products and that it took roughly two seconds and change (on my computer). Now refresh the page to see that the products are cached.

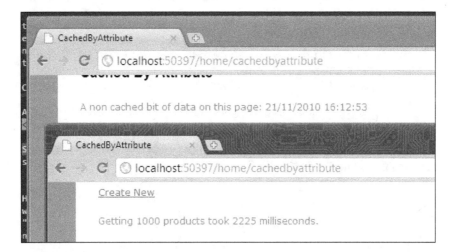

10. Uh oh...they didn't cache! That is because the output cache attribute on a view that is rendered as a child of another view (such as when using `RenderAction`) is ignored.

    Now, let's look at another approach to caching the products listing.

     This is a total hack and should be addressed in the MVC futures project, as well as the next release of the MVC framework.

11. In this approach, we need to render a partial view as a string. We will then cache that string for future use and return it to our view to be rendered. We will use a common shared partial view to do the `RenderAction` for us, to which we will pass the name of an action and its controller, so that we can reuse this approach anywhere in our site.

12. First, we need to create the shared partial view that will handle our product's view rendering. This view will be called `CachedView.ascx` and will be placed in the `Views/Shared` directory. All this view does is call `RenderAction` on the passed-in action and controller names.

Views/Shared/ChacedViewChacedView.ascx:

```
<%@ Control Language="C#"
   Inherits="System.Web.Mvc.ViewUserControl<dynamic>" %>
<% Html.RenderAction(ViewData["ViewName"].ToString(),
   ViewData["ControllerName"].ToString()); %>
```

13. Now we can create a static class called `ControllerExtensions` and place it in the `Controllers` directory. This class will be responsible for rendering our views to a string. Let's create a method called `RenderViewToString`. It will use the `CachedViews` partial view that we created as the handler of the partial view to render.

Models/ControllerExtensions.cs:

```
private static string RenderViewToString(HttpContext httpContext,
   ControllerContext context, ViewDataDictionary viewData) {
  string pathToView = "~/Views/Shared/CachedView.ascx";
}
```

14. Next, we need to create a `StringBuilder` and a `StringWriter` to capture the rendered view.

Models/ControllerExtensions.cs:

```
//Create memory writer
var sb = new StringBuilder();
var memWriter = new StringWriter(sb);
```

15. We then need to create a faked `HttpResponse`, `HttpContext`, and `ControllerContext`.

Models/ControllerExtensions.cs:

```
//Create fake http context to render the view
var fakeResponse = new HttpResponse(memWriter);
var fakeContext = new HttpContext(httpContext.Request,
   fakeResponse);
var fakeControllerContext = new ControllerContext(
  new HttpContextWrapper(fakeContext),
  context.RouteData, context.Controller);
```

16. With all of these variables in place, we are ready to get to work. All we need to do now is to create an instance of `HtmlHelper` to which we will pass all of our faked instances, as well as create some new inline instances of other required classes. Then we can call the `RenderPartial` method (you will need to add a reference to the `System.Web.Mvc.Html` namespace) on the `HtmlHelper` and pass in the path to our `CachedView` partial view, as well as any passed-in `ViewData` (such as the action and controller name...more on this in a sec).

Models/ControllerExtensions.cs:

```
//Use HtmlHelper to render partial view to fake context
var html = new HtmlHelper(new ViewContext(fakeControllerContext,
    new FakeView(), new ViewDataDictionary(),
      new TempDataDictionary(), memWriter),
      new ViewPage());
html.RenderPartial(pathToView, viewData);
```

17. Notice that we created an instance of a `FakeView()` in the previous code. It didn't make much sense to mention this until now. But we need to create the `FakeView` class, which will implement `IView`. This is a requirement for creating an instance of `HtmlHelper`. Here is that class—notice that there actually isn't any implementation in this class.

Models/ControllerExtensions.cs:

```
public class FakeView : IView {
  public void Render(ViewContext viewContext,
      System.IO.TextWriter writer) {
      throw new NotImplementedException();
  }
}
```

18. When we called `RenderPartial` on the `HtmlHelper`, we rendered our view to the `StringBuilder` we created at the top of this method. We can now do some clean up and return our view as a string.

Models/ControllerExtensions.cs:

```
//Flush memory and return output
memWriter.Flush();
string result = sb.ToString();
return result;
```

19. Technically, this is all that is needed to render our view to a string, which could then be cached pretty easily. But we want to make this easier to work with. To do this, we will add a couple of extension methods. The first one is called `RenderViewToString` and it will extend the `Controller` class (so that we can use it from within any class that derives from `Controller`). This method will take in the name of the view and controller that the user wants to render. It will then put those strings into view data to be passed to the `CachedView`. And of course, it will take care of all the dirty work that our `RenderViewToString` method requires.

Models/ControllerExtensions.cs:

```
public static string RenderViewToString(this Controller
controller, string viewName, string controllerName) {
  controller.ViewData.Add("ViewName", viewName);
  controller.ViewData.Add("ControllerName", controllerName);

  string result = RenderViewToString(
    System.Web.HttpContext.Current,
    controller.ControllerContext,
    controller.ViewData);
  return result;
}
```

20. The next extension method will also extend `Controller`. This method is very similar to the last extension method we created, but it will take in a couple of other parameters. This method will hide our caching concepts. It will take in a `DateTime` to set an absolute expiration value and it will take in a `TimeSpan` to allow us a way to set a sliding scale. It will also set the controller and view names into `ViewData` for use by the `CachedView`. Then we will check the cache to see if this view has been cached before (by its view name). If it has, then we will return the cached view. If the item hasn't been cached before, we will get the view as a string, stuff it in the cache, and return it.

Models/ControllerExtensions.cs:

```
public static string RenderViewToString(this Controller
  controller, string viewName, string controllerName,
  DateTime absoluteExpiration, TimeSpan slidingExpiration) {
  string result = "";

  controller.ViewData.Add("ViewName", viewName);
  controller.ViewData.Add("ControllerName", controllerName);

  if (System.Web.HttpContext.Current.Cache[viewName] != null)
    result = HttpContext.Current.Cache[viewName].ToString();
  else {
    result = RenderViewToString(System.Web.HttpContext.Current,
      controller.ControllerContext, controller.ViewData);
```

```
HttpContext.Current.Cache.Add(viewName, result, null,
    absoluteExpiration, slidingExpiration,
    CacheItemPriority.Default, null);
}

return result;
}
```

21. Now we need to put our view renderer into action. To do this, we need to create a new action in our home controller called `CachedAsString`. This action will call our `RenderViewToString` method and pass in caching parameters (a sliding scale of one hour) to use the caching implementation of our string render. Then we will pass the rendered view down to our `CachedAsString` view via `ViewData` as `CachedProducts`. (I have also added some stopwatch data for us to track how long the cached version takes.)

Controllers/HomeController.cs:

```
public ActionResult CachedAsString() {
    Stopwatch sw = new Stopwatch();
    sw.Start();

    string products = this.RenderViewToString("Products",
        "Home", DateTime.MaxValue, new TimeSpan(0, 1, 0, 0));

    sw.Stop();

    ViewData["CachedProducts"] = products;
    ViewData["CachedStopwatch"] = sw.ElapsedMilliseconds;

    return View();
}
```

22. Now right-click on the new action and add a new view. This will be an empty view. It will simply render our `CachedProducts` string and the stopwatch data.

Views/Home/CachedAsString.aspx:

```
<asp:Content ID="Content2" ContentPlaceHolderID="MainContent"
    runat="server">
    <h2>Cached As String</h2>
    <p>A non cached bit of data on this page: <%= DateTime.Now %>
    </p>
    <%= ViewData["CachedProducts"] %>
    <%= "Getting 1000 products took " + ViewData["CachedStopwatch"]
        + " milliseconds."%>
</asp:Content>
```

23. Now run your application and browse to `/Home/CachedAsString`. You should see that the product's partial view took a little over two seconds to render. Now refresh the page. 0 seconds to render! Not too bad.

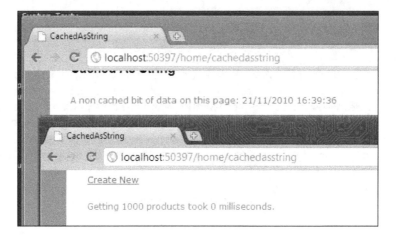

How it works...

The power for this recipe comes in two fashions. It was very important that we get the `Html.RenderAction` method to work as this method calls an action on a controller, which means that the data for the view being rendered is handled outside of the view that is doing the rendering. This means that we can easily reuse this logic without having to duplicate it. This is an important distinction. All other forms of rendering a view inline require that you also create the data that the view needs in the controller for the parent view. This can quickly become very complex and ugly.

In order to use the `RenderAction` method, we had to find a way to get it to execute in a manner that is copasetic for the MVC framework, but that would return something that we could cache in a more manual fashion. Looking at the Web, you will find all sorts of methods to render a view as a string. Not all of them are the same. Most of them didn't work in the manner in which they are advertised. And even fewer of those would actually work with the `RenderAction` method. I did find one post on Lorenz Cuno Klopfenstein's blog, which gave me my basic implementation for rendering a view to a string. Here is that post: `http://www.klopfenstein.net/lorenz.aspx/render-partial-view-to-string-in-asp-net-mvc`.

Once you get the `RenderAction` to be exposed as a string, it is really just a matter of creating some basic MVC components such as the **Products** view and the pass through view, which we used for the `RenderAction`. We also used the standard cache that is built into the framework to cache the view string. This is the one place where I would ask you to think a bit further. Adding dependencies in your code to a framework that you don't own is usually not a good idea. If nothing else, I would suggest that you put a wrapper around the cache usage.

Exposing an application API to your presentation layer

If you work in a team of varied levels of skill, you might find the need to make some of the more complex aspects of your application easier to consume. While you could create a series of wrapper classes, factories, and repositories, junior developers might find their lives to be easier if they had a single point of entry to your application. It is surprisingly easy to create a super wrapper for all the functionality of your application and then expose it throughout the presentation layer of your website. Creating such an API is the topic of this recipe.

How to do it...

1. Create a new default ASP.NET MVC 2 application.

2. Then we will create several base classes, which we will use to insert an extension point between our views, partial views, master pages, and controllers. We will start by creating a base class for our controllers. Create a new class called `BaseController.cs` in the `Models` folder, which inherits from `Controller`.

   Models/BaseController.cs:

   ```
   public class BaseController : Controller {


   }
   ```

3. Next, we will create a base class for our view pages. This base class will be a bit different from the controller base class—in that we have two different types of view pages to inherit from.

   ```
   public class BaseViewPage : ViewPage {


   }


   public class BaseViewPage<T> : ViewPage<T> {


   }
   ```

4. We can create a `BaseHttpApplication`, `BaseViewMasterPage`, and `BaseViewUserControl` to provide further points of extensibility. These classes will go into the `Models` directory also.

   Models/...:

   ```
   //BaseHttpApplication.cs
   public class BaseHttpApplication : HttpApplication {


   }
   ```

```
//BaseViewMasterPage.cs
public class BaseViewMasterPage : ViewMasterPage {


}

public class BaseViewMasterPage<T> : ViewMasterPage<T> {


}

//BaseViewUserControl.cs
public class BaseViewUserControl : ViewUserControl {


}

public class BaseViewUserControl<T> : ViewUserControl<T> {


}
```

5. Once we have all these base classes created, we can start to weave them into our application. They will provide us with a place to easily slip in extended functionality as we need to. All that we need to do is add the word `Base` in front of the MVC framework pieces. An example of this would be in our `Site.Master` page, which originally inherited from `ViewMasterPage`. We will make our master page inherit from `BaseViewMasterPage`. Do this with all the view pages, controllers, and user controls in the application.

Views/Shared/Site.Master:

```
<%@ Master Language="C#" Inherits="
   StateExamples.Models.BaseViewMasterPage" %>
...
```

6. Now we can create some application bits for our demonstration. In this case, we will create some configuration values in our `app.config`. We will create values such as `ContactEmail`, `ContactPhone`, `RootUrl`, and `SiteName` in the `Web.config`.

Web.config:

```
<configuration>
  <appSettings>
    <add key="ContactEmail" value="asiemer@hotmail.com" />
    <add key="ContactPhone" value="(661) 123-4567" />
    <add key="RootUrl" value="http://localhost:50981"/>
    <add key="SiteName" value="www.MvcCookbook.com"/>
  </appSettings>

...
```

7. Now we will create a wrapper class for accessing these config values. This will be a new class called `Configuration`. This class will keep all the aspects of the `ConfigurationManager` class hidden away from our application by exposing these values as properties of the `Configuration` class. Also, as this class will expose the same data to all users of our site, we will make this class using the singleton pattern.

Models/Configuration.cs:

```
public sealed class Configuration
public sealed class Configuration {
    #region Singleton
    private static volatile Configuration instance;
    private static object syncRoot = new object();

    private Configuration() { }

    public static Configuration Instance {
        get {
            if (instance == null) {
                lock (syncRoot) {
                    if (instance == null)
                        instance = new Configuration();
                }
            }

            return instance;
        }
    }
    #endregion

    public string RootUrl {
        get {
            return GetString("RootUrl");
        }
    }
    public string ContactEmail {
        get {
            return GetString("ContactEmail");
        }
    }
    public string ContactPhone {
        get {
            return GetString("ContactPhone");
        }
    }
```

```
      public string SiteName {
        get {
          return GetString("SiteName");
        }
      }

    private string GetString(string key) {
      if (ConfigurationManager.AppSettings[key] != null)
        return ConfigurationManager.AppSettings[key].ToString();

      throw new ConfigurationErrorsException(key + " was not found in
        the configuration");
    }

    private int GetInt(string key) {
      if (ConfigurationManager.AppSettings[key] != null)
        return Convert.ToInt32(
            ConfigurationManager.AppSettings[key]);

      throw new ConfigurationErrorsException(key + " was not found in
        the configuration");
      }
  }
```

8. Now we are ready to create our wrapper class, which we will use to expose our site's API to the developers of our application. This class will be called `Website` and will be placed in the `Models` directory. We will also use the singleton pattern when creating this class. This class will have a property on it called `Configuration` and will return an instance of the `Configuration` class.

Models/WebSite.cs:

```
public sealed class Website {
  #region Singleton
  private static volatile Website instance;
  private static object syncRoot = new Object();

  private Website() { }

  public static Website Instance {
    get {
      if (instance == null) {
        lock (syncRoot) {
          if (instance == null)
              instance = new Website();
          }
```

```
        }

        return instance;
      }
  }
    #endregion

  public Configuration Configuration { get {
      return Configuration.Instance; } }
}
```

9. With our `Website` class created, we are technically ready to consume its values from anywhere in our site. As the `Instance` property on the `Website` class is static, we can easily use this class as we wish and where we wish. For example, on the home page, we can easily display the e-mail address at which we can be contacted.

Views/Home/Index.aspx:

```
<asp:Content ID="Content2" ContentPlaceHolderID="MainContent"
  runat="server">
  <h2><%: ViewData["Message"] %></h2>
  <p>To learn more about ASP.NET MVC visit
     <a href="http://asp.net/mvc" title="ASP.NET MVC Website">
        http://asp.net/mvc</a>.
  </p>

  <p>Please feel free to contact us at
    <%= StateExamples.Models.Website.Instance.Configuration.
       ContactEmail %>
  .</p>
</asp:Content>
```

10. However, this class would be a touch easier to use if it were exposed as a property from the various locations that we work in, such as controllers, views, partial views, and master pages. If only we have an easy way to expose such a property. Oh wait...our base classes. We can easily expose a `Website` property in all of our base classes.

Models/BaseViewMasterPage.cs:

```
public class BaseViewMasterPage : ViewMasterPage {
  public Website Website { get { return Website.Instance; } }
}

public class BaseViewMasterPage<T> : ViewMasterPage<T> {
  public Website Website { get { return Website.Instance; } }
}
```

11. With this, we can update our `Site.Master` page to use the API. All that this means is that we can remove the `Instance` property from our call. But this tends to make our code easier to read.

    Views/Shared/Site.Master:

    ```
    <p>Please feel free to contact us at
      <%= Website.Configuration.ContactEmail %>
    .</p>
    ```

12. You can now run the application and you will see that the data is brought up and out of the `web.config` file, through the configuration class, and out of the `Website` instance and on to our web page. This one line of code hides away a great deal of complexity (albeit simple complexity in this case).

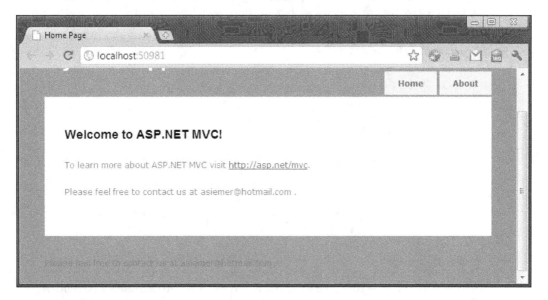

How it works...

All that we have done in this recipe is created a very high level set of objects that wrap a level of complexity, which in turn wraps another level of complexity. Each set of classes that we put deeper behind our API serves to hide a level of complexity. This brings a certain degree of uniformity to our application. It also simplifies our presentation layer code by quite a bit!

Index

MvcSiteMap
 using, for breadcrumbs implementation
  204-206
 working 206
MVC Turbine 40
MyControllerFactory class 84

N

Name property 12
NBuilder
 data layer, mocking 232
 NBuilderabout 8
nested master pages
 about 117
 creating, steps 117, 118
 working 118
NService Bus 198
NVelocity
 using, for view template loading 35
 working 39, 40
nyroModal 148
nyroModalManual function 152

O

OnActionExecuted event 112
OnActionExecuted method 112, 113
onchange event 177
OnClick event 142
OnPreInit event 111
OnPreInit method 110
OrderBy method 136
OutputCache attribute 294
output caching
 about 292
 limitation 295
 using 292-294
 working 295

P

pageable data set
 about 130, 131
 working with 130-132
pagination
 managing, in URLs 89-94
 working 95

partial view
 Html.RenderAction method, working 304
 obtaining, RenderAction method used 296-
  303
 RenderAction method, using 304
 using, for view code segmentation 22-29
 working 29
PDF order summary
 generating, steps 63-65
 starting with 63
 working 66
permalink 82
Person class 212
Plain Old CLR Object. *See* **POCO**
POCO 250
portable area
 about 192
 creating 192-197
 example 198
 working 197, 198
previous visitor
 about 282
 remembering 283-286
product catalog
 about 287
 caching 287-291
 working 292
Product class 46
ProductName property 13
ProductRepository.GetProducts() method 132
ProductRepository class 120, 126
ProductService class 31, 293
progressive enhancement 174

R

radio button array
 about 128
 handling, steps 128, 129
 starting with 128
 working 129
ReadAll method 267
Read method 266
record deletion
 about 137
 jQuery delete link, using 140
 starting with 137

Thank you for buying
ASP.NET MVC 2 Cookbook

About Packt Publishing

Packt, pronounced 'packed', published its first book "*Mastering phpMyAdmin for Effective MySQL Management*" in April 2004 and subsequently continued to specialize in publishing highly focused books on specific technologies and solutions.

Our books and publications share the experiences of your fellow IT professionals in adapting and customizing today's systems, applications, and frameworks. Our solution based books give you the knowledge and power to customize the software and technologies you're using to get the job done. Packt books are more specific and less general than the IT books you have seen in the past. Our unique business model allows us to bring you more focused information, giving you more of what you need to know, and less of what you don't.

Packt is a modern, yet unique publishing company, which focuses on producing quality, cutting-edge books for communities of developers, administrators, and newbies alike. For more information, please visit our website: www.packtpub.com.

Writing for Packt

We welcome all inquiries from people who are interested in authoring. Book proposals should be sent to author@packtpub.com. If your book idea is still at an early stage and you would like to discuss it first before writing a formal book proposal, contact us; one of our commissioning editors will get in touch with you.

We're not just looking for published authors; if you have strong technical skills but no writing experience, our experienced editors can help you develop a writing career, or simply get some additional reward for your expertise.

ASP.NET 3.5 Social Networking

ISBN: 978-1-847194-78-7   Paperback: 580 pages

An expert guide to building enterprise-ready social networking and community applications with ASP.NET 3.5

1. Create a full-featured, enterprise-grade social network using ASP.NET 3.5

2. Learn key new ASP.NET topics in a practical, hands-on way: LINQ, AJAX, C# 3.0, n-tier architectures, and MVC

3. Build friends lists, messaging systems, user profiles, blogs, message boards, groups, and more

4. Rich with example code, clear explanations, interesting examples, and practical advice €" a truly hands-on book for ASP.NET developers

ASP.NET Site Performance Secrets

ISBN: 978-1-849690-68-3   Paperback: 456 pages

Simple and proven techniques to quickly speed up your ASP.NET website

1. Speed up your ASP.NET website by identifying performance bottlenecks that hold back your site's performance and fixing them

2. Tips and tricks for writing faster code and pinpointing those areas in the code that matter most, thus saving time and energy

3. Drastically reduce page load times

4. Configure and improve compression – the single most important way to improve your site's performance

Please check **www.PacktPub.com** for information on our titles

www.ingramcontent.com/pod-product-compliance
Lightning Source LLC
LaVergne TN
LVHW062305060326
832902LV00013B/2061